CREATION'S TESTIMONY

His Invisible Attributes Clearly Seen,
Understood by the
Things that Are
Made

Jeffrey Weitzel

CREATION'S TESTIMONY

*His Invisible Attributes Clearly Seen,
Understood by the
Things that Are
Made*

Text and design: Jeffrey Weitzel, 2025

No Artificial Intelligence (AI) was used in the writing or design of this publication.

Scriptures used are taken from the New King James Version® (NKJV), except where noted. Copyright©1982 by Thomas Nelson, Inc. Used by Permission. All rights reserved.

Green's Literal Translation (LITV). Scripture quoted by permission. Copyright©1993 by Jay P. Green Sr. All rights reserved. Jay P. Green Sr., Lafayette, IN. U.S.A. 47903.

Scriptures are also quoted from the World English Bible (WEB), which is in the public domain. First published in 2020 by eBible.org. Web: worldenglish.bible

Emphasis and [brackets] within quotes are added by the author throughout, unless noted.

Jeffrey Weitzel has no responsibility for the persistence or accuracy of URLs for external or third-party Internet Websites referred to in this publication and does not guarantee that any content on such Websites is, or will remain, accurate or appropriate.

Library of Congress Control Number: 2026904703
ISBN (Hard Cover): 979-8-9923728-0-9
ISBN (Paperback): 979-8-9923728-1-6
ISBN (Digital): 979-8-9923728-2-3

Contents

Introduction 1

PART ONE: THE CREATION 5

1. In the Beginning, Without Excuse 7
2. The Other Creation 16
3. The Voice of God 23
4. God Is Not Perfect (Because He Is Perfect) 30

PART TWO: THE BODY 41

5. Introduction to the Body 43
6. The Temple Is a Body 45
   - The Ark 48
   - The Mercy Seat 51
   - Table of the Showbread 54
   - The Lampstand 57
   - The Curtains 60
   - A Covering of Goat's Hair 64
   - Ram Skins and Tachash Skins 65
   - The Boards 67
   - The Bars 70
   - The Veil 71
   - Screen Door 74
   - The Altar of Burnt Offering 75
   - The Court 78
   - Altar of Incense 79
   - Laver 82
   - Identity 86

The False Tabernacle 91
Summary 93

7. YOU ARE YOUR OWN ANALOGY 94
Foundations 98
Demons and Rats 101
My Green Book 105

PART THREE: THE SKY-CLOCK, GOD'S CALENDAR 113

8. A LITTLE HISTORY 115
The Sabbath 117
Christmas 120
Easter 121

9. THE HANDS OF THE CLOCK 124
The Sun 128
The Moon 132
The Stars 144
Conclusion? 149

10. MUSIC OF THE CALENDAR 158
Intervals and Harmony 160

11. APPOINTED TIMES AND THE MEANING OF LIFE 164
The Sabbath 165
Passover 166
Unleavened Bread 170
Feast of Weeks/Pentecost 175
Memorial of Teruah 184
Atonement 195
The Feast of Tabernacles 203
The Eighth Day 207

PART FOUR: THE TEN ORDERED MATTERS   211

12. THE ORIGINAL CONTRACT 213
13. ONE: NO OTHER GODS ABOVE..219
14. TWO: IMAGES – GATEWAY TO DECEPTION........................221
      Lessons from Banjos..234
      Medicine 242
15. THREE: DON'T BEAR THE NAME OF YAHWEH IN EMPTINESS 259
16. FOUR: THE SABBATH IS FOR RELATIONSHIP........................265
17. FIVE: HONOR YOUR FATHER AND MOTHER.........................274
18. SIX: MURDER – NEPHILM VS JESUS....................................281
19. SEVEN: ADULTERY – IDOLATRY PART 2...............................291
20. EIGHT: DON'T STEAL – EMMANUEL....................................301
21. NINE: NO FALSE WITNESS – THE LAND CRIES OUT..............309
22. TEN: DON'T COVET, GIVE THANKS......................................315

PART FIVE: THE END   319

23. THE GOSPEL OF DEATH..321
24. LOVE 326

Introduction

Shortly after you were born, your mother lay down and rested. It was exhausting work bringing you into the world! And there you were, a new creation. If you could have talked, you'd have had something to say about the experience of being born, for sure. But your life didn't end there. You grew up and did lots of amazing (and likely some stupid) things that have filled out your story to get to where you are today, and now you *can* talk about it. And since you are still here, there will be more to your story before it is over.

Likewise, the creation's story did not end with day 7 after it was born and the Creator rested. It has had a long life, full of adventure, heartache, joy and hope for a better future. Its life has not yet ended either, so there will eventually be more to its story. But in the meantime, it has a story to tell, just like you do.

A person's testimony is one of the most powerful tools he or she has for sharing the gospel. The gospel story is the same for everyone but the effect it has on every individual is unique and personal. Yet it is personal in a way that allows others to be able to relate to it in their own lives, which is what makes it so powerful.

This book is my own testimony at least as much as it is my attempt to tell the testimony of the creation. I know my own story a lot better. But it happens that my story involves discovering that the creation itself actually has a story to tell. Paul was the one to let me in on it:

Introduction

> For the invisible things of him since the creation of the world are clearly seen, being perceived through the things that are made, even his everlasting power and divinity; that they may be without excuse. (Romans 1:20 WEB)

Since I discovered that, I've been trying to listen to what creation has to say and record what I've been told. I ask questions of it, too and sometimes I even get answers. At this point, I think I only know a very small portion of its story, but the small bits I've been privileged to hear have amazed and inspired me. I know there is a ton more out there to discover.

It's my hope that my story will inspire you to start asking your own questions of creation. Because your story is different from mine, I'm quite sure you'll be told different parts of creation's story than I was. And if you do, please share what you discover with me; I'd love to hear it!

Some Functional Tidbits to Help in Reading This Book

- Learning to listen to nature, the creation, does not in any way replace knowing the Bible, but acts as another witness in addition to it and the Holy Spirit, a third leg to give balance. As such it gives much greater clarity on how the writers of Scripture saw the world they lived in, and why their analogies almost exclusively revolved around the natural world.

- Some parts may sound simply more like my testimony or a Bible study than anything related to the creation. You will be correct in that observation. But I found those parts necessary to get the larger-scale picture. In the end, it is becoming increasingly difficult for me to separate Bible study, my personal life, and what creation speaks, because they all start to say the same thing (and that is kind of the point)!

Introduction

- I change up the names I use for the Creator and the Messiah. Some places I use God and others Yahweh. Sometimes I say Jesus and others I say Yeshua. I have grown comfortable in the diverse assemblies I meet with using any of the above names and more. I've seen miracles performed in the name of Jesus and in the name of Yeshua, so am of the opinion that the Messiah must not put the weight on the issue that many of His followers do. Yet I also understand that learning how to pronounce our Hebrew husband's name better might be a small sign of wanting to know Him better. After all, I have done so with my Japanese wife's name, which many have a difficult time saying correctly. And I'm sure I am still not pronouncing perfectly on either account.

- "He who answers a matter before he hears it, it is folly and shame to him" (Proverbs 18:13).

- In the end, this book is not meant to change the world. It has already been changed, and that is the problem—the obfuscation of the world as it was originally created. Fortunately, the solution has also already taken place or is at least on offer through the blood of Messiah. Yet because of creation being so obscured today, many cannot see the offer to accept it. So, if this book offers anything to the reader, it is simply to learn how to see through the fog of modernity in a new way. And by that, I mean in an old way. In the way that people once did when everything was new and there was no choice but to attach meaning to it all, because that much was obvious.

PART ONE
The Creation

In the Beginning, Without Excuse

Yahweh's creation has always been and continues to be sufficient for human existence in both physical and spiritual senses. It is alive and sustains life. It cannot lie or deceive but it is what it is. By that I mean that if you observe a natural, created thing, it will only do what it was designed by the Creator to do. All created things are consistent in that way, so that we can make observations and learn a thing or two about how they work.

Everything in Yahweh's creation is also interconnected to everything else in His creation, in that they are not isolated things functioning independently of each other. Water is nothing without the soil and rocks that contain it and the sky that it evaporates into, or without every creature and plant that drinks it and is made up of it. A flower is also dependent on both the water and soil, on both decaying and living organisms that feed it and pollinate it, on the sun and stars, the heat and cold and the human that stops to ponder its beauty. Insects and birds understand and require the sun, moon and stars for their travels, and have taught men their navigational skills. There is nothing that Yahweh created that we cannot look at and learn wisdom from. It will never and can never lead us astray, because it is what it is and cannot lie.

Part 1: The Creation

The garden of Eden was a picture of this sufficiency. All of creation was said to be good. Yet Yahweh did a remarkable thing and decided to make one thing in His creation differently. He made man in His own image. He would have the power of free will, to make decisions, either good or bad. He did this simply by giving humans rules that they could either follow or not follow. No other creature was given rules or laws, but only man. At first it was only one rule, "But of the tree of the knowledge of good and evil [or 'bad,' the opposite of good] you shall not eat, for in the day that you eat of it you shall surely die." Had Yahweh given this command to any of the other creatures, they would also have suffered the same fate of mankind. But He gave them only instinct instead. This instinct might have told them not to touch the tree, but regardless of if they touched it or not, they would not have been cursed because the rule did not apply, so they could not be deceived. But man was able to be deceived, as the rule was not in our hearts (instinct), but given outside of us.

When the tempter came, they were easily overcome. It is usually thought that it was the fruit of the tree that allowed Adam and Eve to know good and bad. But it seems to me that the tree likely had no special magical properties to dispense knowledge. Although there is much meaning and symbolism behind this tree, for the simple mechanism of dispensing knowledge it was inconsequential that the rule referred to a tree. It was far more critical that they had let the adversary's will enter them. By going against the rule, they suddenly found warring factions, opposing natures, inside of them—natures that want to please their Creator, and others that want to please only themselves. Guilt and shame were the result, and the rest is history. The sinless state could never be recovered (at least not until the arrival and death of Messiah).

From this point, we see the beginning of a pattern of man wanting to hide nature and hide from nature—both our own nature, and the nature of creation. Immediately Adam and Eve tried to hide their natural bodies, as guilt had pricked something inside of them that made them ashamed of who they were. They sewed fig leaves to cover themselves and hid in the trees. Maybe Yahweh wouldn't see them and know that they had done wrong! Of course, He did find them, and after giving them their respective curses, gave them animal skins from the very first atoning (the definition of which is "covering") sacrifice with which to cover themselves.

Sometime after this, Adam and Eve's firstborn, Cain, killed his younger brother, Abel, in jealousy (Genesis 4). God drove him away to be a fugitive and vagabond.

Cain's response was to build a city to dwell in. The term *city* does not mean what we think of today as a large urban center but was simply the term for a walled enclosure. He surrounded himself and his family with a wall to protect themselves from outsiders who might think to harm him, even though Yahweh had already put a mark on him to this end. Cain did not trust Yahweh and so hid himself from Him, closing himself off from the natural world, relying on his own inventions instead. In essence, Cain started his own form of creation, under the guidance of the adversary. Humanity has been doing the same thing ever since.

Evil quickly spiraled out of control, so that by Genesis chapter 6, verse 5, we hear that,

> Yahweh saw that the wickedness of man was great in the earth, and that every intent of the thoughts of his heart was only evil continually. And Yahweh was sorry that He had made man on the earth.

Yahweh decided that the best route forward was to start over with the last righteous man left, Noah.

After the flood, however, it didn't take long for things to go downhill again, and Noah's grandchildren started building the Tower of Babel. This tower put Cain's city to shame. Its goal was to build a tower up to the throne room of Yahweh and challenge His claim to rulership of the earth. They did not look to the natural things of the

Part 1: The Creation

creation but used their own contrivances to show their independence from it.

We see it over and over again. The righteous patriarchs Abraham, Isaac, and Jacob, lived in tents as nomadic people, in harmony with the land, while most of the unrighteous lived in cities. The bigger the city, the more evil it was, with Nineveh, Sodom, Gomorrah, and Babylon being prime examples. Cities were places that were separate from the creation. One could buy and sell instead of being dependent on what you could grow yourself. You were, for the most part, protected from dangerous wild animals. The time spent living in and studying the natural world was far less than that of the nomadic people, and the result was a psychological state reliant on self instead of on God.

These trends have continued to the present day and are indeed accelerating. We have been fast-tracking a society that hides and destroys the natural world in every way possible. Over half of the world's population and more than 80 percent of the people in the United States now live in cities. Just 200 years ago those numbers were well under ten percent.[1]

These cities are flooded with artificial light hiding the stars and removing a sense of connection with the day and night. They are built with artificial man-made materials: plastics, concrete, asphalt, and metal. We move around them at unnatural speeds in motorized vehicles.

Even farmland now bears little resemblance to nature, with huge tracts of monoculture (cultivation of a single crop) farmed by enormous machines with minimal numbers of humans involved. With only 0.8 percent of the U.S. population working on farms (2.6 million of 332 million total population)[2], almost everybody finds

---

[1] https://www.statista.com/statistics/269967/urbanization-in-the-united-states/

[2] https://usafacts.org/topics/agriculture/

their food only in grocery stores, packed in boxes with no sense of where it came from.

Nature is removed from every area of life possible. We work at jobs where we spend more and more of our time simply staring at a lit screen. We talk to people who are not in the same city, state or country exactly like we talk to people who are in the next room. Information is instantaneously available; never does it have to be worked for or earned. We go to schools where we learn by sitting at a desk for hours on end, while looking at screens that tell us about a world we have never seen and probably never will see, and most of the information is deceptive if it contains any truth at all.

The very nature of the family and our own bodies is under attack. No longer is it an obvious fact to many that it takes a male and a female to create a new human, because there are multitudes of genders and it is a simple matter of choice which one we would like to be, with surgery and artificial hormones available as an easy option if we want to physically become another gender.

Our clothing is less and less natural. Have you tried to find 100 percent natural clothes lately? Yes, they are still available, but are fewer and farther between, and usually saturated in toxic chemicals with the prices skyrocketing. We are covered in plastics which surround our bodies with static, then the soles of our feet have a barrier of rubber between them and the ground so that the static cannot safely discharge. It used to be that bare feet or feet shod with leather were able to be electrically grounded. It is a phenomenon that some are starting to link to myriads of health issues.

It hasn't stopped at the unnatural exterior covering of our bodies. We are also wanting to inject and insert artificial things into our insides: medicines and vaccines that carry all sorts of chemicals, unclean animal and human parts, and now even self-assembling nano-chips. We replace malfunctioning body parts with artificial ones or even ones from unclean animals, and people are being convinced that it will be more convenient to have our computers

Part 1: The Creation

embedded into our bodies rather than carry around the cumbersome cell phone all day. Since our bodies are the temple of the Holy Spirit, does it make sense why some say these things could become the intrusion of the abomination of desolations into the holy of holies?

It is almost as if there were a conspiracy to hide something from us.

What does the adversary not want us to see? If we were to spend our time in what is left of the ever-diminishing forest lands and natural areas, what would we find? If we lived where there was no artificial light, where we could see the sky full of stars every night, what could we re-learn? If schooling took place outside, living in nature and observing natural processes, how would our children's behavior change?

The answer is that we just might find some truth, seeing the signature of the Creator on every created thing, which would give us the ability to find God and so discover who we really are. We would not suddenly be sinless creatures, because Adam and Eve had the same opportunity, and we know how that worked out.

But even though they also had the advantage of Yahweh walking in the garden with them, we have some advantages now that they did not. First, we have hindsight, mostly in the form of the Bible. It is the ability to learn from history. Since there is nothing new under the sun, we should be able to avoid a few of their mistakes.

The other, more important, thing we have is the victory of Messiah. We are able to fight now as an actual part of His body because the battle over death has already been won, if we can only accept the truth of that.

This book is dedicated to the idea that we do actually still have the ability to look at the creation and learn tremendous things. The Bible is an incredible gift to mankind that the Creator has given us. But learning through the lens of another culture and tongue, with translations that have often been tampered with, we can easily be misled into incorrect doctrine and thought.

We are told to "test all things; hold fast what is good" (1 Thessalonians 5:21), and "test the spirits, whether they are of God" (1 John 4:1), but what is the method for doing so? Looking at the creation is the method that has best helped me to discern the spirits. Romans 1:20 says, "For since the creation of the world His invisible attributes are clearly seen, being understood by the things that are made, even His eternal power and Godhead, so that they are without excuse."

Friends, we are without excuse! The "things that are made" are still with us. We do not need to uproot and move into a tent in the forest to find most of them. I live in a moderate-sized city, and although I do often long for the refreshment of a hike in the woods, it is the mindset of looking at the created things that we need, not necessarily to be constantly surrounded by nature.

The more we can be in contact with nature, the better, but created things are with us everywhere. Even in a metropolis we can still see the sun and moon, can still bake bread to understand the meaning of leaven, and can still raise our families using the same patterns that God uses to raise His family (hint: He shares the same frustrations we do!). Most importantly, we still have our bodies, which are perhaps the greatest of analogy we have to work with, as we are made in the image of God.

This idea of analogy is used throughout the Bible. We read lots of parables in the Bible that are meant to tell God's people something and hide it from the rest. Most of these parables use analogies from the natural world to build their case: seed, tares, leaven, pearls, vineyards, sheep, fig trees. The rest use the nature of human behavior: vinedressers, sons, virgins, servants and masters, fools and kings.

When we think of parables, we automatically think of the New Testament teachings of Yeshua, but in reality, the Old Testament is full of them, too, because actual historical events can also be parables.

The exodus, though an actual event, was also a parable to glean information from, and was, in many ways, the story of bringing us out of "worldly" ways (those of human creation) and back into Yahweh's creation. Egypt was a modern, advanced civilization of the day. It had big cities, beautiful temples, and a powerful military. They also employed the slavery and subjection that can go hand in hand with civilization, and eventually Israel became the subject of that slavery.

When Yahweh brought them out of that nation, He was very particular about the order that things happened in. First, He saved them with His mighty hand when the nation of Israel had done nothing to deserve it except cry out to Him. They were then led through the Red Sea, which we are told was their baptism (1 Corinthians 10:2). It was after their salvation and baptism that they arrived at Mt. Sinai to receive the law, which was given to them to show them the proper way of life to live in response to the salvation they had already received.

Their salvation did not come from the law; it came beforehand, as a free gift to Israel. And even after their salvation and receiving the law, they were not yet at the destination they needed to get to. The promised land was close, but because of unbelief in the power of their Savior, they were afraid to go in and ended up with a forty-year trial instead. Yet they did catch a glimpse of it before their wandering in the wilderness, and it was a natural wonderland with giant-sized grapes (and also giants...). They were not inheriting a land of walled fortresses with which to defend themselves (Yahweh actually collapsed the walls of Jericho, the first fortified city they came to), but a land of milk and honey, symbols of all the best that nature has to offer. God was offering to take them back to the garden of Eden if they would but obey Him.

This is all an analogy for the process of our own salvation. We have been saved through no works of our own. We accept that salvation by receiving baptism in water to cleanse us of our sins, and we learn the law to show obedience and love to the Father: "If you love me, keep my commandments," John 14:15. Yet even after this, we still must live a life full of trials and tests to see if our faith is enough to stop our reliance on our own creations in order to enter his promised land and return to the natural world He originally gave us in Eden.

2

The Other Creation

Satan is just the Hebrew word for adversary, or opposer, not a proper name. It can, at times, refer to the head of the fallen angels, but it is also often used in reference to humans who oppose, or stand in the way of others. Either way, it is a spiritual concept that we must understand occurs everywhere we turn. One who opposes is standing opposite, facing the exact opposite direction, like a mirror image. If you raise your right hand, the opposer will raise his left. He looks a lot like you, but he is not you. Even Peter was seen as a "Satan."

> From that time Jesus began to show to His disciples that He must go to Jerusalem, and suffer many things from the elders and chief priests and scribes, and be killed, and be raised the third day. Then Peter took Him aside and began to rebuke Him, saying, "Far be it from You, Lord; this shall not happen to You!" But He turned and said to Peter, "Get behind Me, Satan! You are an offense to Me, for you are not mindful of the things of God, but the things of men" (Matthew 16:21–23).

When Yeshua told Peter to "get behind Me, Satan," He was telling him that he was acting in opposition to the Father's will for Him to be killed as the Passover lamb. He was not calling him names or thinking that the head of the fallen angels had taken over his body. Peter was simply acting with a human understanding, which is filled with an adversarial spirit toward the ways of God. It is understandable that Peter would not want Yeshua to be killed, and we would have thought the same. But it was a thought that was directly opposed to the Father's will.

In the last chapter, we saw how the downfall of man quickly spiraled out of control. It did so because, from the initial disobedience, man's will was in opposition to God's. It led Adam to eat the fruit in direct opposition to Yahweh's command. Later, Cain slew his brother in direct opposition to Yahweh's will for him to "do well," then he built a walled compound in opposition to Yahweh's gift of a mark for his protection.

It was this spirit of opposition that started dwelling in men, and it compelled them to start building their own creation, covering over the one that Yahweh had made for them. The result is the world we live in today—a world which despises nature, covering every inch of Gods soil with concrete and asphalt, ingesting artificial chemicals for food and medicine instead of the plants that God made, replacing trees with skyscrapers and Yeshua with computer screens.

This second creation is a counterfeit. Everything the adversary does is meant to mimic something the Creator does, but it is done in a way that appeals to our carnality instead of edifying our spiritual faith. Where Yeshua sends the Holy Spirit, Satan sends New Age spiritualism. Where Yahweh heals us from the inside, Satan's medicines suppress symptoms on the outside, leaving the disease to fester. Where God created the marriage covenant and the beauty of two becoming one, Satan created pornography, adultery and fornication. Where God created man in His own image and beasts to cover the earth, Satan created idols to cover the earth in the image of men and beasts.

These idols are the antithesis of Yahweh's creation. If the creation cannot lie, then idols, the man-made objects of the counterfeit creation, are not capable of telling the truth. As we will see later in this book, idolatry encompasses much more than we realize today. All ten commandments can be boiled down to the battle between the true creation and the false creation.

Our modern sensibilities like to imagine that we have risen above idolatry in the days since "science" has become the greatest possessor of truth, yet a closer look will show most science to be nothing more than idolatry masquerading itself with the sole purpose of hiding God. We will see that science has become the occult religion of blind faith that cannot be questioned, and that the real teaching of the Bible is to test everything and hold fast only that which is good.

It is unfortunate that our churches today have bought into the bait and switch, hook, line, and sinker. The way of life of Jesus' disciples bears little resemblance to what we call Christianity today, which has become at its best a way to improve yourself, and at its worst a den of wolves in sheep's clothing.

In the time of Christ, there were no denominations of Christians. You were either Jewish and therefore continued being Jewish with the understanding that the Messiah taught about in Judaism had actually arrived, or you were Gentile and accepted that that same Messiah had come to save you as well. Both believed every teaching put forth by Jesus and the disciples not by blind belief, but by seeing the works that were done as proof of the power of the one true God and by searching the scriptures for themselves.

Today there are between 33,000 and 45,000 denominations of Christianity worldwide, depending on what research you look at. They are divided along every possible doctrine one can imagine, yet almost invariably follow the same format of one pastor (possibly a few at larger churches) teaching a congregation what and how to believe based on written articles of faith. However, there are no biblical examples that this is how a church is supposed to be run. In many, possibly a majority of these denominations, you will be asked to leave if you question the beliefs put forth by the leaders of the corporate body. The reliance is on the human leadership, not the power of God.

Interestingly, God has even put the idea of an impostor into His creation. There are many plants that look very much like other plants, and usually they even grow in the same habitat. Evolutionists like to think of this as an "adaptation," as if they used to be different and somehow changed themselves over millennia to create an advantage. The real reason they are that way is because Yahweh created them that way to tell us something.

The Bible talks of tares growing up with the wheat. These tares were a grain called darnel that looks similar to wheat until the head produces its grain to reveal a useless imposter. We are even given wisdom in dealing with them: Do not try to identify and pull them early on, but let them grow up to maturity, then bundle up the tares and burn them and gather the wheat into the barn (Matthew 13:24–30).

The tares were sown by the enemy, and this is all symbolic for the impostors we will run into in the course of our lives. We will not always recognize them at first as they will look very much like someone we should trust. They may be a teacher or a friend who tries to get you going down a path that looks promising. The only way to recognize them for what they are is to let them remain in your life until you can see their fruit. Was their teaching edifying to the body of Christ, or did it cast doubt and create fear? In the end, those found to be tares will be dealt with by God and His angels, who will gather them together and burn them in the fire.

We can also look at certain animals that look like their environments to the point that they blend in. Some are dangerous and some are not because there are different reasons for their camouflage. Some are blending in to avoid being eaten, and some are doing so to catch something to eat.

These can show us the need for discernment when dealing with new people who present themselves in our lives because they will always blend in with our life situation. Are they to be trusted and invited into our homes—people we can help, or are they preying on our kindness in order to take advantage of us or throw us off course?

Yet another example in nature is the dangerous impostor that God can redeem for good. Where I live there is a lot of poison oak and it usually grows where real oak grows. I'm pretty good at identifying it, but there are places where it grows among the real oak saplings, and a sapling oak and a mature poison oak shrub can look very similar if you don't know exactly what to look for. It is a sneaky plant and is poison even in winter when there are no leaves, which can make it very difficult to stay out of on a hike.

There were many times in my childhood where I had to deal with the itchy rashes that come from touching it. On one occasion it covered most of my body. At that time, I would have had a hard time thinking that such a plant could be redeemed for anything good. But amazingly, in the spring, bees visit the short-lived flowers and create the most flavorful honey from it. It is very difficult to find, but a few times my wife, Sanae, and I were able to procure some. It tasted probably better than any other honey we've tasted, and eating it was rumored to impart immunity to poison oak.

It was one of those things that would get into liability issues if anyone ever made such a medical claim, but one thing I can say is that neither Sanae nor I have had any poison oak rash since we ate that honey many years ago. I cannot prove that it was from the honey, and we are generally very careful about not getting ourselves into poison oak, but even so I do know we have been in it more than once without ill effects.

This is all to say that God can take an evil impostor and redeem it for His use, giving us something good from it and making the evil of no effect.

As Joseph said to his brothers in Egypt, "And you, you intended evil against me, but God meant it for good, in order to make it as it is this day, to keep a great many people alive" (Genesis 50:20).

As we go through different topics in this book, I think it is important to keep this thought of redemption in mind. God is able to take any evil thing and use it to His purposes and often has. The city was introduced as an evil concept, but God redeemed it with Jerusalem, the city of God. Earthly kings were seen as evil because they took the power and glory that was supposed to be reserved for God almighty and gave it to a man. Yet God allowed Israel to have one when they asked, redeeming the idea of kingship with David, the man after God's own heart. God redeemed the pagan temple with the tabernacle of meeting.

So, when we look at our modern times, we can see the same thing. I truly believe that all modern technology comes from the adversary for the purposes of evil. Yet here I sit on a computer writing this book dedicated to Yahweh, because He can redeem that technology for His use. You'll read later how I believe the modern medical system to be based on witchcraft, yet I know that it can be redeemed as well, with actual permanent healing taking place at times. But just like the kingship, where being redeemed required the utmost care taken to keep it holy, technology, medicine and other inventions of our modern world still have many inherent dangers that must be avoided while using them. And I would still be stupid to go roll around in the poison oak.

From all of my talk of nature being covered over by the adversary, one could start to come to the conclusion that I am advocating some sort of nature worship—that we should drop out of civilization and become one with the earth. This is not at all the case! There is a big difference between being in awe of creation, finding how it points to the Creator, and worshipping creation itself.

Part 1: The Creation

We look to it to admire the handiwork of and learn more about Him who made it.

Our modern culture even tries to proclaim its own counterfeit version of preserving the creation by painting it as a victim. While it is true on many levels that nature is the victim of humanity, the danger with this view is that not only are we seen as the problem for poor, defenseless nature, but we are then also propped up as the solution to the problem, which makes us into gods of sorts, having its fate in our hands.

Yes, we should be good stewards of the land entrusted to us, but nature was made self-sufficient, and it still is. Man was made to "fill the earth and subdue it" (Genesis 1:28), meaning to cultivate, tend, and nurture it for our own use. But that doesn't mean it requires our intervention to survive! Wherever civilizations have died off, it has not been very many years before nature has completely reclaimed the ground, covering over any sign that man had lived there. Nature isn't going away, with or without us, until the One who made it to begin with declares that its time is up. And from reading the book of Revelation, it looks like there will still be nature even after the new heaven and new earth replace the old.

3

The Voice of God

"In the beginning, Elohim created the heavens and the earth." Two-thousand-four-hundred-fifty-one years later, Yahweh gave the written law. In the meantime, Adam, Enoch, Noah, Abraham, Isaac, Jacob, Joseph, and Moses knew the will of God. They understood His ways and worshiped Him in truth.

How did they know what Yahweh wanted if it had not been told to them? Adam walked with Him in the garden and apparently spoke to Him directly, but what about the others? Noah was already righteous before Yahweh appeared to him telling him to build an ark, so how did he come to comprehend righteousness?

Abraham was spoken to by Yahweh Himself, yet he also was righteous beforehand, giving a tithe of the spoils to Melchizedek. How did he know about tithing 500 years before the law was given at Sinai? When these patriarchs sacrificed animals, how did they know the rules that would make an acceptable sacrifice? What gave them their knowledge of obedience? Did they all speak directly with Yahweh as Adam had without those conversations being recorded in the Bible? Was it all carefully handed down from Adam? These are certainly possibilities, but is it possible they had another method?

The answer lies in the opening chapter of the Bible. The Creation. That is what they had. It spoke many things to the patriarchs and all of the ancients. The world they lived in was all they had and all they knew. And it was real. There were no thoughts that the world had always been there or that they had descended from monkeys which had descended from slime. They were immersed

Part 1: The Creation

instead in a creation which not only spoke of its Creator but shouted about Him from the top of its lungs!

In those ancient times, when lightning struck, it was seen as a sign from God. He was speaking. See Job 37:2, Job 40:9, and Psalm 77:18. That there was a spiritual realm was unquestioned. Even the pagan nations understood that. They just misattributed the things that Yahweh spoke to other "gods" that represented only a portion of the creation. Thus, they gave the glory to the creation itself instead of the Creator.

Today we attribute lightning and other natural phenomena to the mechanisms of science. Because we have searched out the causal phenomena required for the occurrence of lightning, for example, static, weather patterns, or high and low pressure systems, we think we understand something and can reduce the lightning to the simple sum of its parts. If A, B, and C meet the right conditions then lightning will strike. Even those who consider themselves Christian think in this manner. But really, this is just giving glory to the creation instead of the Creator.

The reality is that lightning is an intrinsically spiritual thing, not a physical one. What makes A, B, and C happen to line up at any particular time? The glory goes to the Father because it is His voice, based on His thoughts, just as the ancients saw it.

When we think about our own voices, it becomes clear. Our speech happens as a result of A, air from our lungs being pushed through B, our vocal cords, then C, being articulated by our tongues and lips. But is this really the cause of speech? No, it is just the physical hoops that are required for our thoughts to be manifested to others, and our thoughts are intrinsically spiritual.

Science can't even make a valid guess as to where our thoughts originate from. If it weren't for the obvious fact that we have free will, science could say that thoughts are chance connections of neurons in our brains. Yet it is impossible to deny that we have at least some control over the connections they make. And if we have even some control over them, then they are not chance, which means that our thoughts cannot originate solely in the physical makeup of our bodies. There must be some nonphysical force driving our thoughts. And if this is true of our own selves, then why should it not be true of God, in whose image we are made?

Of course, God's voice was found in more than just thunder. In 1 Kings 19:11–12, Elijah fully expects God's voice to be in the strong wind, the earthquake, and the fire, but He shows Himself in a still, small voice instead. Others have heard Him speaking in dreams and visions. Some have heard him through the voice of prophets, and still others have heard him without hearing a sound at all.

Today, at least in most of westernized society, we have trouble hearing God's voice. In fact, we have so many things to listen to at all times of the day that we never even get a chance to sit quietly with our own thoughts. For many, silence is extremely uncomfortable. We prefer to have music on, or the TV or a podcast or some form of background noise. Anything to keep away the silence. If there is nothing making sound, then we have to have something to read or a phone to look at to occupy the empty space.

Why do we dread the silence? And by silence, I mean removing all forms of external input from our brains, including reading, or put another way, not listening to others' thoughts. Silence is the only time we can process all of the things we have heard. Never having silence is like eating constantly and never being able to digest. Silence is when we can have our own thoughts for organizing all the things we have heard and seen. We don't even necessarily have to organize consciously; our subconscious seems to do a lot of it for us, just as our stomach digests our food without our conscious direction.

And just as fasting from food is a great spiritual exercise, fasting from external input—especially the media in all forms—is very edifying. No matter how much we listen to others, we will never properly understand any of it without time to digest. This is the time our brains compare what we have read or heard with what we know

Part 1: The Creation

from experience. And if we cannot put all the pieces together of the information we take in, the puzzle of the world around us cannot be completed, errors will never be detected, and we become easily indoctrinated with lies. But when all of that information is well digested and ordered, and the nonsense has been discarded, we just might be able to hear the still, small voice that is not our own—the voice of God. Isaiah speaks of fasting this way:

> 'Why have we fasted,' they say, 'and You have not seen? Why have we afflicted our souls, and You take no notice?'

> "In fact, in the day of your fast you find pleasure, And exploit all your laborers. Indeed you fast for strife and debate, And to strike with the fist of wickedness. You will not fast as you do this day, To make your voice heard on high. Is it a fast that I have chosen, A day for a man to afflict his soul? Is it to bow down his head like a bulrush, And to spread out sackcloth and ashes? Would you call this a fast, And an acceptable day to Yahweh?

> "Is this not the fast that I have chosen: To loose the bonds of wickedness, To undo the heavy burdens, To let the oppressed go free, And that you break every yoke? Is it not to share your bread with the hungry, And that you bring to your house the poor who are cast out; When you see the naked, that you cover him, And not hide yourself from your own flesh? Then your light shall break forth like the morning, Your healing shall spring forth speedily, And your righteousness shall go before you; The glory of Yahweh shall be your rear guard. Then you shall call, and Yahweh will answer; You shall cry, and He will say, 'Here I am.'

> "If you take away the yoke from your midst, The pointing of the finger, and speaking wickedness, If you extend your soul to the hungry And satisfy the afflicted soul, Then your light shall dawn in the darkness, And your darkness shall be as the noonday. Yahweh will guide you continually, And satisfy your soul in drought, And strengthen your bones; You shall be like a watered garden, And like a spring of water, whose waters do not fail. Those

from among you Shall build the old waste places; You shall raise up the foundations of many generations; And you shall be called the Repairer of the Breach, The Restorer of Streets to Dwell In" (Isaiah 58:3–12).

There is so much written there, but to keep to the point I'm currently making, fasting of any sort is not about being heard, but about listening to the will of God and spending the time to do it. Isaiah lays out that process. Do not make it a selfish thing – "me time". To hear the word of Yahweh, first we must listen. And to listen, we must have a quiet mind and heart. Then when we hear, we must act. Stop burdening others to give you what you want, but instead set free those whom you can, give freely, and share what you have. Take care of the needs of others first, and *then* when we pray for our needs, He will say, "Here I am."

Deuteronomy 8:3 states,

"And He has humbled you, and caused you to hunger, and caused you to eat the manna, which you had not known, and your fathers had not known, in order to cause you to know that man shall not live by bread alone, but man shall live by every Word that proceeds from the mouth of Jehovah." (LITV)

When we do without something that we normally think of as necessary to our survival, we need to find something else to lean on, and God's voice is really the only option that works. Our bodies go into a state of submission that is finally receptive to God's voice. When we are filled with physical nourishment, we have no need for spiritual nourishment. But when that food goes away, in our need to fill that space we become receptive to spiritual nourishment. We can do that by intentional fasting, or God can do it for us, as He did to the Israelites in the above passage.

He states that "He has humbled you, and caused you to hunger." Humility is the natural state when we are doing without a physical

Part 1: The Creation

necessity, and it is the only state that God can speak to. So, let's take some time away from food, but also away from the constant noise of the devices of the imposter. Turn off the phone, the TV, the computer, and the stereo, and listen to the silence. Take in the lack of nourishment coming into our ears. Just as not eating can be very uncomfortable, so can the lack of verbal input. But without that lack, God's voice may simply be too faint to hear.

I grew up in a house where, if anyone was home and awake, the television was on. It was on while getting ready for school in the morning, and at night after I went to bed. When I went off to college in 1990, I did not have a TV to bring, nor did my dorm-mate, and this was before most students had their own computers. Even though I had a lot of homework, I found myself with a lot of time to kill and a strange sensation that kept coming over me that I hadn't really experienced much before. I never actually felt bored, though.

When my friends were not available and my homework was caught up, I found myself simply going out for walks, especially at night. I would sometimes walk for two or three hours, just exploring the city. I never did that growing up and couldn't figure out why I loved it so much. Until it finally dawned on me that the feeling I was having was peace. It was also freedom. Freedom to think. And think, and think, and think! It was years later that I realized how starved my mind had been for the ability to simply think straight without being interrupted by the constant chatter of the TV.

I remember looking around at that time and noticing how stressed people were. They'd talk about the Gulf War and the possibility of a draft, or whatever negative, fear-inducing news was on. Or they'd talk about how much stress they had from their classes. But I really didn't care. Even when I was invited to watch something at another student's room, I would usually turn it down. People would ask me how I would keep up with what was going on in the world if I didn't watch TV.

My response was, "If something really important happens I'll hear about it." And it was true. I heard the important things and was able to save lots of time by not worrying about the bulk of the news that was nonsense.

By ridding myself of the nonsense and having faith I would hear what I needed to hear, I also started to hear, however gradually and slowly, what I didn't even realize until much later was the voice of God.

4

God Is Not Perfect (Because He Is Perfect)

Perfect: (from Merriam-Webster.com)
1) a: being entirely without fault or defect: Flawless
   b: satisfying all requirements: Accurate
   c: corresponding to an ideal standard or abstract concept
   d: faithfully reproducing the original specifically: Letter-Perfect
   e: legally valid

2) Expert, Proficient

3) a: Pure, Total
   b: lacking in no essential detail: Complete
   c: obsolete: Sane
   d: Absolute, Unequivocal
   e: of an extreme kind: Unmitigated

4) obsolete: Mature

5) of, relating to, or constituting a verb form or verbal that expresses an action or state completed at the time of speaking or at a time spoken of

6) obsolete
   a: Certain, Sure
   b: Contented, Satisfied

7) of a musical interval: belonging to the consonances unison, fourth, fifth, and octave which become augmented or diminished when raised or lowered by a half step

8) a: sexually mature and fully differentiated
   b: having both stamens and pistils in the same flower

As shown on the previous page, the modern definition of perfect is to be flawless—an ideal that cannot be improved upon. If we think of a perfect circle, we think of a circle drawn with a compass or some mechanical means that will not introduce any mark outside of the exact radius given. If I think of a pentagonal shape, a perfect one will exist with five sides of equal length spread by five perfectly equal angles.

Then I can think of something in nature, God's creation, that we would think of as circular, say an apple viewed from above or below—its cross-section. If we slice that apple in half at its thickest, roundest point and then lay it on a piece of paper on which is drawn a "perfect" circle of the same radius as the apple, they will not match: There will be some wobbles on the apple. We can also notice on that apple, where we sliced it, the seeds make up a star pattern—five points. If we were to take those five points and draw lines from one to the next, so as to form a pentagon, we would also notice that they would not be equal lengths, and thus the angles would also not match.

In every instance of nature, we would notice the same thing. Crystal structures, which we think of as God's use of symmetry, are not "perfectly" patterned out. Each crystal grown in a cluster will vary slightly, and sometimes greatly, from its neighbor in angle and size. The pattern of seeds in a sunflower, held up often as the ideal use of a Fibonacci sequence (a number series in which each number is obtained by adding its two preceding numbers) in nature, will stray from mathematically computed and drawn versions of the same form.

Even a perfectly straight line cannot be found in God's creation. The line of the horizon, no matter how flat the landscape, is broken up by subtle hills and punctuations of rocks or vegetation. The surface of a body of water, no matter how calm and undisturbed it is, will be corrupted by ripples from the breeze or the jumping of a

Part 1: The Creation

fish or a water-skipper. Every upright growing tree or plant fails to match the perfection of a metal flagpole.

What else are we to conclude, then, other than man is more perfect than God? Man can take a widget and figure out how to replicate it a billion times with each replication identical in every way to the others. But looking in my jar of cashews, which is sitting on the table, each nut is similar to the others, but nowhere near perfectly alike. Some are more curled or twisted or textured or darker colored; in fact, every one is unique, like snowflakes and fingerprints. We know that every human is also unique. How could it be seen as perfect if we were all the same? Isn't God's perfection within us individually? Because we are fearfully and wonderfully made, right? But He doesn't even make us symmetrical! If you take a frontal photo of someone's face who you know, split it down the middle and duplicate and flip it so that it is a perfectly symmetrical picture, you can hardly recognize them; that's how asymmetrical we are!

Is perfection in our hearts, then? But we are all sinners! We aren't perfect in any way! The deeper you look, the more flawed we become! We are all weak, prone to illness and injury, full of spots and wrinkles, thinning hair, body odor, and crooked teeth. We lie, cheat, and steal; we hurt the ones we love most, and are selfish and stiff-necked!

Yet Moses was inspired to write, "He is the Rock, His work is perfect." How could he say that? Nature screams imperfection from its core! It is unruly and unordered! Plants sprout up wherever they may, one here another there, with weeds between everything, plants growing on plants, fighting with each other for light and water. Animals kill each other to survive, picking on the weak.

Our definition of perfection must be skewed if God is perfect. Moses continues in his song saying,

> for all His ways are justice, a God of truth, and without injustice. They have corrupted themselves; They are not His children, because of their blemish; A perverse and crooked generation.

So, He defines His perfection as justice and truth. And if we look at older definitions of perfection, we see that indeed, its meaning has changed; its meaning is no longer "perfect."

Webster's 1828 dictionary defined "perfect" as:

Per'fect, adjective [latin Perfectus, perfico, to complete; per and facio, to do or make through, to carry to the end.]

1. Finished; complete; consummate; not defective; having all that is requisite to it's nature and kind; as a perfect statue; a *perfect* likeness; a *perfect* work; a perfect system.
2. Fully informed; completely skilled; as men *perfect* in the use of arms; *perfect* in discipline.
3. Complete in moral excellencies.
   Be ye therefore perfect, even as your Father who is in heaven is perfect. Matthew 5:48
4. Manifesting perfection
   -*My strength is made perfect in weakness.* 2 Corithians 12:9
   -Perfect chord in music, a concord or union of sounds which is perfectly coalescent and agreeable to the ear, as the fifth and the octave; a *perfect* consonance.
   -A *perfect* flower, in botany, has both stamen and pistil, or at least another and stigma.
   -Perfect tense, in grammar, the preterit tense; a tense which expresses an act as completed.

Then we can go back to the meaning of the word in Hebrew. The main word used in Hebrew is Strong's[3] H8552, *Tamiym*.

Strong's says, "entire (literally, figuratively or morally); also (as noun) integrity, truth; - without blemish, complete, full, perfect, sincerely (-ity), sound, without spot, undefined, upright (-ly), whole."

---

[3] Strong, James. *Strong's Exhaustive Concordance of the Bible.* Hendrickson Publishers, 2004.

Part 1: The Creation

Brown-Driver-Briggs [4] definition is mostly the same, but adds, "what is complete or entirely in accord with truth and fact."

The Ancient Hebrew Lexicon of the Bible [5] says, "Whole; KJV; without blemish, perfect, upright, without spot, uprightly, whole, sincere, complete, full." From the root word "Tam: Fill: Whole: Someone or something that is whole, complete, or full. One who is mature and upright as one who is whole."

Distilling these definitions a bit will allow us to see the contrast of our modern thought vs. what was originally meant to be conveyed. Today the stress of the meaning is on "Flawless, without defect, and corresponding to an ideal standard or abstract concept," whereas the original concept was, "whole, full, complete, and mature; in accord with truth, fact, and integrity."

This difference is made real to me when I put myself into it. If God is asking me to be perfect, even as He is perfect, I am faced with the sheer impossibility of the modern concept. There is no way that I can be flawless or become an ideal standard for others to measure up to. But can I be mature in my faith, or be whole and complete, living entirely in accord with truth and fact? It still sounds daunting, but maybe possible, especially when part of that complete knowledge and maturity is knowing that I don't do it alone: I am filled with the Holy Spirit and made whole by the forgiveness of my sins. I am made mature not through my flawlessness, but through the growth and humility that comes from having made mistake after mistake. Something full was once empty. Something complete was started and in process in prior times. Something mature was at one point in its infancy. This wholeness and maturity is what makes us able to act righteously, with justice and based firmly in truth, which

---

[4] Brown, Francis, et al. *The Brown-Driver-Briggs Hebrew and English Lexicon.* Hendrickson Publishers, 1996.

[5] Benner, Jeff A. *The Ancient Hebrew Lexicon of the Bible.* Ancient Hebrew Research Center, 2021.

is what Moses wrote in the song he sang to commemorate finishing the writing of the book of the law:

> He is the rock, His work is perfect [how do we know that?]; For all His ways are justice, A God of truth and without injustice; Righteous and upright is He. [so how would God describe someone who is not perfect?] They have corrupted themselves; they are not His sons; it is their blemish; they are a crooked and perverse generation (Deuteronomy 32:4–5).

This is all finally in line with what nature told us at the beginning. We reach God's perfection not through the flawless ideal, but through the completed whole that has matured from its infancy. We are not perfect because we are incapable of error, but because we have recognized our insufficiency with all humility and so grasped on to the only thing in the universe that can make us complete—Yeshua the Messiah!

The creation was made intentionally "imperfect" so that we could see our need for help. With that help, we are made complete. And since the time of creation, Satan has been putting it in people's minds that there is a better, *more* perfect way that we can attain on our own. And we have worked tirelessly to attain it, building perfectly square boxes that can be stacked one upon another, filled with unvarying mass-produced widgets, and lived in with a sense of complete isolation from God's own imperfect creation. Satan measures his perfection in tolerances of ten-thousandths of an inch. Yahweh measures His in the ripeness and nutrition packed into the tomato. It may be ribbed, warped and have haphazardly placed seeds, but it is a *whole* food, *complete* in nutrition and *full* to bursting with flavor, having matured that way from a flower to a small, hard, green fruit and finally into one that a has seed that can reproduce itself.

But you know what? That isn't enough. That plant still cannot bear fruit without outside help. It is insufficient on its own. It needs pollination brought to it from a bee or other insect, or perhaps the wind, to start the process that leads to mature fruit. A woman is the

Part 1: The Creation

same; she cannot bear fruit without a husband, can she? And aren't we, the church, called a woman, a bride? We can also do nothing without Yeshua our husband.

Satan tells us that the perfect wife has soft, smooth skin, is unreasonably thin (except in the breasts), is always young and willing to satisfy all our desires, and if she doesn't, then go ahead and trade her in for a new one who does. God says to look only at her heart and to love and cherish her in good times and bad and that her love and devotion to you and God will make her worth far above rubies.

The further in time we go, the greater the difference between God's and Satan's perfections. Satan has created perfectly smooth roads upon which to roll perfectly round tires at 70 mph so we can get to work faster, to the grocery store to buy food that is perfectly presented, chemical-filled and preserved into eternity, and when the car fumes and pesticides make us sick, to the stark white, perfectly sanitized hospital with all urgency. God gave us our own two dirty feet to walk slowly on the lumpy ground, upon which we labor the day long, tending our gardens and herds, the result of which is healthy, nutritious food, bodies fit and muscular, and sound sleep every night, which will keep us away from illness and disease, and then says He only requires us to bathe once in our lifetime and to wash our feet only once per year.

God writes His music with harmonies made up of divisions of fifths and thirds that are different in every key, but Satan takes those keys and makes them all have the same intervals, perfectly spaced, but with harmony rendered away from beauty and into the realm of the mechanical. He does the same with the rhythm, quantizing all the notes into a robotic procession of energetic "perfection" but no sense of emotion, spirit, or life to it.

Squares, and similar shapes built with 90° corners are a human contrivance, inspired by Satan. When you divide up land by drawing a line from here to there, there are now corners that weren't there before. That is a human thing to do. God did not make nature in that way. If you take a stone and put a chisel to it, breaking off a chunk, you are left with a sharp edge, or corner that did not initially exist before the human interaction. This is why God said not to touch a rock with a chisel when building an altar for Him. Humans build houses in square shapes to live in and we put things in square boxes to ship them because square is a very convenient shape for these types of human activities. It is a useful shape, but it is not natural in any way. You can hunt high and low in nature and not find a cube or square. You may find a leaf, flower, or fruit with four lobes, but they will always be set in a rounded form without sharp corners. Crystalline structures can have some semblance of squareness, but they never create a larger form of a true square or cube, but always an irregular mass of imperfect angular crystals. Also, look at the cross. It is two perpendicular lines creating four corners, and what was it used for? Death.

Satan cannot improve upon God's perfection because God's perfection is imperfect by design! God's version brings eternal life while Satan's version brings death. Satan's mistake was to think that his own value was in his perfect beauty. But that is the perfection that breeds pride, the pride he has sought so hard to pawn off on all of us. We should have no part in it! Indeed, let us accept our imperfections with all humility, so that we can also accept Christ, letting Him perfect us!

I have thought long and hard about where the idea of a Savior, or Messiah, is found nature. It evaded me for a long time, and I don't think I am alone, but He is there, all over the place. Let me explain.

There are many, many people out there who can readily accept that God exists. They can see that a world such as ours cannot exist without a Creator. They may not understand that the Creator wants a personal relationship, but they at least know that God must exist in some form.

Part 1: The Creation

Yet if you start talking about Jesus to them, they will immediately turn you away, offended that you are now starting to sound too "religious." This is why 1 Corinthians 1:23 says, "But we preach Christ crucified, to the Jews a stumbling block and to the Greeks foolishness." He is a stumbling block because they cannot see the need for Him.

Their idea of God is that a Creator God must have created things perfectly by default. It makes no sense for a perfect God to need to send a Son to clean up the mess that He made. Of course that is not exactly the way it went, but when we start to confuse the two versions of perfection, that is how we start to think. It's where questions like, "Why does God let bad things happen?" start to creep in, and if left unanswered for too long the very existence of God is then denied, which is a tragedy.

The answer is that God created things imperfectly on purpose, and for a very good reason. Things are not Satan's version of perfect because his version is not beautiful. Things are not God's version of perfect (bad things can still happen) because they are not complete. We see Jesus, Yeshua the Messiah, in nature every time we see something that needs help. He created man in need of a helper and had to give him woman saying, "It is not good that man should be alone; I will make him a helper comparable to him."

He created plants that need to be pollinated with outside help to continue the species. He created the moon in need of the sun in order to make it visible, and the sun in need of the moon so that the sun's light can shine even when it isn't present.

He created every living thing in need of food and water for survival, otherwise it would all perish in short order. Everything in creation is incomplete on its own, in need all the time, and that is the story of Messiah in nature. "Man cannot live on bread alone."

Jesus is the bread of life. He is the Bridegroom coming for His bride, which is us. He lived a perfect sin-free life, but apparently even He was incomplete in that His bride was not yet ready for Him. But

He is perfecting her and will come back for her soon. This will be the new heaven and new earth because all will be completed, finally back in the garden of Eden, but no snake, no pride and no Satanic version of perfection, because God is not perfect, but He is complete.

This is the extent of His love for us, to create us imperfect, sinful, and full of shame, then find a way to complete us in order to make us part of His family, one with His Son. "Therefore a man shall leave his father and mother and be joined to his wife, and they shall become one flesh." Completion, fullness, perfection.

PART TWO
The Body

Introduction to the Body

The human body is perhaps the greatest marvel of all creation because it was made in the image of God. As such, it can inform us about God in many ways if we just study ourselves!

When I was an art student, my favorite class was figure studies. It was a sculpture class where there was a nude model in the center of the class and the students all surrounded him or her in a big circle with our modeling stands and plasteline clay.

Our professor, Paul Buckner, was one of the best figurative sculptors and teachers in the country, and he would explain which muscles were doing what to keep them in that pose, pointing to where those muscles showed up on the model. We would usually spend 9 to 15 hours (3 to 5 classes) with each pose, then we would tear down our models and start over with another one.

There was something intensely gratifying about studying the model and translating that information to the clay with my fingers and modeling tool. It was all about the process, not the finished product, so that I never had any issue when it came time to tear down the old model. I took that class every term for about three years.

I was also taking classes in metal casting. One term I had a figure study that I thought turned out well enough that I decided to cast it in aluminum for a project. The casting turned out decently, and I have had it ever since, but I never liked having that sculpture around.

Part 2: The Body

Something bothered me about looking at this metal body hanging around my house.

At some point, I took it out from display in my living room and put it in storage in the garage, where it remained until very recently when I took it to the dump (along with all of my molds from the last 35 years). As I will explain in more detail in a later chapter, it took me a long time to figure out why I loved the process and hated the result.

The short version is that by studying the figure I was also studying my Creator. I learned to see the connection between form and function and patterns that recurred throughout our bodies. I did not know at that time that I was seeing God's fingerprints and signature. Paul (we never called him Professor Buckner) once said that everything you need to know about the figure and all of nature can be found in the human face, and I don't think he was wrong.

The following chapters will take this concept to heart, because God has certainly taken it to His heart: He designed the tabernacle in our image and designed meaning into our own lives that is unique to each individual.

The Temple Is a Body

> Or don't you know that your body is a temple of the Holy Spirit who is in you, whom you have from God? You are not your own, for you were bought with a price. Therefore glorify God in your body and in your spirit, which are God's (1 Corinthians 6:19).

Most people are familiar with this verse stating that your body is a temple. In fact, it has become a well-known saying bordering on a cliché meaning that you need to treat your body well and respect it. While this is true, it does not even scratch the surface of the meaning that the apostle Paul was trying to convey to us.

This section starts with the question, "If it is true that the body is a Temple, then is the converse also true, that the Temple, or tabernacle, is a body?" The Bible does not use words in a light-headed way.

It was the Elohim who spoke the world into existence with words in Genesis 1. And John 1 goes so far as to say that it was Jesus/Yeshua who was this Word. He was with God and He was God. Words are very important, and every one of them in scripture was inspired by the Holy Spirit. So, when I looked at the phrase, "Your body is a temple of the Holy Spirit who is in you," it seemed legitimate to investigate the same in reverse. After all, there must have been a reason Paul chose the words that he did in 1 Corinthians.

Part 2: The Body

What I have found is that, yes, the tabernacle/temple was most definitely designed as a body, and that the meaning conveyed in the journey to arrive at that answer is both fascinating and eye-opening in our understanding of who we are as members of the body of Christ/Messiah.

I'll be focusing on the tabernacle instructions that were given to Moses in Exodus 25–27 and 30, as they were the first and most complete descriptions we have. The temple of David and Solomon, although it was based loosely on the tabernacle design, has no indication that its design was ever divinely revealed to David or Solomon, nor was its design completely laid out in the Bible.

The temple of King Herod that was around at the time of Christ/Messiah has very little biblical design information given and was likely inspired more by politics than any divine command. Detailed divine instructions are given for the construction of Ezekiel's temple, but it is a future temple that has not yet been built and certainly has different design and symbolic requirements that will not be revealed until its time. So, we are left with the original tabernacle as the best example to use for any meaning that has been revealed by Yahweh.

I'll also only be paying minimal attention to the actual physical assembly of the tabernacle, how it fits together as an architectural unit. Many have done that, so I will not be focusing on what it actually looked like thousands of years ago. I do have some ideas of what it looked like and believe it to be either round or oblong/oval. I can back that up even though many will disagree. We'll get into that a little bit. But, in the end, it really doesn't matter. Its actual shape doesn't change one bit of what I'm looking into here. What we will see is that the tabernacle is still very much with us today, so what it looks like currently is of far more importance.

The instructions begin back in Exodus 24:12 just after Moses, Aaron and his sons, and the seventy elders ate a covenant meal with Yahweh. Yahweh told Moses to "Come up to Me on the mountain and be there; and I will give you tablets of stones and the law and commandments which I have written, that you may teach them." This law and commandments are central to the entire design of the tabernacle, in a very literal way, for they will be placed inside the ark of the covenant, which is placed in the holy of holies in the center of the tent. Keep this in mind.

Another thing to keep in mind is that the idea of a house (or temple or tabernacle) of worship was in no way unusual or unique to Israel. All of the surrounding nations had them, too, including Egypt, from which they were escaping. And that is really the main point of God giving these instructions. He is in effect saying, "You have seen the temples of Egypt, the gods that they represent, and the sacrifices that they require. I have seen your desire to worship physical things in a physical place. I will give you what you desire, but My ways will not be like the ways of the heathen. Here is what My temple will look like, and how you will be expected to worship and sacrifice to me."

Chapter 25 opens with Yahweh asking for offerings from Israel with which to build the tabernacle and all of its furnishings. "Speak to the children of Israel, that they bring me an offering. From everyone who gives it **willingly with his heart** you shall take My offering". Already Yahweh is separating Himself from the surrounding nations. Back in Egypt they saw firsthand how the Egyptians would be treated if Pharaoh (their gods' representative on earth) wanted something built. There would be forced labor involved, no questions asked, and Israel likely would have been a big part of that labor. Yahweh is telling them here that He will not force anything on them. It will only take place with a willing heart. This apparently had a profound effect on Israel, because in Chapter 36:5–7 they were offering so much that "the people were restrained from bringing, for the material they had was sufficient for all the work to be done—indeed too much."

Then we learn the purpose for this project in verse 8, "And let them make Me a sanctuary, that I may dwell among them." He will come and live with them. What an offer! No other nation had their gods actually living among them. It was not possible because they did not exist. Yahweh's very name means the self-existent one and He was coming to dwell among His people. This was a promise for both Israel at that time and also for the eternal future. How it would happen eternally was about to be laid out in the very design of the tabernacle He was building to dwell in.

When an architect is going to design a house, he or she generally starts with thinking about the interior—what is going to be housed inside of it. The architect needs an idea of the functional aspects. Where will the bathrooms and kitchen be? What kind of furniture is desired? What will the flow of traffic look like? Form follows function. During the construction phase, it is reversed and the framework, exterior, walls, and roof are done first, then the interior can be worked on. Yahweh used the same idea. Exodus 25–30 is the design phase and it is all about the function. He starts on the inside and works His way out. Exodus 36–38 is the construction phase, and it starts from making the parts for the exterior structure and then moves inwards.

When we think about it, isn't this how our lives are? Yahweh designed us from the inside, but throughout life, we work first from an understanding of our physical outward parts, and gradually as we mature, learn about our inner spiritual functions that are the far more important ones. We'll be focusing on Yahweh's design phase here.

THE ARK

> And they shall make an ark of acacia wood; two and a half cubits shall be its length, a cubit and a half its width, and a cubit and a half its height. And you shall overlay it with pure gold, inside and out you shall overlay it, and shall make on it a molding of gold all around. You shall cast four rings of gold for it, and put them in its four corners; two rings shall be on one side, and two rings on the other side. And you shall make poles of acacia wood, and overlay

them with gold. You shall put the poles into the rings on the sides of the ark, that the ark may be carried by them. The poles shall be in the rings of the ark; they shall not be taken from it. And you shall put into the ark the Testimony which I will give you (Exodus 25:10–16).

Yahweh starts His design then with the very interior, because it is the most important part of its function, the heart of the tabernacle, which is the ark of the covenant. If we are going to start thinking of this tabernacle as a body, then the heart seems like an obvious place to start, as it is also at the center of our bodies and has arguably their most important function.

There is language indicating that the ark is a heart throughout this description. There are four corners with four rings with two poles for carrying it. The poles will have two ends going into the rings and two ends coming out. A heart has four sections with two veins coming in and two arteries coming out. The heart's veins and arteries function is carrying blood. What are the ark and its poles carrying? The Ten Commandments (literally, ten words). Leviticus 17:11 says, "For the life of the flesh *is* in the blood." So, the Ten Commandments are the lifeblood! They give life to this body that we are describing.

> But this *is* the covenant that I will make with the house of Israel after those days, says Yahweh: I will put My law in their minds, and write it on their hearts; and I will be their God, and they shall be My people (Jeremiah 31:33).

I'm going to take an aside here about the law because I believe it is important, but it will also relate to the body here and later. The ten words were written by the finger of God (Exodus 31:18). The whole of the law was not. Exodus 34:28 tells us only the Ten Commandments were written on the tablets of stone. This then begs two questions: Who wrote the rest of the law and where was it kept? Deuteronomy 31:24–31 gives us both answers:

Part 2: The Body

> So it was, when **Moses had completed** writing the words of this law in a book, when they were finished, that Moses commanded the Levites, who bore the ark of the covenant of Yahweh, saying: "Take this Book of the Law, and put it **beside the ark** of the covenant of Yahweh your God, that it may be there as **a witness against you;** for I know your rebellion and your stiff neck."

Moses wrote it. And that part of the law was never meant to be written inside of the heart. It was put outside of the ark as a *witness against them* because of their rebellion and stiff necks. We see the same language used by Paul in regard to the law being "wiped out" in Colossians 2:13–14:

> And you, being dead in your trespasses and the uncircumcision of your flesh, He has made alive together with Him, having forgiven you all trespasses, having wiped out the handwriting of requirements that was **against us**, which was contrary to us. And He has taken it out of the way, having nailed it to the cross.

These are the requirements on the side of the ark. The Ten Commandments were written inside of the heart/ark and *were not taken out of the way*. This is a very important thing that is missed by both Christians who believe that the Sabbath and holy days do not need to be kept, and by Christians who believe the whole body of the law remains untouched. Satan attacks both sides of every issue, so discernment needs to be at the forefront of our studies and prayers.

To be clear, I am not saying that this external law has no relevance anymore, because Yahweh does not change, and there is much evidence that even after Jesus/Yeshua's death, His disciples continued to keep it. There is still tremendous benefit from both studying and keeping these laws where possible. But it certainly has no more penalty attached to it, which is a huge change.

Paul says in Romans 5:13, "For until the law sin was in the world, but sin is not imputed when there is no law." If this was the case before the law was in the world, it is also the case after it has been removed. There is still sin, it is just not imputed (charged to our account). The law has gone from being a curse because it is impossible to keep perfectly to being a blessing when keeping it with a heart that does so out of wanting to know Christ better.

Back to the ark…

The ark is covered with gold, as are many other parts of the tabernacle described later. Gold has always been given its value from the fact that it does not corrode. This speaks to the incorruptibility of the heart after the law has been written on it. Even the wood that the ark is built from speaks to this incorruptibility. Acacia (shittim) wood is drought and fire resistant while living, and as a harvested wood it is very strong and both rot and insect resistant.

It is God's law that gives these characteristics to the heart. We may not think of fire or insect resistance as heart characteristics, but think of Isaiah 43:1–2, "Fear not for I have redeemed you; I have called you by your name; You are Mine…When you walk through the fire, you shall not be burned, nor shall the flame scorch you," and look back at the plague of flies upon the Egyptians, and how no flies came into the land of Goshen, for Yahweh set them apart to make a distinction.

No, Israel was not yet incorruptible, but Yahweh was showing them what was to come, and this is where it would all start, with the creation of a heart made pure and incorruptible through the blood of the law, the Ten Commandments, flowing through it.

THE MERCY SEAT

> You shall make a mercy seat of pure gold; two and a half cubits shall be its length and a cubit and a half its width. And you shall make two cherubim of gold; of hammered work you shall make them at the two ends of the mercy seat. Make one cherub at one

end, and the other cherub at the other end; you shall make the cherubim at the two ends of it of one piece with the mercy seat. And the cherubim shall stretch out their wings above, covering the mercy seat with their wings, and they shall face one another; the faces of the cherubim shall be toward the mercy seat. You shall put the mercy seat on top of the ark, and in the ark you shall put the Testimony that I will give you. And there I will meet with you, and I will speak with you from above the mercy seat, from between the two cherubim which are on the ark of the Testimony, about everything which I will give you in commandment to the children of Israel (Exodus 25:17–22).

Mercy seat is a pretty bad, or at least very non-literal translation. The Hebrew word for Mercy Seat is *Kapporeth* (Strong's 3727), which comes from the same root as Atonement, meaning to cover. Basically, in this context it just means a lid. Pretty boring. But we're going to see something very exciting about this lid. Obviously, its design is anything but boring with two large angelic beings with outstretched wings surrounding the whole thing. Most importantly, this is going to be where Yahweh will meet with and speak with Israel. When He finally makes His appearance there in chapter 40, He shows up as a cloud, the same pillar of cloud by day and of fire by night that has been leading them in the wilderness thus far.

Think about this in terms of a human body. Surrounding the heart we have two long wing-shaped objects called lungs that are in charge of our breath. Our breath is moist air, just the same as a cloud is. On a cold day, you can even see this breath when you breathe out as a cloud-like vapor.

Our breath has multiple functions. It not only supplies oxygen to our blood in critical relationship with the heart, but is also responsible for our voices, our speech. It is not surprising that this "lid" to the ark has a critical relationship with it and is also the place where Yahweh will speak with Israel. What will He speak about? "About everything which I will give you in commandment to the children of Israel." Or, as Jesus/Yeshua said in Luke 6:45, "Out of the overflow of the heart the mouth speaks." He will speak about those things which are written in the heart, the blood, the commandments. This speech will be teaching and commenting on the application of those laws. You can think of them as "overflow" of the heart, and as stated in the aside previously, they would be written down by Moses and placed outside of the ark, as if overflowing it.

In Hebrew the word for breath is *ruach* (Strong's H7307). It is the same word that is used for the wind and the spirit. Its Greek counterpart is pneuma, the word used when talking of the Holy (set apart) Spirit. Putting this all together we see this "mercy seat" as a picture of the residence of the Holy Spirit. It is no wonder then that Yahweh *spoke* all of creation into existence; *breathed* the breath of life into Adam; Yeshua *spoke* words of healing in the new covenant as acts of mini re-creation; and demons were cast out through the *spoken* command of the disciples, causing them to proclaim "even the demons are subject to us in Your name!"

If you look throughout the Bible, especially the New Testament, you will see that the acts of the Holy Spirit are always closely linked to speech in some way. During the outpouring of the Holy Spirit at the Pentecost in Acts 2, it was "tongues of fire" that landed on men and the gift of speaking in tongues was granted. Look at the list of gifts Paul talks of in 1 Corinthians 12: 8–11 and see how many of these gifts rely on speech and words.

> For to one is given the **word** of wisdom through the Spirit, to another the **word** of knowledge through the same Spirit, to another faith by the same Spirit, to another gifts of healings [always performed by the **spoken word**] by the same Spirit, to another the working of miracles [again performed through **speech**], to another prophecy [defined as the **speaking** of the **words** of Yahweh], to another discerning of spirits, to another different kinds of **tongues**, to another the interpretation of **tongues**. But one and the same Spirit works all these things, distributing to each one individually as He wills.

Part 2: The Body

It should also be no wonder then that He sat here in the lungs of the tabernacle *speaking* to Israel about the commandments placed in the heart of the body.

TABLE OF THE SHOWBREAD

> You shall also make a table of acacia wood; two cubits shall be its length, a cubit its width, and a cubit and a half its height. And you shall overlay it with pure gold, and make a molding of gold all around. You shall make for it a frame of a handbreadth all around, and you shall make a gold molding for the frame all around. And you shall make for it four rings of gold, and put the rings on the four corners that are at its four legs. The rings shall be close to the frame, as holders for the poles to bear the table. And you shall make the poles of acacia wood, and overlay them with gold, that the table may be carried with them. You shall make its dishes, its pans, its pitchers, and its bowls for pouring. You shall make them of pure gold. And you shall set the showbread on the table before Me always (Exodus 25:23–30).

There are features both here and in other fixtures of the tabernacle that are of the same design as the ark, with rings and poles for carrying, made of the same wood and overlaid with gold. They speak to the same traits of incorruptibility and of having blood carried to them. All parts of our body require blood, after all.

To really understand what is going on here, we need to get into the Hebrew language and see what some of these things are referring to. The best place to start is with the showbread. When I hear the term *showbread*, I personally get a little confused. Did Yahweh just put it there for show? Highly doubtful. In the Hebrew it is two words: *Lechem* (Strong's 3899) meaning bread, and *Paneh* (Strong's 6440) meaning "Face." Face bread! Face, as in English, can refer to the face of a man, one's countenance, one's presence, the face of the earth, or of the forward-facing part of any object. In all forms it refers back to its basic meaning of "face." It is used extensively in

Exodus 33, which takes place after the instructions for the building of the tabernacle have been given, but before it is actually built.

> So the LORD spoke to Moses **face** to **face**, as a man speaks to his friend. And he would return to the camp, but his servant Joshua the son of Nun, a young man, did not depart from the tabernacle. Then Moses said to the LORD, "See, You say to me, 'Bring up this people.' But You have not let me know whom You will send with me. Yet You have said, 'I know you by name, and you have also found grace in My sight.' Now therefore, I pray, if I have found grace in Your sight, show me now Your way, that I may know You and that I may find grace in Your sight. And consider that this nation is Your people." And He said, "My **Presence [Face]** will go with you, and I will give you rest." Then he said to Him, "If Your **Presence [Face]** does not go with us, do not bring us up from here. For how then will it be known that Your people and I have found grace in Your sight, except You go with us? So we shall be separate, Your people and I, from all the people who are upon the **face** of the earth." So the LORD said to Moses, "I will also do this thing that you have spoken; for you have found grace in My sight, and I know you by name." And he said, "Please, show me Your glory." Then He said, "I will make all My goodness pass before you, and I will proclaim the name of the LORD before you. I will be gracious to whom I will be gracious, and I will have compassion on whom I will have compassion." But He said, "You cannot see My **face**; for no man shall see Me, and live." And the LORD said, "Here is a place by Me, and you shall stand on the rock. So it shall be, while My glory passes by, that I will put you in the cleft of the rock, and will cover you with My hand while I pass by. Then I will take away My hand, and you shall see My back; but My **face** shall not be seen" (Exodus 33:11–23).

After Moses saw Yahweh's glory, in Exodus 34:29–34, it is Moses' own face that shines, so that he has to cover it with a veil while appearing to Israel. Moses then again shows up in the gospels during the transfiguration while the face of Yeshua is shining like the sun.

Part 2: The Body

Remember these shining faces when we get to the next section, as they will be explained more. But for now, there are a few more interesting details to explore.

The table itself has dimensions that are roughly the same ratio as the human head and neck. Perhaps this table is the head on which the face sits.

There are some other items on this table/head, too: the dishes, pans, pitchers, and bowls. First, I need to point out that I am certainly not attempting to analyze every point of information listed in these chapters of Exodus here. It is certainly all important, but not all of it may be relevant to the tabernacle being a body. My focus is on the big picture design considerations, so I am only using the information given that speaks to that. So, when thinking of these utensils on the table, at the risk of looking like I'm stretching things to make a point, I'll just throw out the information I found and some possibilities it brings up, and you can make your own conclusions.

When we look at the Hebrew words for these utensils, we do find some interesting things. At this point I was expecting other facial features like a nose, ears, mouth, eyes, etc., but that is not what showed up. The word for dishes just means a hollowed-out container. Nothing too exciting to me. Pans is *kaph* (Strong's H3709) meaning the palm of the hand or other things so shaped, like the sole of the foot or a spoon. So, there are a couple of body parts there.

Next is pitchers, in Hebrew *qasaw*, translating to a cup, from the root meaning a cover. Again, not exciting. And finally, bowls, which is *menaqqiyth* (Strong's H4518) meaning "Bowl: From the shape of a bowl that holds liquids like a breast that holds milk," (*Ancient Hebrew Lexicon*) from the root word meaning breast. Now, that is interesting!

None of these have to do with what we would see on a face, yet if we consider one of the other meanings that face has, we see all of them relating to the front-facing side of the body. The palm of the

The Temple is a Body

hand is considered its front (as opposed to the "back" of the hand), and the breasts are certainly on the front.

Functionally, these utensils are all for holding things. Think of the palm of the hand holding anything and the breasts holding the milk. Apparently, they are for things other than just the showbread, which is the only actual food-related item on the table. A plate or pan would be the only thing needed for the bread, but we have quite a variety of other things here, too, as if the table is set for a whole meal.

I don't have an answer and so can only speculate on why that would be, but it is interesting, nonetheless. Perhaps we are seeing bowls of olive oil for dipping the bread and cups for wine, foreshadowing the Passover meal Christ shared with the disciples, the eating of His body and drinking of His blood. Maybe we're looking at containers for the milk and others for some honey, bringing us into the promised land. Most certainly, this bread refers to the body of Yeshua on some level.

One more thought before we move on. Proverbs 27:19, "As in water face reflects face, so a man's heart reflects the man." All parts of our bodies are interconnected. It is not a coincidence to use the analogy of the face to talk about the heart.

THE LAMPSTAND

> You shall also make a lampstand of pure gold; the lampstand shall be of hammered work. Its shaft, its branches, its bowls, its *ornamental* knobs, and flowers shall be *of one piece*. And six branches shall come out of its sides: three branches of the lampstand out of one side, and three branches of the lampstand out of the other side. Three bowls *shall be* made like almond *blossoms* on one branch, *with* an *ornamental* knob and a flower, and three bowls made like almond *blossoms* on the other branch, *with* an *ornamental* knob and a flower—and so for the six branches that come out of the lampstand. On the lampstand itself four bowls *shall be* made like almond *blossoms, each with* its *ornamental* knob and flower. And *there*

shall be a knob under the *first* two branches of the same, a knob under the *second* two branches of the same, and a knob under the *third* two branches of the same, according to the six branches that extend from the lampstand. Their knobs and their branches *shall be of one piece;* all of it *shall be* one hammered piece of pure gold. You shall make seven lamps for it, and they shall arrange its lamps so that they give light in front of it. And its wick-trimmers and their trays *shall be* of pure gold. It shall be made of a talent of pure gold, with all these utensils. And see to it that you make *them* according to the pattern which was shown you on the mountain. (Exodus 25:31–40).

This is often called the menorah, which is its name in Hebrew meaning light, lampstand, or candlestick. Again, I'll focus on the design considerations that speak to its function as part of the body. I mentioned in the last section to remember the shining faces of Moses, Yeshua, and Yahweh. They are shining for a reason. They have been lit up by something. More information is given on the placement of the lampstand and the table for the showbread in chapter 26:35. "You shall set the table outside the veil, and the lampstand across from the table on the side of the tabernacle toward the south; and you shall put the table on the north side."

The lampstand is placed directly across from the table for the showbread, in order to shine its light on it, to light up the face. So what body part is the lampstand? Luke 11:34 tells us, "The lamp of the body is the eye. Therefore, when your eye is good, your whole body also is full of light. But when your eye is bad, your body also is full of darkness." It is the eye, and it lights up the face, as well as the whole body.

In Exodus 25:33, we see the shape of the individual lamps, "made like almond *blossoms*." But the word *blossoms* is added to the translation. It's not actually there, which is why it is italicized in many translations. All of the italicized words are added by the translators of the NKJV in the above quote for the sake of clarity, but sometimes they simply add words out of assumption. Consistently throughout, what the original Hebrew says is simply almonds.

What shape is an almond? Whether still in the shell or the nut itself, it is shaped exactly like the eye and has often been used as a poetic description of the eye for centuries. I had never seen a photo of the almond fruit before, so looked it up and was fascinated to see that when it ripens, it splits open on one side to reveal the shell of the nut, and it looks very much like eyelids surrounding the eye.

The description also talks about "knobs" and "flowers." The knobs are the Hebrew *kaphtor* (Strong's H3730) which is an architectural term. Strong's says of it, "Probably from an unused root meaning to encircle; a chaplet; but used only in an architectonic sense, that is, the capital of a column, or a wreath like button or disk on the candelabrum: - knop, (upper) lintel." I'm thinking that these knobs encircling the almond bowls are modeled after the eyelids of the almond fruit and used on the lampstand as a capital atop the branches of the stand.

The word for flowers is *perach* (Strong's H6525) meaning a bud, from the root word meaning "bursting out." I love the imagery of "bursting out" for how a flower bursts out in a showy display just like light bursts out from the sun, or from Yahweh's face.

The orientation of the lamps is to be "so that they give light in front of it." Sounds like the placement of our eyes to me. Yahweh's designs are used over and over in nature, almost as if He wants us to see something in them. We saw earlier how the placement of the lampstand was in the south. The sun is another great light that is placed in the south, at least for those in the northern hemisphere, which includes the majority of the earth's population, and certainly all of Israel.

> The heavens declare the glory of God; and the firmament shows His handiwork. Day unto day utters speech, and night unto night reveals knowledge. There is no speech nor language where their voice is not heard. Their line has gone out through all the earth,

and their words to the end of the world. In them He has set a tabernacle for the sun, which is like a bridegroom coming out of his chamber, and rejoices like a strong man to run its race (Psalm 19:1–5).

It seems that our whole earth, complete with the sun, moon, and stars set in the firmament, may be a large-scale picture of the same thing. Throughout time, people have seen a face in the moon, and the fact that it reflects the light of the sun really brings the picture together. The moon is the bread and the face. The sun is the lamp and the eyes. Certainly, there is a heavenly reality that all of this is picturing, and Yahweh is telling us about it with these visual images made with words.

And it keeps coming back to the heart as well. If we just keep reading the above passage, in verse 8 it says, "The precepts of Yahweh are right, rejoicing the heart. The commands of Yahweh are pure, giving light to the eyes." These of course are the commandments found in the heart of the ark, and they are what gives the light to the eyes, lighting up the lampstand so that it can light up the face.

THE CURTAINS

Moreover you shall make the tabernacle with ten curtains of fine woven linen and blue, purple, and scarlet thread; with artistic designs of cherubim you shall weave them. The length of each curtain shall be twenty-eight cubits, and the width of each curtain four cubits. And every one of the curtains shall have the same measurements. Five curtains shall be coupled to one another, and the other five curtains shall be coupled to one another. And you shall make loops of blue yarn on the edge of the curtain on the selvedge of one set, and likewise you shall do on the outer edge of the other curtain of the second set. Fifty loops you shall make in the one curtain, and fifty loops you shall make on the edge of the curtain that is on the end of the second set, that the loops may be clasped to one another. And you shall make fifty clasps of gold,

The Temple is a Body

and couple the curtains together with the clasps, so that it may be one tabernacle (Exodus 26:1–6).

The curtains will be the covering for the sides of the tabernacle. They are acting as the skin, if you will, and they are covered in blue, red and purple, with designs of cherubim. Our own skin, if you look closely, especially in certain areas, is also covered in similar colors. We can see our blood vessels under the skin in a network of blue (no oxygen), red (full of oxygen), and purple (the color much of it becomes when viewed through the skin).

Why cherubim? We saw them used before in the lungs, so is there a common thread? One of the main purposes of the blood is to carry oxygen to the body, and that oxygen originated in the lungs. Cherubim are creatures of the air, being winged, so it seems we are looking at their symbolic purpose here. The cherubim of the lungs were representing the breath of the Holy Spirit, so it appears that this spirit will be spread throughout the body.

When we talked about the heart, we mentioned Leviticus 16 where it said, "The life of the flesh is in the blood." Now we are adding another dimension to it. If the Ten Commandments are the blood, then the cherubim are the oxygen that gives life to the blood. The life is *in* the blood. The cherubim are in the lungs and in the veins.

Oxygen is really a life-giving force to our bodies. We previously correlated the cherubim to the Holy Spirit; now we can get more specific and call the oxygen the Holy Spirit that transports life through our blood. In Genesis 2, we see that Adam had no life until Yahweh breathed life into him, "And Yahweh God formed man of the dust of the ground, and breathed into his nostrils the breath of life; and man became a living being."

Here is a succinct summary of the process of oxygen in our bodies, taken from *oxygen-review.com*[6]:

---

[6] As of publication, this article and website has been removed from the internet

Part 2: The Body

In the human body, oxygen uptake is carried out by the following processes:

Oxygen diffuses through membranes and into red blood cells after inhalation into the lungs. The heme group (that consists of an iron) of hemoglobin binds oxygen when it is present, changing haemoglobin's color from bluish red to bright red.

A liter of blood can dissolve 200 cc of oxygen gas, which is much more than water can dissolve.

After being carried in blood to a body tissue in need of oxygen, O2 is handed-off to an enzyme (monooxygenase) that also has an active site with an atom of iron.

The enzyme uses oxygen to catalyze many oxidation reactions in the body (metabolism). Carbon dioxide, a waste product, is released from the cell and into the blood, where it combines with bicarbonate and hemoglobin for transport to the lungs. Blood circulates back to the lungs and the process repeats.

This exactly describes the process I just covered, down to the colors of the embroidery in the curtains (bluish-red sounds like purple to me!).

At some point in this study, it seems appropriate to ask the question, "If the tabernacle is a body, whose body is it?" We've seen a few clues so far, but no direct answer. We've seen that whoever it is has the commandments written in their heart, the holy spirit in their lungs, and a face illuminated by the light in his or her eyes, which narrows it down to exclude the non-converted or pagan populations, but we would expect as much.

Up until here, it might be logical to say that it is pointing toward Yeshua/Jesus. Then we also saw the possibility, in the utensils on the table, of hands and breasts being mentioned. Could this be a female, or was the reading of breasts a little far-fetched? We'll have to gather some more information.

Another thing to note with the curtains is that they are coupled together in two groups of five (verses 3 and 5). Five on one side and five on the other. If we look at our bodies, we have five fingers and five toes on one side and five of each on the other. We are symmetrical creatures, and it appears that the tabernacle is too.

Verse 6 says, "and couple the curtains together with the clasps." The word *together* here in the NKJV is very easy to overlook, which I initially did. But then I saw the Literal Version from the Interlinear Bible[7], "And you shall join the curtains, each to her sister, by the hooks." That's quite a discrepancy. So, I looked up the Hebrew words. The translation "together" is actually a combination of three Hebrew words. First, *ishshaw* (Strong's H802), meaning a woman or wife. Second, *el* (Strong's H413) is an article meaning toward or to. And third, *achoth* (Strong's H269), meaning sister. Literally we then have "woman toward sister." It didn't have to be worded that way, but Yahweh chose those words. These curtains of the tabernacle are certainly female, stronger evidence pointing toward a female body here.

There's one more connection I'd like to make. Psalm 122 is about David going up to Jerusalem to visit the house of God (the tabernacle) and praying for its peace. It shares some pertinent information.

> I was glad when they said to me, "Let us go into the house of Yahweh." Our feet have been standing within your gates, O Jerusalem! Jerusalem is built as a city that is compact together, where the tribes go up, the tribes of the LORD, to the Testimony of Israel, to give thanks to the name of the LORD. For thrones are set there for judgment, the thrones of the house of David. Pray for the peace of Jerusalem: "May they prosper who love you. Peace be within your walls, prosperity within your

---

[7] Green, Jay P. *The Interlinear Bible Hebrew-Greek-English*. Sovereign Grace Publishers, 1986.

palaces." For the sake of my brethren and companions, I will now say, "Peace be within you." Because of the house of the LORD our God I will seek your good (Psalm 122).

The word *compact* in verse 3 is *chabar* (Strong's H2266), meaning "To bind by coupling together" (*Ancient Hebrew Lexicon*) and is the same word in Exodus 26:3 and 6 where the curtains are coupled together. Why would Jerusalem be coupled together? The context in verse 4 is that Jerusalem is coupled, or joined to the tribes, the 12 tribes of Israel, because that is where they go up to the testimony (the law that is in and beside the ark). Why is this pertinent? Because Jerusalem is also many times referred to as a woman. Could we be looking at Jerusalem for our identity?

A Covering of Goat's Hair

You shall also make curtains of goats' hair, to be a tent over the tabernacle. You shall make eleven curtains. The length of each curtain shall be thirty cubits, and the width of each curtain four cubits; and the eleven curtains shall all have the same measurements. And you shall couple five curtains by themselves and six curtains by themselves, and you shall double over the sixth curtain at the forefront of the tent. You shall make fifty loops on the edge of the curtain that is outermost in one set, and fifty loops on the edge of the curtain of the second set. And you shall make fifty bronze clasps, put the clasps into the loops, and couple the tent together, that it may be one. The remnant that remains of the curtains of the tent, the half curtain that remains, shall hang over the back of the tabernacle. And a cubit on one side and a cubit on the other side, of what remains of the length of the curtains of the tent, shall hang over the sides of the tabernacle, on this side and on that side, to cover it (Exodus 26:7–13).

The first set of curtains were described as enclosing or surrounding the tabernacle; whereas this set is said to be "a tent *over* the tabernacle." These are the next section just above the first ten linen curtains and are made of goat hair. There are eleven of them so that they can be doubled up "at the forefront of the tent" and still only have ten sections exposed (ten being the number we get when coupling five fingers or toes on both sides). There is also a section on the opposite end that will "hang over the back of the tabernacle." Again, we have words relating this to the body. "Forefront" is a combination of three Hebrew words (Strong's H413, H4136, and H6440) meaning *toward, front,* and *face* (the same word for face we saw with the showbread); it is *toward the front of the face.* The word for "back" in Hebrew is *achor* (Strong's H268), meaning, "the part of the body that is behind." Seeing as these curtains are made up of goat's hair, I am getting a picture of a woman's hair here. Only women had long hair in the Bible, as it was not proper for men to have such, and it seems that this hair is long. It is doubled over in front of the face, as long hair is usually brushed or pinned back over itself to keep it out of the eyes. And it hangs down over the back and sides just like long hair.

Song of Solomon 4:1 and 6:5 use goat's hair as an analogy for the beautiful Shulamite's hair, "Your hair *is* like a flock of goats, Going down from Mount Gilead." Although this analogy is far from what our modern culture would use to suggest beauty, it is evident that Solomon saw it as a perfect picture of long, flowing hair. "Going down," according to Strong's is probably more accurately stated as capering, as goats do when playing. I like that picture better personally, as I can visualize the way hair bounces and flies around when in motion. And Mount Gilead, of course, pictures his lovely Shulamite's head.

RAM SKINS AND TACHASH SKINS

> You shall also make a covering of ram skins dyed red for the tent, and a covering of badger skins above that (Exodus 26:14).

Part 2: The Body

Two parts, but very short and sweet. We're not given much information, so we only have a few descriptive words to go on. First, ram skins dyed red.

The only reason I can think of for dying something red is to symbolize blood. It is also a covering. Relating these few clues to the body, they seem to point to the muscle, the flesh. Muscle is where the majority of our blood is pumped, so that when the skin is removed, muscle appears bloody red. Muscles also cover the entire body.

The second section calls for "a covering of badger skins above that." It is highly unlikely that badger skins were used. The Hebrew word is *tachash* (Strong's H8476) but refers to an unknown animal. Some translations call it a dugong, which is a sea cow or manatee. This seems even more unlikely for a people many miles inland in a desert. Strong's says, "Probably of foreign derivation; a (clean) animal with fur, probably a species of *antelope.*" Antelope or other members of the deer family seem like the best option because they are both clean and available. I can't see Yahweh prescribing the use of an unclean animal for holy purposes. In researching the different species of deer/antelope in the region of the exodus I found that there is a species of deer that is called the "red deer," named for the reddish-brown color of its hide, as opposed to the grayish brown found in most deer. It is still found throughout much of Europe and was historically found in the area of the exodus although it is now extinct in that region. I can't say for sure this was the animal referred to by tachash, but it seems likely because of how intricately linked it is to the red-stained ram skins: These two parts are pointing to a single function, and it seems obvious that the theme of the color red has to do with blood. Linking that with the idea of a covering, we see the covering of Yeshua's blood on our own selves. On a physical level, we could say that these two coverings are referring to multiple layers of muscle—ram skins to internal muscles and tachash to the superficial muscles, or something like that. However, regardless of

The Temple is a Body

their description of the human body, we need to focus on the covering of blood that forgives our sins. This is then one of the most critical details in this body!

THE BOARDS

> And for the tabernacle you shall make the boards of acacia wood, standing upright. Ten cubits shall be the length of a board, and a cubit and a half shall be the width of each board. Two tenons shall be in each board for binding one to another. Thus you shall make for all the boards of the tabernacle. And you shall make the boards for the tabernacle, twenty boards for the south side. You shall make forty sockets of silver under the twenty boards: two sockets under each of the boards for its two tenons. And for the second side of the tabernacle, the north side, there shall be twenty boards and their forty sockets of silver: two sockets under each of the boards. For the far side of the tabernacle, westward, you shall make six boards. And you shall also make two boards for the two back corners of the tabernacle. They shall be coupled together at the bottom and they shall be coupled together at the top by one ring. Thus it shall be for both of them. They shall be for the two corners. So there shall be eight boards with their sockets of silver—sixteen sockets—two sockets under each of the boards (Exodus 26:15–25).

If we are already looking at this structure as a body, it is a fairly easy thing to see these wooden uprights as ribs. But there are a couple of things that may not be obvious and will make it even more apparent. First is their number—twenty on each side. We do not have twenty ribs on each side. But we can look closer at what is said. Verse 17 said, "Two tenons *shall be* in each board for binding one to another." The term for tenon (Strong's 3027—yad) literally means an open hand, and the phrase "binding one to another" is the same exact one we saw with the curtains that were coupled together; literally "woman toward sister," or "each connected to her sister," as the interlinear translation has it. So not only is this again pointing to the female nature, but it also seems to point to these boards being paired up.

There are different ways to imagine how this pairing can be accomplished in the design. The actual tabernacle's construction is far from a settled matter; there just is not enough detail given in the Scriptures to make any dogmatic decisions. Yet there is a basic picture most people have of how it looked, being a rather rectangular box.

There are, however, alternatives, and I would like to present one of them because it has helped me greatly to free my mind from the rectangular box. I still maintain that the important basis to my study is to focus on the *words* that are given in Exodus, not the visual picture. But there is some importance in knowing that the design we are coming up with could actually be physically possible within the given instructions, especially given a radical rethinking of the standard ideas.

There is a man by the name of Andrew Hoy, who has done extensive work with a re-envisioning of the tabernacle structure based on the starting premise that the curtains could be coupled along the short sides instead of the long ones. What that does is to make the outer edge of the tabernacle much, much larger, which of necessity also changes the structure of everything else. Since exactly how the different parts are connected together is not given sufficiently in Scripture, but only vaguely, there is no reason his method cannot be considered.

In his design, the tabernacle becomes a giant, round, yurt-like structure. He is also a Hebrew scholar and has found much of the language that gives rise to a rectangular shape has been mistranslated. I have studied his work and find his ideas to be very plausible even if I do not agree with all of his conclusions. You can look at his work at his website *Project314.org*. The 314 comes from the number Pi (3.14159...), which is arrived at from the dimensions of the courtyard when those curtains are coupled the long way.

The Temple is a Body

I can agree with his idea for coupling the curtains, however, I see no need to make the shape perfectly round. The descriptions in Exodus talk about distinct "sides" and "back corners," language that is hard to use when talking about a perfect circle. But if you look at the oblong shape of the rib cage, there are certainly distinct sides as well as a differentiation in what would be the front and the back (or top and bottom), yet it still holds a mostly roundish shape.

In Hoy's design, he also notes the coupling of the boards, each to her sister, but takes it further and "couples" together four boards for each upright member, making only five uprights on each side. His engineering seems to work, but it does not take into account the possibility that the boards represent the human rib cage with ten ribs on each side.

If we couple each board to her sister, and only to her sister (not her three sisters), then we will have the ten true ribs per side our rib cages require. They will be coupled so that the lower part is vertical, and the upper part will be angled toward the center of the structure like a pitched roof, mimicking the arched shape of our ribs.

In addition to the forty boards for the rib cage, there are eight more boards mentioned—six for the west side and two more for the corners in the west side. The word for west (*yam*, Strong's H3220) actually means "the sea." But it can also be used to mean "toward the sea" meaning to the west, as the Mediterranean Sea was to the west of the Israelites.

Looking to the west, then, we find the very back side of the tabernacle, or as I picture the orientation, the side of the torso to which the head would attach. On this end of the rib cage there are two main additions, the collar bones and the shoulders. I believe this is what we are seeing in this western end. These six boards are uprights representing the shoulders—three each, perhaps showing the triangle of the scapula. Then there are two more boards for the "corners." I see these representing the clavicles. They are "coupled together at the top and…at the bottom by one ring."

Part 2: The Body

If we were to look at the ribcage and shoulders from above (minus the head), we would see a ring formed by the bones of the upper ribs, shoulder blades and clavicle forming a circular opening. How these eight boards and ring actually function in the tabernacle structure is unclear to me because the description in Exodus is vague. I've sketched out a number of ideas, all of which could work, but I cannot be certain to state, "This is it!" Again, we are looking at meaning, not blueprints.

THE BARS

> And you shall make bars of acacia wood: five for the boards on one side of the tabernacle, five bars for the boards on the other side of the tabernacle, and five bars for the boards of the side of the tabernacle, for the far side westward. The middle bar shall pass through the midst of the boards from end to end. You shall overlay the boards with gold, make their rings of gold as holders for the bars, and overlay the bars with gold. And you shall raise up the tabernacle according to its pattern which you were shown on the mountain (Exodus 26:26–30).

These bars are the beams at the peak of the tabernacle that the boards connect to. Their job is to act as an attachment point to the boards to give strength to the structure. In our rib cages, this job is done by the sternum. All twenty of our ribs connect to it. The top part of the sternum is the manubrium, a roughly five-sided shape to which the clavicles connect. So there would be five bars connected end to end on one side of the sternum, the same on the other side, and five on the western manubrium end which would support the eight boards of the western wings. There is also one middle bar going from end to end. This would be the very peak of the tabernacle and another structural piece giving rigidity to the fifteen bars that surround it.

At some point I may add illustrations for how this looks (my interpretation of it), but for now I really want to stress these things as ideas, not an actual blueprint. Or maybe it would be better said that I am not creating the blueprint because it has already been made in the human body.

In verse 30, Yahweh told Moses to build these things "according to its pattern which you were shown on the mountain." We don't know exactly what He showed Moses, but it was not just the words written down in Exodus. The word *show* or *shown* is *rah* (Strong's H7200), meaning "To see or perceive something or someone. Also to see visions," (Ancient Hebrew Lexicon). It seems that Moses was shown a vision. He literally saw what it was to look like, then was also given the words to write down. It is quite possible that Yahweh showed Moses a vision of a human torso! Moses was fasting for forty days, so another possibility is that while Yahweh was speaking, He told Moses to look down at his own very exposed ribs, telling him that this is what he is to build! Just a thought!

THE VEIL

> You shall make a veil woven of blue, purple, and scarlet thread, and fine woven linen. It shall be woven with an artistic design of cherubim. You shall hang it upon four pillars of acacia wood overlaid with gold. Their hooks shall be gold, upon four sockets of silver. And you shall hang the veil from the clasps. Then you shall bring the ark of the Testimony in there, behind the veil. The veil shall be a divider for you between the holy place and the Most Holy. You shall put the mercy seat upon the ark of the Testimony in the Most Holy. You shall set the table outside the veil, and the lampstand across from the table on the side of the tabernacle toward the south; and you shall put the table on the north side (Exodus 26:31–35).

Here we are back to the region of the heart again. This veil has the same blue, purple, and scarlet thread and artistic designs of cherubim as the curtains. The proximity of the veil to the heart only reinforces what I already stated about the cherubim representing the oxygen in our blood, and the function of the Holy Spirit. There are four pillars as well, again speaking to the four chambers of the heart.

There is, of course, an analogous covering around our own hearts. The *pericardium* is a protective layer surrounding the heart. According to *healthline.com*[8], it has the following functions:

- It keeps your heart fixed in place within your chest cavity.

- It prevents your heart from stretching too much and overfilling with blood.

- It lubricates your heart to prevent friction with the tissues around it as it beats.

- It protects your heart from any infections that might spread from nearby organs like the lungs.

We can draw analogies to the purpose of the veil.

- It will guard the ark with a barrier, keeping it in its place. As Exodus stated, "a divider for you between the holy place and the Most Holy."

- It will guard against others placing items inside the heart that are not meant to be there (overfilling), or from stealing from inside of it. As Deuteronomy 4:2 states, "You shall not add to the word which I command you, nor take from it."

- Yahweh needs His privacy in there! Any outside interference (friction) would be unacceptable.

- It protects it from infection from nearby organs like the lungs. Could the lungs, symbolizing the Holy Spirit, infect the heart? If we are drawing spiritual analogies, we should realize that there are counterfeits for everything and the Holy Spirit is not an exception.

---

[8] Watson, S. (2018, March 28). *Pericardium*. Healthline. https://www.healthline.com/health/pericardium

The Temple is a Body

Discerning of spirits was one of the fruits of the spirit listed in 1 Corinthians 12, meaning that there are both good and bad spirits and we need to be careful which we breathe in. If we do accidentally breathe in a bad spirit, it is comforting to know we have this layer of protection.

The best way to discern spirits is to test them according to Yahweh's law. The pericardium is the layer of protection separating the good from the bad, discerning whether the breath that came in through the lungs matches those laws that are contained inside of the ark, keeping them from infection.

This is the part of the temple that was torn in two when Yeshua died. We have to ask ourselves why would we want this protective layer torn? We wouldn't ever want to let evil into the heart, would we? That is absolutely correct. Yahweh also does not want to let evil into the heart of His body.

But the people He has been raising up and nurturing to become one with His Son are inherently evil themselves! This is why the Father sent the Son to die to forgive and cleanse us. No longer would we be an unclean invader into the temple; we would be clean and welcome guests! And since we would be clean, there was no longer a purpose for that protective layer. It was torn in two and we had direct access to the heart of the Father, to His commandments, so that they could be written on our own hearts. This is the circumcision of the heart. The pericardium was the foreskin of the heart, torn in circumcision at Christ's death.

The word for veil is *paraketh* (Strong's 6531), meaning curtain or veil, in the sense of a dividing of space, but it comes from the root *perek* which means to break apart or fracture, as of flesh from a whip: cruelty, severity, or rigor. Yes, the veil breaks apart or separates the space in the tabernacle, but I can't help but think this word must have also been used with foreshadowing of the violent tearing, or fracturing, of the veil when Christ died.

Part 2: The Body

SCREEN DOOR

> You shall make a screen for the door of the tabernacle, woven of blue, purple, and scarlet thread, and fine woven linen, made by a weaver. And you shall make for the screen five pillars of acacia wood, and overlay them with gold; their hooks shall be gold, and you shall cast five sockets of bronze for them (Exodus 26:36–37).

The word for this screen is *masak* (Strong's H4539), meaning a covering, from the same root, *sak*, as the word sukkah, which is the word used for tabernacle when referencing the commanded Feast of Tabernacles. This masak is hiding the interior of the tabernacle from view from the outside. There is no other door mentioned in the construction. There would likely be an open section in the front (east end) of the tabernacle used for the entrance, with the screen placed inside, supported from five pillars blocking all view of the interior, specifically blocking the holy of holies, which if any outsider were to catch a glimpse of, they would immediately die. This type of entryway allows in air for ventilation, but not vision.

Our interior organs are split into two sections—the thorax and the abdomen. In the thorax, or upper section, inside the ribcage, we have the heart and lungs only, the organs needed for sending oxygen throughout the body. Below are all the other organs: liver, kidneys, stomach, bladder, and intestines. The dividing line is the diaphragm.

The diaphragm has two main functions. First, it is a barrier that completely separates the upper and lower organs. If anything were to pass from below into the chamber above, it would be catastrophic. As I am writing this, I know of one brother who is in the hospital with a perforated diaphragm and bowel. It is an extremely dangerous situation because, as you can imagine, material from the bowel can then enter the chamber of the heart and lungs. Think of the spiritual significance of this and you can start to understand the reason for the first function of the diaphragm.

Its second function is the muscle used for respiration, or breathing, expanding and contracting to bring in air to the lungs. This is the ventilation of the tabernacle.

The attachment point of this muscle is—get this—to the lower five ribs, our five pillars on which to hang the screen. Below this connection are all the organs that take care of expelling toxins and uncleanness from the body, and we'll start looking there, outside the tabernacle, next.

THE ALTAR OF BURNT OFFERING

> You shall make an altar of acacia wood, five cubits long and five cubits wide—the altar shall be square—and its height shall be three cubits. You shall make its horns on its four corners; its horns shall be of one piece with it. And you shall overlay it with bronze. Also you shall make its pans to receive its ashes, and its shovels and its basins and its forks and its firepans; you shall make all its utensils of bronze. You shall make a grate for it, a network of bronze; and on the network you shall make four bronze rings at its four corners. You shall put it under the rim of the altar beneath, that the network may be midway up the altar. And you shall make poles for the altar, poles of acacia wood, and overlay them with bronze. The poles shall be put in the rings, and the poles shall be on the two sides of the altar to bear it. You shall make it hollow with boards; as it was shown you on the mountain, so shall they make it (Exodus 27:1–8).

In English, the word *altar* can mean a table-like object used for wide-ranging religious ceremonies or rituals, but in Hebrew (and probably most of the ancient world) an altar (Strong's H4196—*mizbeach*) literally means a place of sacrifice. That is its sole function.

The Exodus instructions contain a lot of information about its construction, but we need only to understand its function to make sense of it within the context of the body.

Part 2: The Body

There is one design consideration I'd like to note, however. No longer are we seeing a gold overlay, but a bronze one. We are outside of the purity of the inner tabernacle. This area outside is concerned with making things clean, but that purpose necessitates contact with things that are *not* clean, so gold is not used.

Functionally, this is where all of the killing occurs. It is a bloody place, located at the very entrance to the tabernacle in the east. We can now squarely identify the body of the tabernacle as that of a woman because a woman's body also has a bloody location at its entrance. Before you think that can't be what is being pictured here, let's look at the function of each.

In Genesis 3:16, woman is given a curse because of her sin. "He said to the woman, I will greatly increase your sorrow and your conception; you shall bear sons in sorrow, and your desire shall be toward your husband; and he shall rule over you." This curse affected her conception and childbearing, of which her monthly period is an integral part.

It is my belief that before the curse, women were meant to conceive and give birth without becoming "unclean" for one week of every month (see Leviticus 15:19) or for forty or eighty days after childbirth (Leviticus 12). Have you ever thought of why Yahweh would call a woman unclean for something she has no control over and that is actually fulfilling His own command to be fruitful and multiply?

It is because of the Genesis curse for sin! It was not meant to be so originally, and one day will no longer be so again. Paul mentions this curse in his first letter to Timothy but adds that women will be "saved in childbearing if they continue in faith, love, and holiness, with self-control." Why? It is a type of sacrifice to cover for her sin, if she does so with humility. This is how it relates to the sacrificial altar. The blood at the altar performs exactly the same function. Animals are being sacrificed as a covering for sin. In both cases, the woman's body and the tabernacle altar, this blood ultimately points to the blood of Messiah poured out for the forgiveness of our sin, which most of us understand. But I think the link between menstruation and sacrifice needs to be made clear.

Blood sacrifice of any kind was only ever necessary because of sin. The first sacrifice ever made was a direct result of it, and it was made by Yahweh Himself. Adam and Eve realized they were naked and hid themselves with fig leaves, but when Yahweh found them, He gave them animal skins to clothe themselves. Those skins came from somewhere; an animal had to be killed to get them. They were a literal covering for sin. Think about that. But there is more.

Yahweh must have known that eventually men and women would forget about the need or significance of a covering sacrifice, so He gave the woman her monthly menstrual cycle as a constant reminder and wrote the meaning of it directly into her body. This cycle is intricately tied to the lunar cycle, but also to the holy days that Yahweh later set forth in Leviticus 23. The beginning of a woman's cycle starts with blood, a visible reminder, and each month starts with a new moon, a visible reminder. The first month also starts the new year on this day, while the seventh month has the memorial of Trumpets on the first day. The woman's cycle continues until day 14 or 15 when ovulation occurs. The 14th of the first month is Passover, and the 15th starts Unleavened Bread. In the seventh month the 15th starts the Feast of Tabernacles.

Both of these feasts begin at the full moon and both Unleavened Bread and Tabernacles last for seven days, which is the same amount of time that fertilization can usually occur in the woman's body. Sometimes fertilization can occur as late as day eight, and in the seventh month we also have the 8th day, or "Last Great Day" as some refer to it, on the 22nd day of the month.

If you are not familiar with these holy days, we will be going over them in the next section of the book. They outline the entire plan for the salvation of mankind. They are a set of convocations, or rehearsals (Hebrew *miqra*—Strong's H4744) that each give us one act of the play. That this play is written into every woman's body is an incredible testimony that the Creator has given us. The entire plan of salvation is given in one story and written in multiple ways for us to receive so as to be without excuse. It is written in the holy days, in the cycle of the moon, in the cycle of the woman, and in the sacrificial system which is typified in the altar of burnt offering set up at the entrance of the tabernacle of the body.

THE COURT

> You shall also make the court of the tabernacle. For the south side there shall be hangings for the court made of fine woven linen, one hundred cubits long for one side. And its twenty pillars and their twenty sockets shall be bronze. The hooks of the pillars and their bands shall be silver. Likewise along the length of the north side there shall be hangings one hundred cubits long, with its twenty pillars and their twenty sockets of bronze, and the hooks of the pillars and their bands of silver. And along the width of the court on the west side shall be hangings of fifty cubits, with their ten pillars and their ten sockets. The width of the court on the east side shall be fifty cubits. The hangings on one side of the gate shall be fifteen cubits, with their three pillars and their three sockets. And on the other side shall be hangings of fifteen cubits, with their three pillars and their three sockets. For the gate of the court there shall be a screen twenty cubits long, woven of blue, purple, and scarlet thread, and fine woven linen, made by a weaver. It shall have four pillars and four sockets. All the pillars around the court shall have bands of silver; their hooks shall be of silver and their sockets of bronze. The length of the court shall be one hundred cubits, the width fifty throughout, and the height five cubits, made of fine woven linen, and its sockets of bronze (Exodus 27:9–18).

The court is made of fine linen, much like the curtains, however there are no instructions for blue, purple and scarlet thread, except for the gate of the court. Remember the colored thread represented

The Temple is a Body

the blood vessels running through the skin. The absence of color says to me that this is not skin, and the court's location outside of the tabernacle proper, surrounding it, says to me that we must be looking at clothing. It makes sense that a body would be clothed, for modesty's sake if nothing else. The fact that the gate does have colored thread just tells us that there is an opening in the garment, as every garment has, that naturally reveals some of the skin.

There is something else that tells us more about what these clothes are, while also giving us a big clue to the identity of the body of the tabernacle. Fine linen is used consistently in Scripture to represent purity. Proverbs 31:22, in describing the virtuous wife, says, "She makes tapestry for herself; Her clothing *is* fine linen and purple."

Revelation 19:7–8 also refers to a virtuous wife, a very specific one.

> Let us be glad and rejoice and give Him glory, for the marriage of the Lamb has come, and His wife has made herself ready. And to her it was granted to be arrayed in fine linen, clean and bright, for the fine linen is the righteous acts of the saints.

So, this linen is not just simple clothing but represents the righteous acts of the saints. Revelation calls these saints the wife of the Lamb. The identity of our woman starts to come into focus!

ALTAR OF INCENSE

> You shall make an altar to burn incense on; you shall make it of acacia wood. A cubit shall be its length and a cubit its width—it shall be square—and two cubits shall be its height. Its horns shall be of one piece with it. And you shall overlay its top, its sides all around, and its horns with pure gold; and you shall make for it a molding of gold all around. Two gold rings you shall make for it, under the molding on both its sides. You shall place them on its two sides, and they will be holders for the poles with which to bear it. You shall make the poles of acacia wood, and overlay them with

gold. And you shall put it before the veil that is before the ark of the Testimony, before the mercy seat that is over the Testimony, where I will meet with you. Aaron shall burn on it sweet incense every morning; when he tends the lamps, he shall burn incense on it. And when Aaron lights the lamps at twilight, he shall burn incense on it, a perpetual incense before Yahweh throughout your generations. You shall not offer strange incense on it, or a burnt offering, or a grain offering; nor shall you pour a drink offering on it. And Aaron shall make atonement upon its horns once a year with the blood of the sin offering of atonement; once a year he shall make atonement upon it throughout your generations. It is most holy to Yahweh (Exodus 30:1–10).

This altar is also a place of sacrifice of burnt offerings, much like the previous altar, only this one is for burning incense. We're back inside the tabernacle proper again, so again we see the gold overlay. And again, we'll focus only on its function. Every morning and every evening, Aaron will burn sweet incense on it to Yahweh and will make atonement on it once per year. Leviticus 16:12–13 tells us more about how it was used during the Atonement service:

> Then he shall take a censer full of burning coals of fire from the altar before Yahweh, with his hands full of sweet incense beaten fine, and bring it inside the veil. And he shall put the incense on the fire before Yahweh, that the cloud of incense may cover the mercy seat that is on the Testimony, lest he die.

Its placement is just outside the veil, facing the ark and mercy seat. It was necessary that the smoke of the incense would cover the mercy seat when Aaron went in so that he would not die. What is going on there? What is this smoke that it would save Aaron? Let's get a few more clues from elsewhere in the Bible.

> A Psalm of David. Yahweh, I cry out to You; Make haste to me! Give ear to my voice when I cry out to You. Let my prayer be set before You as incense, the lifting up of my hands as the evening sacrifice (Psalm 141:1–2).

> Even them I will bring to My holy mountain, and make them joyful in My house of prayer. Their burnt offerings and their sacrifices will be accepted on My altar; For My house shall be called a house of prayer for all nations (Isaiah 56:7).

What we are seeing with the burning of incense is prayer. Earlier we looked at the mercy seat and the smoke that arose from it and realized it was the breath of Yahweh, the Holy Spirit. The smoke that arises from the incense is the breath of this body which is the tabernacle. These prayers are to be offered every morning and every evening. They mingle with the breath of Yahweh in two-way communication with Him, to become one in the Holy Spirit. This house or tabernacle is a house of prayer. The altar is the mind, or perhaps the brain if we want to look at it as an organ (it does have carrying poles like all of the other organs in the tabernacle after all), whose thoughts show the content of the heart. The word *prayer* literally means to plead. It is an outpouring of the heart to Yahweh, cries for help and mercy, and pleading for intercession for ourselves and others.

This altar is not for strange (foreign) incense, burnt offering, or grain offering (or food offering in some translations), or drink offering. It starts to make more sense, why fasting is done on the Day of Atonement. No food or drink comes into the body so that the prayer is pure, worthy to mingle with the breath of Yahweh. Yeshua, in Matthew 26:41, reminds us to "Watch and pray, lest you enter into temptation. The spirit indeed *is* willing, but the flesh *is* weak." So, we remove the parts of the flesh we can when we really need to be sure that we are able to hear God's voice. Atonement is one of those times, as is any additional fasting done to help our prayer life.

We know that with Yeshua's sacrifice, the veil of the holy of holies was torn, so that we no longer need an intermediary to keep us from death when approaching the throne. Yet these ideas are still pertinent. The need for prayer did not cease, but is now needed more than ever, because it is not only once per year that we can have direct contact with the almighty, but all day every day. At the very least, we should be offering it up every morning and evening as the incense was offered.

LAVER

> You shall also make a laver of bronze, with its base also of bronze, for washing. You shall put it between the tabernacle of meeting and the altar. And you shall put water in it, for Aaron and his sons shall wash their hands and their feet in water from it. When they go into the tabernacle of meeting, or when they come near the altar to minister, to burn an offering made by fire to the LORD, they shall wash with water, lest they die. So they shall wash their hands and their feet, lest they die. And it shall be a statute forever to them—to him and his descendants throughout their generations (Exodus 30:18–21).

The idea of washing in the old covenant is pervasive and important. The way to show respect to any guest or traveler was to wash their feet. Washing was used throughout the Torah as a cure for "uncleanness." Anything mentioned that made a person unclean, be it handling a dead body or leprosy or mold on a garment, at least part of the process of becoming clean was to wash in water.

That washing makes you clean sounds like a bit of a no-brainer, but the biblical idea of cleanliness goes beyond getting the physical dirt off to include spiritual cleanness and that seems unique. Just as the physical body could be soiled, so could the spiritual one. These things were expounded on in the Torah so "that you may distinguish between holy and unholy, and between unclean and clean" (Leviticus 10:10).

To be sure, the body we are building with the tabernacle is a spiritual one, but it is built as a physical one in the image of the spiritual, just as mankind was created physically in the image of the spiritual Elohim. So, the physical parts of the body are built into the

The Temple is a Body

tabernacle, but so are the things that are necessary to maintain the proper functioning of the body for the purposes of holiness that it was created for. Clothing is not part of the actual body, but we saw the court of the tabernacle serving as clothing because clothing is something that serves the proper functioning of the body. Likewise, the laver serves the purpose of bathing this body, both physically and spiritually. Isaiah had a prophetic description of the Israelites who would remain in Jerusalem during the captivity that displays this function beautifully:

> In that day the Branch of the LORD shall be beautiful and glorious; and the fruit of the earth shall be excellent and appealing for those of Israel who have escaped. And it shall come to pass that he who is left in Zion and remains in Jerusalem will be called holy—everyone who is recorded among the living in Jerusalem. When the Lord has washed away the filth of the daughters of Zion, and purged the blood of Jerusalem from her midst, by the spirit of judgment and by the spirit of burning, then the LORD will create above every dwelling place of Mount Zion, and above her assemblies, a cloud and smoke by day and the shining of a flaming fire by night. For over all the glory there will be a covering. And there will be a tabernacle for shade in the daytime from the heat, for a place of refuge, and for a shelter from storm and rain (Isaiah 4:2–6).

Yahweh will wash away the filth of the daughters of Zion and do so in a way that is intricately tied to the idea of the tabernacle. What we are seeing with all this washing is the idea of baptism.

When I first started studying the Bible seriously, I had a hard time understanding where baptism came from. It seemed out of the blue for John the Baptist to start his ministry in such a way. I could not understand why people wanted to be baptized by some preaching stranger when there seemed to be no precedent in the old covenant. Others tried to explain to me that the precedent was the ritual washings in the Old Testament, yet it didn't seem the same

Part 2: The Body

thing to me. But I also didn't really understand the idea of clean and unclean the way the Israelites did.

Now that I'm understanding the role that cleanliness and holiness played, it is finally starting to make perfect sense that John the Baptist was really doing nothing new. He was just pointing out that people were unclean and needed to repent and be washed to become clean. This baptism (washing) would have been completely understood and accepted once people were convicted of their need for repentance because they had been taught their whole lives through the Torah that washing to achieve spiritual cleanliness was no different than washing to achieve physical cleanliness.

In John 3:1–8, Jesus told Nicodemus that you must be born of both water and the Spirit:

> There was a man of the Pharisees named Nicodemus, a ruler of the Jews. This man came to Jesus by night and said to Him, "Rabbi, we know that You are a teacher come from God; for no one can do these signs that You do unless God is with him."
>
> Jesus answered and said to him, "Most assuredly, I say to you, unless one is born again, he cannot see the kingdom of God."
>
> Nicodemus said to Him, "How can a man be born when he is old? Can he enter a second time into his mother's womb and be born?"
>
> Jesus answered, "Most assuredly, I say to you, unless one is born of water and the Spirit, he cannot enter the kingdom of God. That which is born of the flesh is flesh, and that which is born of the Spirit is spirit. Do not marvel that I said to you, 'You must be born again.' The wind blows where it wishes, and you hear the sound of it, but cannot tell where it comes from and where it goes. So is everyone who is born of the Spirit."

Being born of water is the birth of the flesh. Water is that which gives earthly life. What happens when we are born of the womb? The mother's water breaks. The child has been surrounded by it in the womb (the child's world for nine months), then comes out to breathe air. *Ruwach* (Hebrew). *Pneuma* (Greek). Both words refer to Yahweh's breath—words used to describe the Spirit. We breathe in for the first time at birth, a symbol of the breath of eternal life in the Spirit that will happen when we pass through this world. Then what's next? "The whole creation groans and labors with birth pangs," we are told in Hebrews 8:22. The symbolism is on many levels, including even the earth (the whole creation) on which we are living, which is a womb, surrounded by amniotic fluid, with waters below and waters above the firmament! (Genesis 1:7)

When we are baptized, we pass through the watery grave, dead to this world, alive to the next. Being completely immersed in water, we come out and have hands laid on us, just as a father catches the child during birth. The Spirit is imparted, and we take our first Ruwach or Pneuma. Then we are newborns suckling on the milk of the Word until the day we are weaned, having gradually attained the ability to digest solid food and meat. When we finally die in the flesh from this world, we will also pass through the waters of the firmament to attain to the heavenly realm as children in the family of Yahweh.

As we come out of the womb, we are also coming from darkness into the light. So, too, in baptism we are coming out of the darkness of sin into the light of Christ. Paul tells us it is the same difference between this world and the next: "For now we see through a glass, darkly; but then face to face: now I know in part; but then shall I know even as also I am known" (1 Corinthians 13:12). The pattern is all laid out for us in creation, so that we are without excuse!

The need to be washed clean, then, is so important as to be designed into the functional hardware of the tabernacle, representing the womb of rebirth. It is the only process that can be used to cleanse one who has repented. It is this washing of baptism that offers new life, eternal life, free from sin. It is the womb that offers this baptism to the child entering the world so it can arrive in a pure, clean state.

This water is mentioned elsewhere in Scripture as well. John 7:38, "The one believing into Me, as the Scripture said, out of his belly will flow rivers of living water," (LITV). This just said, "as the Scripture said," however there is no place in the Old Testament (the Scriptures that Yeshua and John had) that said anything about living waters coming out of a belly (the Hebrew word for belly means abdominal region, or a hollow cavity. Some translations incorrectly say heart).

Could the "Scripture" Yeshua referred to have simply been the design of the tabernacle? I think it is likely, because the water in the laver is indeed referring to the waters of life. These are the waters that came out of Yeshua's side (part of His abdominal section) when it was split with the spear, which was also a foreshadowing of the waters of Revelation 22:1 and 17, "And he showed me a pure river of water of life, clear as crystal, proceeding from the throne of God and of the Lamb." And "Whoever desires, let him take the water of life freely." The throne of God was originally symbolized in the tabernacle, the waters of life flowing out of its entrance to make all who will partake clean. Isaiah 12:2–3, "'For Yah, Yahweh is my strength and song; and he has become my salvation.' Therefore, with joy you will draw water out of the wells of salvation" (WEB).

Identity

There is much more to be said. I have not mentioned the holy anointing oil, which is used to set apart all parts of this body to Yahweh, and how the human body makes its own oils, similarly covering all parts of it. I have not talked about the composition of the incense itself and the herbs that make it up. Surely their individual properties will say much about the prayer we are to be offering. I have not talked about the garments for the priests, their design similarities with the tabernacle, and what it all represents, which could be another volume on its own. But we have enough information now to make some conclusions as to who this tabernacle actually represents.

The Temple is a Body

We've already gotten a lot of good clues, but first, let's make this even easier by quoting more of what Scripture has to say about it.

> Look upon Zion, the city of our appointed feasts; your eyes will see Jerusalem, a quiet home, a tabernacle that will not be taken down; not one of its stakes will ever be removed, nor will any of its cords be broken (Isaiah 33:20).

> Or don't you know that your body is a temple of the Holy Spirit who is in you, whom you have from God? You are not your own, for you were bought with a price, therefore glorify God in your body and in your spirit, which are God's (1 Corinthians 6:19).

> What agreement has a temple of God with idols? For you are a temple of the living God. Even as God said, "I will dwell in them, and walk in them; and I will be their God, and they will be my people." Therefore "Come out from among them, and be separate," says the Lord. "Touch no unclean thing. I will receive you. I will be to you a Father. You will be to me sons and daughters,' says the Lord Almighty." (2 Corinthians 6:16–17 WEB).

> Now, therefore, you are no longer strangers and foreigners, but fellow citizens with the saints and members of the household of God, having been built on the foundation of the apostles and prophets, Jesus Christ Himself being the chief cornerstone, in whom the whole building, being fitted together, grows into a holy temple in the Lord, in whom you also are being built together for a dwelling place of God in the Spirit (Ephesians 2:19–22).

> Wives, submit to your own husbands, as to the Lord. For the husband is head of the wife, as also Christ is head of the church; and He is the Savior of the body. Therefore, just as the church is subject to Christ, so let the wives be to their own husbands in everything. Husbands, love your wives, just as Christ also loved the church and gave Himself for her, that He might sanctify and cleanse her with the washing of water by the word, that He might present her to Himself a glorious church, not having spot or

Part 2: The Body

wrinkle or any such thing, but that she should be holy and without blemish. So husbands ought to love their own wives as their own bodies; he who loves his wife loves himself. For no one ever hated his own flesh, but nourishes and cherishes it, just as the Lord does the church. For we are members of His body, of His flesh and of His bones. "For this reason a man shall leave his father and mother and be joined to his wife, and the two shall become one flesh." This is a great mystery, but I speak concerning Christ and the church (Ephesians 5:22–32).

He who overcomes, I will make him a pillar in the temple of My God, and he shall go out no more. I will write on him the name of My God and the name of the city of My God, the New Jerusalem, which comes down out of heaven from My God. And I will write on him My new name (Revelation 3:12).

Then I, John, saw the holy city, New Jerusalem, coming down out of heaven from God, prepared as a bride adorned for her husband. And I heard a loud voice from heaven saying, "Behold, the tabernacle of God is with men, and He will dwell with them, and they shall be His people. God Himself will be with them and be their God" (Revelation 21:2–3).

There are a few themes that come forward when looking at these scriptures written by Isaiah, Paul, and John. They equate the tabernacle with Jerusalem, with the church and with the bride of Christ.

Revelation 21:2–3 is my favorite because it associates all four in one place. The word *church* is not mentioned there, but "with men" and "His people" refer to the same concept. Let's look at the "church" for a minute. It is the Greek word "Ekklesia" (Strong's G1577), which literally means "called out." Out of what? Out of the world (John 17 is a good place to read about this). Holiness is all about this concept, meaning to be set apart out of the world. Called out and set apart are the same thing. The church is the called out and set apart people of God.

The Temple is a Body

"His people" referred to in Revelation 21:3 was quoted from Leviticus 26:11–12 and is talking about exactly these called out and set apart people. The quote is referring to the reason for the building of the tabernacle, that Yahweh intended to dwell there among His people. John is revealing what the ultimate fulfillment of this will look like, calling it "the holy city, New Jerusalem," and "a bride adorned for her husband."

When we talked about the curtains we saw where Jerusalem was referred to as "a city coupled together." I have heard others teach that this coupling is about the two covenants, and I don't think that is necessarily wrong, but the Bible often contains multiple layers of meaning. For our purposes here, I will say that Jerusalem is the bride of Christ who is coupled to her Husband, Yeshua/Jesus. Reading through the book of Song of Solomon will give you a glimpse of the relationship between Jesus (the Beloved) and His Bride in very romantic, even sensual language. The love and longing between them is forefront. And it all takes place in Jerusalem, with all of the "daughters of Jerusalem" looking upon them. In ancient times, a city was defined by the walls around a population center. Size did not matter. The unwalled villages surrounding a city were called "daughters."

Ephesians 5 also takes us through the relationship between Christ and His people, but here His people are called the church (again, Ekklesia—called out ones). Paul really understood the relationship of Christ to the Ekklesia, which he calls a body, just as the tabernacle pictures. The Ekklesia is the body of which Christ is the head (verse 23).

Our bodies do what the head instructs them to do. They submit willingly because they are of the same body and so have the same will. If the body resists what the head instructs, we call it illness. The head, in return, does not make unreasonable requests of the body, or require it to do functions that it cannot reasonably perform. I would not tell my arms to lift 2,000 pounds because they cannot do that. I

Part 2: The Body

would also not tell a part of the body to perform a function that belongs to another part of the body, such as telling my knee to taste some food because the knee would not know how. This is what Paul tells us,

> So husbands ought to love their own wives as their own bodies; he who loves his wife loves himself. For no one ever hated his own flesh, but nourishes and cherishes it, just as the Lord *does* the church. For we are members of His body, of His flesh.

All our Head asks of us is in 2 Corinthians 6:17 is to "Come out from among them, and be separate,' says the Lord. 'Touch no unclean thing. I will receive you."

Speaking of the Head, I questioned for a while why we see parts such as a face, eyes and a table with the dimensions of the head and neck inside of the torso of the body instead of atop it where they would seem to belong. But the answer became clear when I realized that these items were the ones that represented Jesus as the Head. They didn't belong to the body of the woman, whose torso this temple is. This is a picture of Jesus indwelling His bride. He rules this body from the region of the heart, not from the region of our brains. He spared no detail in the picture He created in the tabernacle!

Yes, our bodies are temples/tabernacles, and we know this because Yahweh showed the pattern to His people in the deserts of Sinai. The surrounding nations would have temples of wood and stone to house idols of wood and stone, but His people, His bride, would have temples made of flesh to house the living God. And this bride, this temple or tabernacle called the New Jerusalem, is you and me! The tabernacle pictured in the Old Testament of the Bible is pointing to your very own body today!

The False Tabernacle

Of course, for every beautiful thing that Yahweh creates, the adversary crafts a counterfeit, and the tabernacle is no exception. The concept for this study came from putting together 1 Corinthians 6:19 (Don't you know your body is a temple of the Holy Spirit) with Ezekiel 36:26 (I will take the heart of stone out of your flesh and give you a heart of flesh.) If that heart of stone was the commandments in the ark, then what else might the tabernacle represent?

One thing I noticed while considering certain parts of the tabernacle was that if I just used my mind to think hard about it, I would get off on a trail that led to the way of the flesh, and it would just feel wrong. But when I prayed about it and let the Spirit lead, a better way would appear.

One example of this was with the entrance to the tabernacle. When considering the entrance to a woman's body, it is easy to start thinking of things in a sexual context (at least for men…). This would be where the priest enters in, which could be seen as a sexual act of sorts. Then he enters the holy of holies, which could be seen as a womb being impregnated. I have actually seen this analogy used elsewhere. Was it correct? Our bodies certainly have a sexual aspect to them, but there is also a reason that intercourse is treated as an unclean act biblically, and nothing unclean can enter the holy of holies.

The idea didn't sit well, but I couldn't completely disprove it. I prayed about it, and it immediately came to me that Jesus/Yeshua was born of a virgin. Intercourse was not part of it! He was clean in every way. If we are to be part of His body, we too should have nothing to do spiritually with sexual uncleanness. Is not the bride also referred to as a virgin?

This is when I realized the difference between the furniture inside the tabernacle and outside the tabernacle, separated by the screen door. Inside was completely clean and outside was for *becoming* clean. The upper organs maintain the oxygen, or life, in the body and the lower organs, separated by the diaphragm, cleanse the body of uncleanness.

It is this lower part of our bodies that often becomes a false tabernacle. It is responsible for most of our strongest fleshly desires. Our stomach dictates our lives to a large extent. Do we live to eat or eat to live? Our sexual organs are also in the lower body and the lusts that they put ourselves through can wreak all sorts of havoc. Both types of desire lead to indulgence and a lack of self-control, an essential fruit of the Spirit.

Religious practices have often been corrupted with temple prostitutes and fertility worship as an excuse for sexual indulgence and have used practices involving excessive alcohol consumption and gluttony during feast times. These things all originate in the region below the diaphragm.

Those individuals and religious leaders who have recognized problems in these areas have sometimes resorted to extremism at the opposite end of the spectrum. They have promoted asceticism and living lives of complete abstinence, even forbidding marriage. Both of these practices may have certain benefits in the short term and the Bible even promotes fasting and speaks of those who have become eunuchs for the kingdom of heaven's sake. These are both done for the sake of self-control. But in the long term there is a danger for those who maintain lifestyles of not just self-control, but of constant self-denial. Their focus in such cases actually remains on the stomach and/or sexual desire, as abstinence becomes their whole identity. Our proper focus is meant to be on the heart. Real self-control comes from the heart and nowhere else. When our Head told us how to behave, He wrote it on our hearts, so that is where we look!

I am grateful for the clarity that this study has brought to me, as it reveals our proper identity in the body of Messiah, as well as the proper behavior that is fitting for one of such identity. It also gives perspective to clean and unclean, holy and unholy, and an understanding of the created marvel that is our physical bodies, the true temples of the Holy Spirit and place of residence of our Creator.

> And let them make Me a sanctuary, that I may dwell among them. According to all that I show you, that is, the pattern of the tabernacle and the pattern of all its furnishings, just so you shall make it (Exodus 25:8–9).

> But this is the covenant that I will make with the house of Israel after those days, says Yahweh: I will put My law in their minds, and write it on their hearts; and I will be their God, and they shall be My people (Jeremiah 31:33).

Summary

Ark	Heart
Stone Tablets/Law	Blood
Mercy Seat/Cherubim	Lungs/Oxygen
Table of Showbread	Head/Face
Lamp stand/Light	Eyes
Curtains	Skin
Covering of Goats Hair	Hair
Ram Skins and Tachash	Muscles/Blood Covering
Boards	Ribs
Bars	Sternum
Veil	Pericardium
Screen Door	Diaphragm
Altar of Burnt Offering	Menstrual Cycle
Court	Clothing
Altar of Incense	Prayers
Laver	Womb/Baptism

7

You Are Your Own Analogy

Part of my studies of the human figure back in art school was studying anatomy. Paul Buckner taught the anatomy for artists class as well. It was taught almost as in-depth as a medical school anatomy class but focused only on the superficial muscles and bones (and we had a *live* nude model in the class, which I'm sure they did not get in med-school…). The human anatomy fascinated me—not just what it looked like, but how it all worked together.

In my senior year, I had an idea for a sculpture that was an anatomical study of the human head, except in place of all of the facial muscles I used small human figures performing the actions of the muscles they represented. It was painstaking to sculpt because of all of the details, but my teachers were amazed. It is still probably my favorite sculpture that I have ever made. I titled it, "You Are Your Own Analogy." Now, years later, that title holds true and even means much more to me.

If the tabernacle is analogous to the body of the bride of Christ, then maybe there are other analogies hidden in the Bible as well. I started looking at some well-known biblical characters and found something interesting; their early lives foreshadowed their later lives.

The most obvious case is Jesus, especially if you think of His time being known as Yahweh, the God of the Old Testament, as being His early life. The entire Old Testament speaks of the coming of Messiah: the sacrificial system, the story of Abraham and Isaac, the Passover in Egypt, Jonah in the belly of the fish, and many lines spoken by the prophets. In the New Testament, though, we are only given one real glimpse of Jesus as a youth, yet the only quote from Him at that time speaks volumes, "Don't you know I must be in my Father's house?"

But there are many other examples besides Jesus as well. Moses was brought up in the house of Pharaoh as a prince, but he gave up that life to help out his real brothers. Eventually that led to his being raised up by God as a sort of prince to his people. His former life had foreshadowed his later one.

Joseph was brought up as the favored son by his father Jacob. As a youth he had dreams that his family would all bow down to him one day. This made his brothers jealous and mad, leading them to sell Joseph into slavery, in part to keep those dreams from coming true. Of course, that action is the one that caused them to come to fruition. He was forced into giving up his life as favored son only to later become the favored servant of Pharaoh, where he was able to save his family from starvation, causing them to willingly bow to him. His former life had foreshadowed his later one.

David was a shepherd boy, skilled at protecting the family sheep from predators. He gave up that life to shepherd the people of Israel as their king. As a boy, he slew a lion and a bear. As God's anointed, he slew a giant and thousands of mighty men. His former life had foreshadowed his later one.

Peter, James, and John were fishermen. When they met Jesus, they immediately gave up that life and became fishers of men. Their former lives had foreshadowed their later ones.

Some cases are directly prophesied. Jacob and Esau struggled with each other even while in Rebekah's womb. When Rebekah sought Yahweh about this, He prophesied to her that the firstborn would serve the younger. When they were born, Esau came out first, but Jacob, the younger, was grabbing his heel, earning his name, which means "supplanter." As they grew, they continued to quarrel, and Jacob eventually conned Esau into selling him his birthright and his father into giving him Esau's firstborn blessing. His former life had foreshadowed his later one.

All of these examples made me think about my own life. If God used these people's early lives to show them their later lives, then what about myself? Would He bother with me?

I've often had strange, vivid dreams that I wondered if there could be meaning to. I've written many of the more striking ones down. One day back in 1997, I had an acquaintance over for some tea. I had known her through a mutual friend in college. She had moved back to her home country of Japan after graduation two years prior and was back to visit friends. Our mutual friend was out of town, so I invited her over for tea, even though I barely knew her myself. We had a very good visit, but nothing romantic.

That night, I had a dream about barely escaping an explosion that would have certainly killed me by making a heroic leap from a fence into a tree. As soon as I set foot in the tree, I found myself in a peaceful, almost magical-looking world, welcomed by others (maybe spirit beings?) who had been awaiting my arrival. I wrote that dream down and wondered at it.

Over the next few days, I was plagued by a voice in my head telling me that I needed to ask the friend I had tea with to marry me. I thought this crazy, of course, because I still barely knew her. But I had also prayed not long before all of this to the God I barely knew at the time, that if He wanted me to find a wife, He would have to send her to me Himself, because I was done trying.

I had had a string of bad relationships and no longer had any trust in my ability to find the right person. So, was this voice God telling me this is the one? Or was it my impatience, realizing I was stupid to think I could get along single for any length of time?

After a week, the voice did not go away and I decided I had to make the leap and write a letter to her in Japan, popping the question. It turned out that on her flight back to Japan, the in-flight movie kept reminding her of me—the way the actor looked and the way the man and woman kept meeting over years but never getting to know each other. Until they finally did get together in the end, of course.

When she received my letter a couple of weeks later, she had been writing me letter after letter only to crumple them up and throw them away each time because they kept turning into love letters. We were married about a year later (and are still today!). Was this my dream?

Not long after getting married, I also started being drawn to study the Bible more. I was brought into a work situation with a boss who had a different understanding of the Bible than anyone I had previously met. I tried to argue with him with my smart-ass college grad attitude, but he actually had biblically sound answers for everything I'd say. He also introduced me to another couple we stayed in contact and studied with after he left the country. It took ten years of study for me, sitting on the fence the whole time about whether the Bible way of life was right or not, but I eventually decided I needed to take the leap and decided to get baptized.

It seems to me that that dream was foretelling some real-world fence-leaping that I would need to do. Both times, it made my life better and actually got me off of paths that could have led to my destruction. The second time, I found some spiritual beings welcoming me as well, as I know the angels in heaven all cheer when another is added to the saved!

When I was first introduced to biblical Christianity, the couple who consistently had us over for Bible study was about my parents' age. The husband had come into the church first and it had been another nineteen years until his wife finally submitted to God.

One of the reasons it took me ten years to take the leap was because Sanae was far less sure of these things than I was. I was probably ready a few years before that if it was just me, but it was a difficult thing to decide, knowing that my baptism could cause even more conflict in our marriage than it already had.

It was not at all easy to bring in Christianity to a wife who grew up in a Buddhist and Shinto culture. She was not personally attached to those religions but was rather skeptical of *any* religion. We had actually discussed before our marriage that neither of us liked religion. Even though we both believed in God, she had said she would be against any deep involvement in religion. She had already given up so much to be with me and I kept adding to the list, which was not easy on her.

It would take her another five years to decide to be baptized on her own. During this time, I often thought it strange, but comforting, that the one couple who helped us learn the Bible also had to go through a similar situation, being "unequally yoked" for a long period of time, foreshadowing our own situation.

Foundations

Sanae and I bought our house in 1999, one year after we got married. We soon discovered that the house had foundation issues. The ground would swell and shrink throughout the year, making doors impossible to close for part of the year.

We found a foundation company who could put helical piers on our foundation, which would screw down into the earth until they hit bedrock. Additionally, they could tie the stem wall together with huge threaded rod that would cinch the foundation together to reverse cracking permanently.

It would be very expensive to do this extensive surgery to our foundation, but I was just starting to understand the biblical concept of building on the firm foundation of Jesus Christ and saw the parallel there. I felt the need for a firm foundation in both cases. Sanae agreed that the foundation needed to be done (actually it was her idea initially), so we bit the bullet and did it with the little money we had at the time. Our foundation has not moved since and has been a great investment. My spiritual foundation took a bit longer to receive the same treatment.

Our son was born in 2007 while I was starting to consider baptism. I took three weeks off of work for the birth and lay around in bed with the new baby for most of that time. But toward the end, I was going stir crazy and felt I needed to do some physical work, so I ordered a unit of soil to be delivered to our driveway and proceeded to try to move the entire unit to the back garden in one day.

If you are not familiar, a unit is 7.5 cubic yards of soil—a huge pile, large enough to overflow the single car driveway. The next day I could not get out of bed. That much exertion after doing nothing physical for two weeks had caused me to herniate my disc. I had had off and on back problems since I was eighteen, but nothing like this.

The backbone is really a foundation in our physical bodies. When this happened, it was showing something else spiritual that was happening inside of me. My spiritual foundation was sick—not broken, but sick. I had also started a job in 2006 where I was on the computer for hours on end every day for the first time in my life. I hated this job for that reason and numerous others, which caused a lot of mental stress.

But the computer also had a built-in coping mechanism that I discovered for the first time—porn. It's not like I didn't know porn was wrong, because I did. I hated using it and tried to control it but could only do so for limited periods of time and when the stress got strong, so did the porn. Satan was trying his best to throw me off course during the time that a I was trying to come to know Jesus. I had a crack in my foundation, and it would take me another fifteen years until that crack was healed.

As I was going through physical therapy for my back, my therapist told me that my posture was bad and had been for so long that the facia at the front of my hips was restricting me from even being able to stand upright properly if I tried. She worked for months to stretch that facia, which was a very painful process. I started to wonder whether there was a link between my spiritual life and my back, knowing there were issues with both. I could not stand in an upright position, nor could I stand upright before God.

The physical therapy did allow me to stand with better posture and it alleviated much of my back pain. But it did not touch the sciatic nerve pain down both legs because the source of that pain, the herniated disc, was still there. So, I ended up having surgery to remove the bulge that was pressing on my nerve. Surgery was an immediate success in that the nerve pain was instantly gone, but that result was short-lived.

Afterwards, I regularly re-injured my back. Sometimes it was through overdoing some work, but other times it just started for no apparent reason. Gradually, however, I started noticing that my back issues tended to coincide with my porn use. It made no sense physically, but I really started wondering if there was something there.

This went on and on for about fifteen years until 2022 when I again injured my back, not even knowing how. The pain just started growing and growing until I again could barely get out of bed. The Feast of Tabernacles was coming up soon, and we had a rental house reserved for ten days. I didn't want to miss it.

I started seeing my chiropractor, who was also a solid Christian friend from church. He put me on three different treatments, but I only had time to see him twice before leaving for the feast, and the pain had not yet gone down substantially. Even though the site was only about three hours away, he strongly advised me not to go so that I could continue being treated.

I requested prayer from some of the brethren we were planning on seeing at the feast, and I decided to go on faith that God would allow me to attend.

I worried about the drive, but we made it there without stopping somehow. Sanae insisted on unpacking the car and I went to bed.

You are Your Own Analogy

The next morning, our friends who we were sharing the house with arrived and without even thinking, I went out and started helping them unpack their car. I didn't even think about my back until Sanae asked me what the heck I was doing. I realized that I did not have any pain. None.

Was it just a temporary reprieve? I kept trying different positions to see if it came back, but it didn't. I made a decision that I had been healed. Twice during the feast, I thought I felt a twinge coming back, but both times I rebuked it and claimed healing from God, and it went away. Since then, I have overworked my back many times, doing things that would have easily put me out of commission before, but I've never had any more than some temporary muscle pain, as if I had worked out at the gym.

So, since my back was healed, was my porn issue also healed? Yes and no. I believe that the foundation of the issue was healed. The part of me that could not let go of it had loosened its grip. I knew I didn't need it to deal with stress anymore. That being said, there were a few occasions afterwards when I gave in, but those times felt different. It is hard to describe the difference, but perhaps it seemed like more of a habitual reaction than a desire. Analyzing only goes so far, though.

But where analyzing fails, God kicks in. Even after giving in, my back has not started hurting again. Instead, God showed me another issue that paralleled my journey with porn. Demons.

DEMONS AND RATS

I am far from an expert in the field of demons, but whether I want to be or not, they are something that has had an effect on my life. Some say there is a difference between demon oppression and possession, others say not so. Some don't use the word *demons* and just call them *spirits*. I don't really know if I was oppressed or possessed or if it matters, but I know that if you are holding on to an issue related to a demon or evil spirit, however lightly, it is not going to go away. The demon/spirit of lust that I had in me held on tight. I wanted it to be gone for years, but there was that small part of me that would miss it if it left.

Around the time my back was healed, I was finally so fed up with my issue that I was ready to completely let go. So, when it came back again, I was upset, angry, and confused. Why and how could it come back when I had finally successfully cast it out?

It turns out that this thing with demons also had a physical parallel in my life. Rats. It is fitting that they should parallel each other, for they act the same in almost every way, infesting dark locations, entering through hidden cracks, and staying out of view at all times, the only evidence being their stench and the waste they leave behind. I hate them both with righteous hatred.

When we had the helical piers put on our house, the contractors installed brackets to fix them to the foundation. But they had to break off the footing underneath the stem wall to attach them. This left perfect access points for rodents to tunnel under. It wasn't an immediate issue, but a couple of years later, we had our floors insulated under the house, and then there was a really nice warm place for rats to want to live.

From then on, it has been a constant battle. I started by plugging entrances to tunnels I found, but they would just burrow next to where I plugged. I trapped and poisoned. The poison just left dead rats to cause an even worse smell. I went under the house and cleaned up old rats' nests, carcasses, droppings and ruined insulation.

Most of the tunnels originated under our deck, which made access to find the holes difficult. So, we hatched a plan to remove our deck and pour a concrete patio along most of the house in the back yard where they came in. I turned that plan into adding a large sunroom as well.

It took me about three years to complete that process, only to discover that the rats still found a way under. They tunneled at least fifteen feet from the far end of the garage where there was no crawl space. I felt defeated but decided to do a major clean out under the house, replacing every bit of contaminated insulation with new material. I also replaced the plastic moisture barrier and sealed off the new floor insulation with hardware cloth (fencing sheet made of crossed wires spaced every quarter inch) so that there was no way for a rat to get into it even if they got under the house.

At the time I was doing this work, our church was offering a workshop on restoration from past hurts. Sanae and I both thought it sounded like a good idea and took the course. It had us dive deep into things from our past that caused us not to trust others so that we could forgive and restore relationships.

It was a fourteen-week course, with each week aimed at a different angle of cleaning out the dark corners of our souls. Although that may not sound directly related to my problem, it certainly got into things like porn use and what causes people to do it. One benefit was helping Sanae understand where I was coming from and that it was never about her insufficiency to me.

Many times, I had been under the house doing insulation or putting up hardware cloth just before going to the workshop. It really led me to see a connection between the two activities. It was a time when I realized that if I wanted results, I had to do real work, and dirty work, too. There was no other way around it. And I did. In prayer, in study with my wife, and under the house.

There finally came a day when I had finished both jobs. I was finally able to use our new patio sunroom and have no rat smell, and I hadn't seen porn in a good length of time! Celebrate and relax!

I wish I could say the story was over then. But shortly after that we took a long trip to Japan to visit and help out Sanae's parents. I love Japan in many ways, yet there are also aspects of being there that are quite stressful to me. Short story, I broke down again for a short time during that trip.

Then, after we came home, we discovered that the rats had again found another way to tunnel under the foundation. There was no evidence that they had found a way through the hardware cloth into the insulation, yet they were under the house. The consistency of these parallels amazed me.

Prayer and repentance again followed, and I battled through my defeat with the rats, discovering where they had found access. It was always close to one of the helical piers that had been installed. So, I dug around every one of them on all sides of the house and poured concrete so that there could be no exposed areas wherever they tried to dig next.

I delayed the cleanup for a while, dreading going under the house again for the dirty job. But finally, I did and didn't find any rat carcasses like I expected, just lots of rat poop and one little spot where they had been able to pull the hardware cloth back to access the insulation again, although nothing was there at the time. I cleaned that section and re-stapled it and swept the entire surface of the moisture barrier to clean up all the poop.

I have always been honest with Sanae about when I had failed in my battle with porn. (Well, almost always. Early on, I tried hiding and lying about it, but soon found out how that backfired, exacerbating the problem.) Even though she did her best to understand and forgive me, there has always, understandably, been a rift in our marriage because of it. However, during this whole battle with the rats, I hadn't ever mentioned any of the parallels I had been finding to Sanae about the rats and my porn. So, the day after I finished the final sweep-up under the house, I was surprised when, seemingly out of nowhere, she told me that she felt that our marriage had been healed. Again, I could not believe the timing. But I do believe it as well, because I know that these things are from God. And because it was my wife who told me, I know I have finally put this chapter behind me.

In the days that followed, I felt like I was falling in love with Sanae again and she noticed renewed energy and optimism. I realized that a spiritual darkness had been lifted off of us. The demons were gone!

But I have also learned my lesson that there is no time for celebration and relaxing. We are in a spiritual battle to the finish, which is when we die. Every day we put on the armor of God. On days I forget to do so, I notice things going wrong.

Maybe that was a long story and more personal that you'd wish to hear. But it is the story that God has given me through my life. I can't speak for anyone but myself in finding parallels in the physical and spiritual walks, yet I would at least encourage anyone reading this to look prayerfully into your own life experiences. Finding parallels and analogies are further evidence of Yahweh being present in our lives, which can be both encouraging and edifying.

MY GREEN BOOK

There is one more story I'd like to share before ending this section. By the time I was in high school, I already knew I wanted to be an artist of some sort, but I was against all of the standard career choices with it, such as graphic design or other commercial work. The more I thought about what I wanted to do, the more I simply wanted to be the best, to make the ultimate art that would blow everyone away, and I started formulating a plan on how to do that.

It would have to be the biggest and best and unique in a way that nobody had done anything like it before. I remember being shown a short animation piece by an animator named Joan Gratz. She painted with clay to make animations unlike anything I had seen. Instead of the standard cartoonish drawings, they were real paintings-come-to-life. It inspired me to study animation.

But my project would have to go beyond the work of Joan Gratz. She only made shorts because of how labor-intensive the process was. I would have to make a feature film. But not only that, I would have to write my own music to it and have it performed live and build all of the instruments from scratch. And I'd have to make my own theater with a 360° screen, or even project onto the inside of a full sphere. It would start out as simple painting, then expand as the film went on, incorporating technology that had not yet been invented. It would be mostly abstract but would be about the ultimate struggle between good and evil, grander than the *Star Wars* saga.

I did calculations and figured out that I could make a two-hour film with a frame rate of twenty-four frames per second (most high-end animation only used twelve frames. Saturday morning cartoons were four to six frames) in about twenty-four years if I could paint twenty-four frames per day, three-hundred days per year. This would be my life's project.

I knew it was overly ambitious, but I thought, *I only have one life, so make it worthwhile.* I took careful notes of everything I wanted to accomplish and ideas that might make it possible. The notes were not just technical in nature, however. A lot of them were just thoughts that would come to me, philosophical or just observations on life. I was very much pondering who God was, and what life was about. Every deep thought I had was recorded, with the intention of incorporating it somehow into the project. All of my notes were kept in a green three-ring binder. I called it my green book[9].

I remember thinking, and even wrote down in the green book, that most of the physical things I could want in life could be taken away, lost, or stolen. But if I put everything into my project, it could not be taken away. I'm not sure why I thought that because now I can think of many things that could destroy it, but at the time it made sense.

---

[9] This has nothing to do with another famous "Green Book" that I just recently discovered, which was written by Muammar al-Qaddafi, leader of Libya from 1969–2011. I actually read this book and find it fascinating. It is his philosophy on government, which is all about giving true power to the people. I can't say I agree with his thoughts 100 percent, but I believe there was a lot to this so-called "dictator" that western nations want to hide, because his philosophies revealed the slavery of the west disguised as democracy.

You are Your Own Analogy

I went to college with the idea of studying animation. There was a college in California, Cal Arts, where I could get a degree in Experimental Animation, but it was way more expensive than my family could afford, so I went to the University of Oregon, hopefully just for the first two years until I could maybe earn a scholarship. There were a few motion graphics classes where I could learn the basics, so I jumped in.

I poured everything I had into those classes, going above and beyond the assignments. I would stay up most of the night in the lab working on the painting with clay method. I couldn't figure out exactly how Joan Gratz did what she did (she did not reply to letters I wrote her), but I ended up discovering my own technique using oil paints on glass that seemed to work well.

In my third year of school, I started an ambitious independent study project. It would only be about a six-minute movie, but that was a lot of work to plan and create. I set up a studio in my rental house and spent all of my time on it. Computers were just starting to be used for animation in those days, but they were cumbersome, and I had no desire to use them, so I worked with an old 16mm film movie camera that the school checked out to me.

Working on film is a big risk because you don't know what you are going to get until the film is developed. There is little room for error. I could get about two minutes on a reel of film. When the first reel was done, I took it in to get developed, then anxiously watched the result. Apparently, the camera body had a light leak that made the movie flicker between light and dark. I could see how the animation itself turned out, which I was fairly pleased with, but it was still unusable and would have to be redone.

The department took the camera in for repair, then I started again from scratch. It was painstaking work, but I didn't mind because I had a goal in mind. After weeks of work, I again had a two-minute roll to develop and watch. I put it in the projector and my heart sank when it showed that the light leak had not been fixed.

I was devastated and refused to continue working on the project. My professor knew the work I was putting in, seeing what I had accomplished, so my grade was not affected, but I felt defeated. I would not try again.

In the meantime, I had started taking some sculpture classes and was really enjoying them. There was a freedom that I did not get while doing animation, which had started to feel more like work. After my devastation, I didn't see where to go with the animation, so I just didn't think about it and did what I enjoyed, which was sculpture.

I didn't forget about my green book, although I sensed that my plans might not proceed as expected. I wondered if I was supposed to learn sculpture and the human figure to do 3-D stop-motion animation, but mostly I just kept studying with less planning than before.

I could have graduated with a BS degree in four years, but I decided to stay on for a fifth year to get my BFA, Bachelor of Fine Arts. The extra year is a year of focused study in one area of art. I chose sculpture.

By the time I graduated, I really didn't have any plan for the future, though. I had no idea what to do with my degree. I didn't want to go to school for two more years to get a Masters, even though I wouldn't have minded becoming a professor. So, I just kind of thought I would make sculpture until I was discovered, and do whatever I could toward my green book project. But internally I was unsettled and a bit panicked.

I needed something big to change, but I didn't know what. I knew that both the girlfriend I was living with and my job at the mall were dead ends. So, on the same day, I both quit my job and broke up with her and started planning a cross-country trip to New York. I had a bunch of pocket-sized bronze sculptures of skulls and hands that I would try to sell while traveling to finance the trip, and I would

You are Your Own Analogy

bring my "You Are Your Own Analogy" sculpture to get into a gallery, too.

I started by going South to California and got a shop in San Francisco to take some of the small bronzes, then headed east, sleeping in the back of my Subaru wagon at night wherever I could find an out-of-the-way place to park it. I loved the isolation driving through the deserts of Nevada and Utah but never stayed anywhere long.

It was early November, and I wanted to get to the east coast with enough time to be back in California to visit relatives for Christmas. I got to Madison, Wisconsin, where I visited my great uncle for Thanksgiving, then pushed on to New York City. I didn't know a soul in New York, but I had the number of a friend of a friend. I looked him up and he let me crash at his apartment for a few days.

One thing I hadn't thought about was parking in New York. I knew that leaving my car on the street, if I could even find a spot, could be risky, so the first night I paid an exorbitant amount to put it in a garage overnight. But I couldn't afford that every night, so the next night I decided to risk leaving it on the street. Dumb move. It was loaded with all my stuff because I didn't feel like asking the friend to hold my junk.

I might as well have put flashing signs on the top saying, "Free Stuff Inside!"

The next day when I went to the car, the side window had been smashed, and everything was gone except for my sleeping bag and a bag of dirty laundry. The "You Are Your Own Analogy" sculpture had actually been placed in a New York gallery already, but that was about all that was spared. Duffel of clean clothes, gone. Box of small bronze sculptures, gone. Art supplies, gone. And my green book, the project that could not be taken away from me, *gone*.

By this time, the green book had about six or seven years worth of notes and thoughts in it. It was everything to me. I couldn't believe that it, of all things, would be taken. Even the dirty laundry should have had more value to anyone other than me. I knew the green book would just be thrown away later by somebody without even being read. But I was forced to start thinking about things differently. Maybe God was saying something to me.

In a strange way, I actually felt relief. For years, my life had been trapped in those thoughts and plans. To make something like that into any sort of reality took a giant mental feat of dedication that meant I couldn't allow myself to even think about giving up on it. But if God was the one taking it away…

The trip back west gave me at least one clue as to my future with art, although I didn't know it at the time. I took the southern route this time, because winter was fast approaching. As I did on the way, except for New York, I avoided big cities, preferring fewer people and more peace and quiet.

While driving along the Gulf Coast, I found myself in the small town of Ocean Springs, Mississippi, when an art museum caught my eye. I went in and was fascinated. It was dedicated to one artist, Walter Inglis Anderson, but he was not your typical artist. In fact, most of his paintings were watercolors done on lined notebook paper. He seemed like someone who would never have chosen to have a museum named after him.

Anderson spent most of his time on Horn Island, where he regularly rowed from his home in Ocean Springs just to observe whatever was there. He painted birds and crabs and the water and the beach around him. Then he took his paintings and burned them in his campfire. He didn't want notoriety or money from his art. He simply felt it was his duty to God to notice the beauty in the creation and record it. But once recorded, there was no reason for keeping anything because the observation had been made.

Any of his paintings the museum owned were there only because his family members occasionally found ones he had not yet burned and held them back. He also kept a log of his time on Horn Island.

I bought a book there that had his entire logs in addition to many of the salvaged paintings.

Why this art moved me so much, I couldn't tell you at the time, but it did. It was meditative for me to read his logs, and I could picture myself in his place observing the beauty of the sea. Now I know it is because he had no pretension, pride, or vanity in making his art. He was simply giving freewill offerings to the Creator because it was all he could do in response to the beauty the Creator had given him. Although I have never made art in that way, the idea has stayed with me.

These two events, being forced to give up the vanity of my life's dream, then being given an example of an artist who never had a hair of vanity on his head, gradually sank into my subconscious. It would take me over a decade to actually do anything about it.

The full story of voluntarily giving up my art will be for a later chapter. But to bring the idea around full circle, years after ending my career as an artist, I have found myself again, quite unintentionally, with another green book, the one you hold in your hands. This time it is one that is dedicated as an offering to God, not to my own vanity. My earlier life has foreshadowed my later one.

PART THREE
The Sky-Clock, God's Calendar

8
A Little History

The calendar is a ubiquitous thing that most of us think very little about. It is something we hang on our walls and refrigerators (or keep on our phones for you modern types) to keep track of what is happening on any particular day. We have come to have complete reliance on it to structure our lives, but how did it come to be? Why is it structured the way it is and how long has it been that way? When the Bible instructs God's people to do something on a particular day, is it possible for us to use our modern calendars to figure out what day He really meant?

It turns out that both what the Bible teaches to do and the way it teaches us to figure out when to do it, are vastly different from what almost everybody does today. We keep different holy days; we have a different structure to the year, to the months, and to the weeks. In fact, we have been influenced on all sides by imposters and frauds that hide the creation's instructions and replace them with man-made counterfeits bent on having us worship anything but the Creator.

History is really the story of man trying to overcome creation, as he has been attempting to do so since the beginning. Part of that has been man trying to come up with a calendar that is more perfect than the one Yahweh gave us in the first week of creation. God's way was perfect, meaning it was complete and mature, as we saw earlier, but it did not resemble the perfection that Satan likes to see. In other words, it was not robotic and infinitely repeatable. It had quirks that

Part 3: The Sky-Clock

made every year unique and made people have to observe the sky to follow it accurately.

Today our calendar looks like this: There are 365.2425 days in a year with twelve months of either 31, 30, or 28 days (29 in leap years); and there are seven-day weeks continually cycling independent of all other cycles. We call this the Gregorian calendar after Pope Gregory XIII, who reformed the prior Julian calendar, which was almost identical except for the way leap years were counted.

Both Gregorian and Julian calendars are based solely on the sun for calculating the length of the year. Months and weeks are abstract inventions not based in nature. We insert into this calendar the high holy days of the Catholic church of Easter and Christmas, as well as lesser days of Lent, Good Friday, etc., with the Lord's Day as a day of worship on Sundays, the first day of the week.

If we look at our Bibles, however, there is no mention of the length of a solar year: Months are not arbitrary, but are based on the cycle of the moon; there is no mention of either Christmas or Easter; and the seventh day Sabbath was instituted as the day of rest and assembly, although when exactly the seventh day is can be argued about, and we'll get to that later.

What happened?

We stopped looking at nature, at the whole of creation as a tool for calculating times, seasons, days and years, and decided to pick and choose, taking aspects of it to worship and raise above others. Genesis tells us that all of the lights in the firmament—the sun, moon, and stars—are there for this purpose. Yet since shortly after the time of Christ, the sun has been the only light to receive any use to these ends, and the reason for that is not random. It was an intentional transition in order to give praise to Sol, the sun god. The sun is indeed a wonderful thing that we all rely on for our very lives. It is also only one aspect of creation, and being a created thing, should not be worshiped. Yet sun worship has abounded throughout history, and if we think our modern society is an exception, we are sadly mistaken because today's calendar revolves around the sun (pun intended).

Most Christians will readily admit that sun worship was an important aspect to many, if not most, pagan cultures. What becomes far more uncomfortable to look at is the historical evidence that it was these pagan cultures that shaped our own most important holidays, and not any biblical reality.

THE SABBATH

The history I'm going to lay out here will be controversial to both those who keep Sunday as the day of worship and those who keep Saturday as a Sabbath. But it is simply based on the honest research I have done. I come across it from the view that nature has always had a say in things, but that does not change the research itself.

History is an inherently dangerous thing to discuss. As Napoleon famously said, "What is history but a set of lies agreed upon?" So, take this history how you will. I am not claiming it as absolute truth, as you will see in the next chapter, but it is certainly history worth examining.

Ancient Rome was a thoroughly polytheistic culture, worshiping gods of every flavor, of which Sol, the sun, was one. These Romans were the ones who held power over Jerusalem in the time of Christ. At that time, Rome kept an eight-day market week, which was very different from the calendar of their Jewish subjects, but they gave the Jews a certain amount of freedom to keep their own customs as they always had. It is quite possible that the Jews at that point still kept the weekly Sabbath in line with the cycles of the moon, not on the repeating seven-day cycle we now know as a week (we will discuss this in more detail later).

In the centuries that followed the destruction of the temple in 70 AD, however, this began to change. Rome, led by Julius Caesar, had conquered Egypt previously in 47 BC, and started being enamored by the astrological week that Egypt had been using (which Egypt had previously imported from Babylon and Greece). The astrological week was one based on the seven known wandering luminaries. Although Rome did not immediately adopt this new calendar, it did gain interest and sway with the Romans and their polytheistic proclivities, so that by the time of Constantine in the early fourth century, the eight-day market week had mostly fallen out of favor.

Christians, for the most part, still did their best to uphold the Jewish calendar they had kept for centuries, although now that there were two different seven-day cycles being used, Rome saw an opportunity to force a unified weekly cycle on all. In 321, Emperor Constantine, who was a devout pagan sun-worshiper at the time (albeit in the guise of a newly converted Christian), made an edict commanding people to worship the sun. He said,

> On the venerable Day of the sun let the magistrates and people residing in cities rest, and let all workshops be closed. In the country, however, persons engaged in agriculture may freely and lawfully continue their pursuits: because it often happens that another Day is not so suitable for grain sowing or for vine planting: lest by neglecting the proper moment for such operations the bounty of heaven should be lost.

This mandate did not directly outlaw traditional Sabbath worship, but it certainly made maintaining that tradition increasingly difficult. Many people think that Constantine was a Christian, as that is how historians generally paint him, yet the reality was that he was simply a sun worshiper who tried to blend the rapidly spreading Christian beliefs in with the long-held pagan beliefs in order to appease everyone in his empire, and thus create a unified populace.

It was at this time that the Jewish week and the astrological week, with their completely different origins, became synthesized into the week we now know. Christians, for the most part, made the transition to this new week, and kept the Sabbath on the newly created day of Saturn, as it was now the seventh day of the astrological week and "the Lord's Day" on the day of the Sun.

Prior to Constantine's edict, Sun-day had actually been the second day of the week, and Saturn's-day had been the first day of the astrological week. But in order to venerate the sun, it was given the "preeminence" as the first day of the week by Constantine, which shifted Saturn's day to the end. When this change took place, they did not have a week that skipped Saturns-day, but rather just renumbered the days of the week to make Sun-day number one.

This fact causes many difficulties to the idea that a Saturday Sabbath has been kept in an unbroken cycle from creation, because it is hard evidence to the contrary.

There were still some Christians, however, who would not give up their traditional Sabbath for the day of Saturn. So less than forty years later, in 364 AD, at the Council of Laodicea, the Catholic Church added their own edict to Constantine's pagan one because they were looking for a way to disassociate Christianity from Judaism. Up until that point many Christians still identified more or less as Jews, just Jews whose Messiah had arrived. The Catholic Church could not stand that idea. The edict stated,

> Christians shall not Judaize and be idle on Sabbath, but shall work on that Day: but the Lord's Day, they shall especially honour; and as being Christians, shall, if possible, do no work on that day. If however, they are found Judaizing, they shall be shut out from Christ.

This was the death blow that finally obliterated the remnant of Christianity keeping the Sabbath as it had been delivered at creation. At the same time, the word *Judaizing* was put into the collective consciousness of Christians, associating anything seen as Jewish as being evil. This included the appointed times, or Holy Days of Leviticus 23.

Part 3: The Sky-Clock

Christmas

Constantine, in his quest to merge the pagan and Christian populations, also started to merge their festivals. But he was not the first to do so. Saturnalia had long been an important winter solstice festival that honored Saturnus, the harvest god, and Mithras, the god of light, with the promise that the sun was being born and would grow during that season. It was a time of celebration and glad tidings that involved gift-giving, sex orgies, and human sacrifice.

The Christian populations generally avoided this celebration, but often still decorated their homes with holly to avoid persecution by the pagans. Up until the early second century, celebrating the birth of Christ was not done in any widespread way, and when it was done, there was no consistency to the time of year to celebrate it, as the date was not mentioned in Scripture[10]. However, Telesphorus, the second Bishop of Rome from 125 to 136 AD, declared that church services should be held in December to celebrate "The Nativity of our Lord and Saviour." This declaration did not seem to convince the Christian populace, however, with many preferring to keep the nativity either during the Feast of Tabernacles in September or October, or at their new year in March, if they kept it at all.[11]

In 320, Pope Julius I declared December 25th to be the birthdate of Jesus Christ, which happened to coincide with the same day that Roman Emperor Aurelian had declared forty-six years earlier to be "Natalis Solis Invicti," the festival of the birth of the invincible sun. Only five years after Julius' declaration, Constantine made Christmas a formal, immovable feast day to take place on that day, completing

---

[10] Even though scripture does not mention a date, the season can easily be inferred through Luke 2:8, "Now there were in the same country shepherds living out in the fields, keeping watch over their flock by night." The only season during the year in which a shepherd would do this is in the spring, when the sheep are giving birth, as it is a dangerous time for the sheep. They certainly would not be out in the open field at night in the winter.

[11] https://didyouknow.org/christmas/history/

the merger of the Christian and pagan, or rather, simply putting a Christian face on an entirely pagan festival.

Even with this new formal institution, most Christians still resisted celebrating it, knowing that it was not biblically ordained. As Christianity spread throughout Europe, Christmas was often either banned, illegal, or despised. Yet it was still pushed by the Catholic Church enough to maintain its place in the church calendar.

It was actually not until very modern times that it became a widespread celebration. After a major push in the mid-19th century to popularize Christmas with various marketing schemes (think "A Christmas Carol") it gradually became a legal holiday in the United States between 1836 and 1907, as the various states adopted it.

Most of the associations we have with its celebration, however still date back to the ancient Saturnalia festivities and related pagan celebrations from other cultures, such as the Scandinavian Yule festivals. These include our image of Santa Claus, whose bag of gifts was originally pictured in history as a bag that carried off children to be sacrificed; the decorated tree which was written about as far back as the book of Jeremiah in the Bible (see Jeremiah 10); the mistletoe, which pagans believed contained magical powers (kissing under the mistletoe being the remnant of the orgies that originally took place); and reindeer guiding a sleigh, bearing a striking resemblance to the hybrid stag-demon Furfur of Celtic mythology.

EASTER

The history of Easter is similarly a story of hybridizing pagan and Christian theology and similarly bears the fingerprint of Constantine, who felt obliged to solidify the timing of it once and for all, because it had been celebrated by Christians at various different times. However, Easter is a bit more subtle to the undiscerning eye than Christmas. Whereas Christmas has zero biblical basis for its existence, Easter seems, on the surface, to have some. Many refer to it as "resurrection Sunday," and the timing of it does indeed coincide

Part 3: The Sky-Clock

roughly with when Christ's resurrection took place. Certainly, there is nothing wrong with celebrating the resurrection of the risen Messiah. The Bible even instructs us about how to keep that day! But these instructions are where the true resurrection day and the institution we know as Easter get off track.

Most Christians understand that the Passover of the Old Testament was foreshadowing Jesus as the Passover Lamb slain for the forgiveness of the sins of the world, but then fail to understand that the instructions given in Leviticus 23 tell us about the entire Feast of Unleavened Bread, which the Jews of the New Testament times called Passover, combining it with the sacrifice that took place the night before the Feast of Unleavened Bread was to start.

In Leviticus 23:10-14, Yahweh instructed Israel about the wave sheaf, which was to be offered the day after the Sabbath during the Feast of Unleavened Bread. The timing is the day after the Sabbath, which in turn is after the Passover sacrifice. This was exactly the timing of Jesus' death and resurrection: The sheaf of the firstfruits of the barley was waved, which is to say it was raised up to heaven, just as Jesus was raised up on the day after the Sabbath.

This is the clear timing given for when to celebrate the resurrection, as well as how. It was given as a harvest festival, as were all three of the biblical festival seasons. But these harvests were all symbolic of the harvest of souls to God the Father at their respective resurrections. We'll get more into these things later.

These instructions bear little resemblance to the Easter of today. First, where do we get the name Easter? The name should be the first clue as to its origins, and many researching this will immediately find associations with the names Ishtar and Astarte, equivalent names of the same ancient near eastern Semitic goddess of war and sexuality.

However, there are also those who adamantly disclaim this, saying that the only association is with the names sounding similar.

Both Wikipedia[12] and Skribbatous.org[13], a pagan historical website, claim that it is only inept research that leads to the connection between Ishtar/Astarte and Easter. They both claim that the real source for the name comes from a different goddess, the West Germanic goddess of spring, Ēostre. Reading further in the same Wikipedia article, however, shows that Ēostre was simply the Germanic equivalent of the Norse goddess Freyja, from whom we get our name for Friday. Freyja in turn is widely known to be the Norse version of the Roman Venus, who, it turns out, was the Hellenized version of… (drum roll, please) …Ishtar!

Ēostre, and thus Easter, was often associated with hares, or rabbits, and eggs, which have both long been used as symbols of fertility and birth. The church's claim that eggs are a symbol of the "rebirth" of the risen Christ is nowhere found in the Bible. Venus and Ishtar are also known to be goddesses of sexuality and fertility and were often worshiped with temple prostitution.

All of this symbolism should be seen as an abomination to the celebration that is supposed to be about the offering of the risen Christ being raised up to the Father and accepted.

It was these three festivals of Christmas, Easter and the Sabbath that the Catholic Church used to gain a strangle-hold in the lives of well-meaning Christians, keeping them focused on pagan rituals and away from the true meaning of His own plan of salvation as laid out in the holy days that God commanded in Leviticus 23 and, it turns out, in nature.

---

[12] https://en.wikipedia.org/wiki/Ēostre

[13] https://skribbatous.org/blog/easter-and-ishtar

Part 3: The Sky-Clock

9

The Hands of the Clock

And God said, "Let luminaries be in the expanse of the heavens, to divide between the day and the night. And let them be for signs and for seasons, and for days and years. And let them be for luminaries in the expanse of the heavens, to give light on the earth." And it was so. And God made the two great luminaries: the great luminary to rule the day, and the small luminary and the stars to rule the night. And God set them in the expanse of the heavens, to give light on the earth, and to rule over the day and over the night; and to divide between the light and the darkness. And God saw that it was good (Genesis 1:14–18 LITV).

This is Yahweh's calendar. Some have called it the *sky-clock*, and I can't disagree with that name. Our modern (non-digital) clocks are modeled after it: If you look up at the sky, the sun and moon rotate around the sky exactly like the hands of a clock in front of the twelve constellations of the ecliptic, which are the twelve hours of the day. But it does more than keep the time of day. It keeps the time of the seasons and years and gives us signs to wonder at as well.

The creation account is the story of Elohim bringing order to an unordered world. The images of Genesis 1:2 (formless, void, darkness) are images of chaos and disorder, which is how the ancients viewed the idea of what we would today likely call nothingness. The remainder of the chapter is how He filled up that emptiness and ordered it. Order is seen as "good." By definition, order has reason and meaning. All that God sets in place can be seen this way. There is no randomness in His actions. Although we may look at the stars and see a random jumble of specks of light, the heavenly bodies are no exception. They are ordered and meaningful.

Wanting to keep God's calendar is a positive thing. Many places in the Bible say, "If you love me, keep my commandments." His appointed times: Sabbaths, new moons, and holy days, figure prominently as part of the commandments that God gave Israel and were all originally to be visible by using God's sky-clock. And even though they are not what gives us our salvation, that being the free gift of God through believing in the life, death and resurrection of Yeshua, they are a way for us to show our love to Him for what He did for us.

Those who have done so will unanimously tell you of the incredible meaning that can be gleaned from them, meaning that cannot be gleaned in the slightest from keeping the pagan days that Christians have been tricked into keeping by giving them pseudo-Christian sounding names and meaning. But it has also become obvious that there is no agreement on the actual timing of these appointed times.

It should not be a difficult thing to do, to look at the sky and know where in the day, week, month, and year we are. Yet it is. There are some basic things that have been lost to us since the time of creation. Some has been lost in much the same way that common sense is no longer common, some lost in cultural constructs that have changed over millennia, but there is more as well—difficulties that no common sense or research can account for. These are the things that those who try their best to keep God's calendar end up arguing about and splitting up fellowships over. And I will tell you right now that my goal is not to tell you what the one true calendar is, because I can't. And anyone who thinks they can, especially those who attack others who see differently, are wrong. More on why that is later.

So, what I'd like to do in this section is go over all the variables that are involved in figuring out time in a biblical way. I can't go over every calendar that men might come up with because the permutations based on the combinations of variables would probably fill a library. But just looking at the variables themselves should be enough to teach us something and at least point toward the basic types of calendars that are in use. And in every one, there is some merit, but also some fault. I'll go into some detail about some of the less familiar models just to point out where they come from, not because I think they are more correct or less correct.

To those who have not been around a church that even thinks about the calendar it may be a surprise that there are people who argue about such things. But believe me, there are many groups that take this very seriously, and I will no doubt offend some of them by writing what I have to say. To all, though, I just encourage you to keep an open mind and consider some things you may not have considered before.

Not everybody reading this will feel that keeping God's holy days is something they are ready to do, for a variety of reasons. Still, going through this information can only help build a greater understanding of the created world.

Others may have started to actually believe what I said about Easter and Christmas being completely pagan with no Biblical basis whatsoever and are wondering where to go next with that information. The next step is to see that God commanded His people to keep certain days "throughout their generations" even if very few people acknowledge them today at all. The one universal thing that all holy day keepers agree on is that they don't just line up on the Gregorian calendar the same way every year. In order to keep these days, then, we need to know how to keep time, how to use the clock that is written in the sky.

Appointed Times & the Meaning of Life

You may ask, if it is that difficult to figure out, then can't we just pick one calendar that is already in use and use that? Don't the Jews already have it all figured out anyway? Yes, you can just pick one, and yes, Judaism has a formula for calculating out the calendar for thousands of years. But even most Jews will acknowledge that their formula is not the way it was done back in biblical times. Back then they actually had to watch the sky and possibly the land before they could make a proclamation of any month or season.

When the last temple was destroyed in 70 AD, their priestly government, called the Sanhedrin, went with it. And without that government to make the decisions on when the moon was sighted, a new system had to be put into place to figure things out. Tradition says that Rabbi Hillel II came up with a series of calculations in the 4th century that can figure out the calendar without the use of the luminaries, and these calculations are still in use today. So, they no longer use the luminaries that were commanded in Genesis. They have also added many of their own rules into their calculations that were not biblically based—things such as "postponements" when a Sabbath and a holy day would combine to form a double Sabbath. These things have caused many to want to go back to using the Bible only (as well as the sun moon and stars) to figure these things out. But like I said, it is no easy task.

When the Bible mentions that a month begins with the new moon, we need to know what a new moon looks like, and trust me, this is not as simple as it sounds. When the Bible says something starts on a certain "day," we need to know when a day starts, and believe it or not, there is no consensus there either. Even the start of the year is a matter of debate. If you think this information should certainly be found somewhere in the Bible, you are both right and wrong. What is there is either not clearly spelled out or often is just *no longer* clearly spelled out. You see, we are reading a Bible that has been translated not just into another language, but into another culture and another time. Things that used to be taken for granted were often not written, so if the information is available at all, it needs to be completely reconstructed from context, which can itself be misleading. Interestingly, the Bible predicted this mess we would be in:

> "Whom will he teach knowledge? And whom will he make to understand the message? Those just weaned from milk? Those just drawn from the breasts? For precept must be upon precept, precept upon precept, Line upon line, line upon line, Here a little, there a little." For with stammering lips and another tongue He will speak to this people (Isaiah 28:9–11).

God knows He is speaking with stammering lips and another tongue to His people. The solution, He says, is to piece things together bit by bit, here a little, there a little, and with diligence we will grow and improve, just like with any skill. He wants us to have to work at it because it shows our hearts and our will to work for the knowledge of His ways.

So, let's approach these three luminaries one at a time to see what issues we have to conquer to come by some semblance of the calendar that God Himself put in place.

The Sun

The sun rules the day (Genesis 1:16). We can then assume that at the very least, the sun will tell us when a day starts and stops. Many people have done studies on the Hebrew words that are translated as "day" in English, and the short version of the story is that the word *day* can refer to either the light portion of the day or the entire 24-hour cycle, much like it does in English. So, when Yahweh commands to "keep the Sabbath day holy," He could be referring to either one. And there are people who do it both ways. By far the most common way is to keep it from sunset to sunset, but it is not the only way it is done. There are also folks who say the Sabbath is only for the light portion of the day. In ancient times, before electric lights lit up our homes at all hours, either version probably amounted to much the same thing, as labor was seldom done during the night to begin with. There are also those who keep a 24-hour Sabbath but start it at sunrise.

During creation week, each new day of creation ends with the phrase, "So the evening and the morning were the ___ day." Jews and the majority of Sabbatarian Christians take that phrase to be referring to the order of a day, that the evening comes first, then the morning and that makes a 24-hour cycle, or day.

However, there is a small but growing group who say this is not at all what the Bible is saying. They point to the Hebrew words and phraseology and conclude it should be translated closer to: "Such and such was created [on that day], then there was evening, then there was morning [the one that starts the next day]. The ___ day." They also point to the fact that on the first day, the first thing God created was the light, and afterward he separated it from the darkness, so that the light came first. Then they look at many other places in the Bible where morning is mentioned in the same breath as the next day, and the places that mention the phrases *day and night* or *morning and evening* vs. the phrases *night and day* or *evening and morning*, noticing that there are at least double the occurrences that mention day or morning first. There are also places that mention something happening "tomorrow" and then noting that that thing would occur in the next daylight portion, not that evening. Numbers 11:18-32 is one such story. They would add to that the sentiment that when we wake up in the morning, it just feels like we are starting a new day.

My point is not to convince you one way or the other, however, but just to point out that even how to start a day is far from a settled matter. Even looking at early historians provides ammunition for both sides, as there seems to be evidence in both directions, and both will pick and choose whatever "proves" their side.

The sun also gives us the period of the year. It follows a regular cycle of raising and lowering itself on its circuit through the sky. In

Part 3: The Sky-Clock

the summer it is high up at midday, more directly overhead, bringing heat and length to the days before gradually falling to its lowest point, closer to the horizon at midday during the winter, bringing with it shorter and colder days. It then begins its journey higher again and repeats the cycle.

At some point in this journey is the beginning of the year, but the sun itself does not tell us where that point is. Low point? High point? Midway between at the equilux (even light and darkness)? Exodus 12:2 tells us only that the month of Abib shall be the beginning of months, which obviously infers the start of the year. The name Abib refers to the state of ripening barley that will be ready for the first fruit wave-sheaf offering during the Feast of Unleavened Bread (Leviticus 23:10). Agriculturally, this puts us in the spring—March or April on our modern calendars. Most Jews, however, celebrate two new years. According to JTSA.com, "Nisan [another name for Abib], the month in which Passover occurs, comes to mark the first in the annual cycle of twelve months, while Tishrei [the seventh month] would herald the onset of a new solar year." The beginning of the seventh month, for most Jews, is a far bigger celebration. Some have done studies that conclude that the first month of creation was actually what we would now call the seventh month, then God changed the times when He proclaimed the first month to be Abib. There are also Jews who, in addition to the first and seventh months, celebrate a separate new year for trees and still another new year for animals. So, when is the new year? Apparently, the answer is not straightforward.

Does the sun also speak of seasons? Its cycle is regular enough that people have used the high and low points (the Solstices) to mark the start of summer and winter, and the days where the sun crosses the equator in between (the equinoxes), where light and dark are twelve hours each, to mark the first days of spring and autumn. So, it does seem to be able to schedule seasons. But are these the seasons that Genesis is speaking of? The Bible does mention summer and winter, but only as the times of heat and cold, not specific "seasons" with start and end dates. The Hebrew for *seasons* is Strong's H4150 *moed'im*, which means "appointed time," or "feast day." The Bible does specify appointed times for feast days and gives great detail on what days they are to be kept on, and they do not line up with "spring, summer, autumn, and winter." They also cannot be calculated simply using the sun. So, I don't believe that the sun can lay claim to the "seasons" of Genesis.

THE ENOCH/JUBILEES/ZADOK CALENDAR

There is a calendar system that many are coming across today, however, that does only rely on the sun for all seasonal calculation. Some call it the Priestly or Zadok calendar, as it supposedly aligns with the priestly rotation of 1 Chronicles 24. It is outlined in the extrabiblical books of both 1 Enoch and Jubilees.

There is much debate going on right now over whether these books should be considered inspired scripture or not. I will not enter that debate here, but I have read them both in their entirety and find them worthy of being read. The calendar they use relies on the equinox or equilux (depending on your interpretation) to start the year. The year is made up of exactly 364 days every year divided into twelve months that are not aligned with the moon. Instead they are assigned a regular amount of days.

Eight months will be thirty days and four will be thirty-one days, every third month being assigned an extra day as the head of each of the four seasons. The year is then also divided into exactly fifty-two seven-day weeks. In this system, the days of the week fall on the same calendar days year in and year out, and holy days will never fall on a weekly Sabbath.

It is all about even mathematical division with the only reliance on the lights in the firmament being the sun for starting the year. To accommodate the obvious difference between the 365.25-day actual solar year and the calendar's 364-day cycle, there are occasional intercalated weeks added. They wait long enough to use full weeks instead of using an extra day or two every year so that it does not throw off the days of the week from the recurring cycle. There are varying methods adherents use to decide when that week will be added, as it is not prescribed anywhere in either Enoch or Jubilees.

The charm of this calendar is that it is fairly simple and straightforward on the surface. As such, I think it is a calendar worthy of discussion in regard to the witness of the sun. If the calendar is something you are moved to research, this could be a rabbit hole worth jumping down. Yet even if you are convinced that Enoch and/or Jubilees are inspired scripture, you may find yourself confused by the apparent conflict with the Bible's instructions for using the moon in starting the months, most holy days and, of course, new moon days.

THE MOON

The moon rules the night (Genesis 1:16). And the controversy around the moon dwarfs that of the sun. The Bible talks about new moons and moons in general as periods of time. The word *month* in the Bible is just a translation of the word *moon*. So, when do we start a month? With the new moon. Simple! Not so fast. Just what *is* a new moon? The U.S. Naval Observatory says it is the complete absence of light on the moon. Zero percent illumination, or the conjunction with the sun. But is that what was meant biblically? The Bible is silent on the topic. Many biblical scholars and Sabbath/Holy Day keepers believe that the new moon historically was the first visible crescent, which had to be sighted to proclaim the start of the month. There is again controversy over whether that history started with creation, in Israel, or during the Babylonian captivity.

Some actually believe that the new moon is a full moon, pointing to the timing of Jesus' crucifixion in which the sun was darkened for three hours. They take that to mean that there was an eclipse at that time, which could only have happened two weeks into the month (the time of Passover) if the moon had been full two weeks earlier, at the new moon. If the sun darkening was a natural phenomenon, then they have a point. However, there has never been a record of the totality of an eclipse lasting for more than 7.5 minutes while the Passover darkening was stated to be for three hours.

Zero illumination, first crescent, and full moon observers also all have their favorite historians to back them up. There are even those (especially those who keep the Zadok/Enoch/Jubilees calendar) who believe the Bible rarely even mentions the moon! They claim that the term *new moon* is actually only the word *renewal* without the word for moon attached, which they say was only added in modern translations, a conclusion you would have to come to in order to reconcile that calendar with the Bible.

But assuming there is an actual new moon in the Bible, the controversy doesn't end with figuring out what a new moon is. There is also the question of *where* the moon should be viewed. This is mostly important to the first visible crescent crowd. Since the sighting is critical, it changes dramatically depending upon where you see it from. Some claim that it must be observed within Israel; some say from within Jerusalem itself. But both cite the reason that the priests at the temple needed to know as soon as possible to proclaim the start of the month so that the sacrifices would not be delayed. Others say local observance is the way to go because most believers do not live in the Holy Land today, and the sacrificial system is not in place now anyway. The Jerusalem crowd will counter with Isaiah 2:3, "For out of Zion shall go forth the law, And the word of Yahweh from Jerusalem." Allow me a quick digression with that one.

THE WORD GOES OUT FROM JERUSALEM

> This is what Isaiah the son of Amoz saw concerning Judah and Jerusalem. It shall happen in the latter days, that the mountain of Yahweh's house shall be established on the top of the mountains, and shall be raised above the hills; and all nations shall flow to it. Many peoples shall go and say, "Come, let's go up to the mountain of Yahweh, to the house of the God of Jacob; and he will teach us

Part 3: The Sky-Clock

of his ways, and we will walk in his paths." For out of Zion the law shall go out, and Yahweh's word from Jerusalem (Isaiah 2:1-3 WEB).

I personally was taught for years that the Word of Yahweh goes out from Jerusalem, and that that is the reason all Sabbaths must start in the time zone of Jerusalem first. I cannot use a local sighting of the moon to start the new month because I may see it before it is seen in Jerusalem and start my month early. The sighting must come from Jerusalem first so that the word can go out from there. But is that really what Isaiah was talking about? I will follow the logic through.

Isaiah 2:3 is set in the latter days (v. 2) in a location that could be the current location, heavenly Jerusalem, or some other location that will be set up at that time. It could even be all spiritual analogy that does not refer to a physical place at all. We just do not know. Yet, for the sake of argument, we will assume that it refers to the current physical location in the modern nation of Israel. Starting every month with a lunar sighting from Jerusalem is effectively establishing an international date line to just east of Jerusalem. Currently the time zone starting at Iraq and Saudi Arabia is the next time zone east, so those countries would need to wait almost a full day, twenty-three hours, until they start their Sabbath so as not to supersede Jerusalem. Maybe that is how it should be, but it seems irrational for those just a few miles away to have to wait almost a full day to start their month or celebrate a Sabbath or holy day.

Genesis 1 says that the sun and moon are made for times and seasons, but did it say that they are only to be looked at from Israel? When Yahweh gave that command, Israel was not yet even a nation, Jerusalem had not been founded, and man had yet to even be created and placed in Eden. Certainly, these lights were meant for all the world to see and use. And if all the world could see and use them, then would they not be keeping the Sabbaths and new moons at their local time?

So, what does it mean for the word of Yahweh to go out from Jerusalem? We first need to know the identity of Jerusalem. Is it just a city or location, or is there more? We just read in the last section that Jerusalem is the name given to Christ's bride! It is a spiritual thing—the spiritual identity of those who are married to Yeshua, the Messiah. During the time talked about in Isaiah 2 and Micah 4, it is Christ's Bride who is teaching the law to all the nations. Revelation 20:6 says, "They will be priests of God and of Christ and will reign with Him a thousand years."

We know these priests are also Jerusalem, or become so, from Revelation 21:2, "I saw New Jerusalem coming down out of Heaven from God, having been prepared as a bride, having been adorned for her Husband" (LITV). She will be His mouthpiece, an extension of Him, and will teach the nations. And wherever she is, she will teach them to keep the Sabbaths and to find them by the sun, moon, and stars, wherever they are!

THE LUNAR SABBATH

To add another layer to the discussion of the moon, there is the notion that some put forward that the moon also dictates, or at least originally dictated, the cycle of the week. The traditional view of the week, of course, is that it has been kept in a perpetual seven-day cycle since the time of creation, handed down unbroken until today. But lately there are many who question this tradition. I gave some of the history of how this Sabbath was changed, if indeed it was the original Sabbath, in the last chapter.

I'd like to spend some extra time on this because I think that it is merited. Very few people have heard of the lunar Sabbath, and of those who have, there is a lack of understanding how it actually works, being dismissed out of hand without investigation, as I did the first time I heard about it. Through my study of finding the Word in nature, however, I decided I might want to look into it further. I now find this method fascinating, as it makes use of the natural world perhaps more fully than any other calendar. It brings us into some unconventional thinking, to be sure, yet with an open mind it does appear to be intellectually honest, thorough, and consistent with the Scriptures. This is not to say I find it perfect or "the one true calendar." Like I said before, I don't believe there is one at this time. Yet I do find it quite possible that the lunar Sabbath originally played a significant role in God's calendar as it *used to be*.

Without its attachment to creation, the week as we know it seems like an artificial construct. The year follows the sun as perfectly today as it always has. The month makes sense, with its connection to the moon, even though we have now detached it in modern society. But what about the week? There seems to be no seven-day repeating cycle in nature. Tradition says that the week is simply the memorial of the seven-day creation that has been kept intact since the creation. But is there actually any evidence that it has never been broken? The correct calculation of the holy days stopped when the temple was destroyed in 70 AD, so is there any reason the Sabbath should have fared better?

As a hypothetical thought experiment, assume that the Sabbath was actually lost, so that we did not know what day of the week it currently was. Would there be a way to regain that knowledge? Would there be anything in nature that would point us toward the correct day? Sadly, as tradition currently understands the Sabbath, no there is not.

As another thought experiment, let's assume there is an unbroken seven-day weekly cycle. Now imagine two explorers setting off in ships from the same location, sailing in opposite directions. Suppose after many weeks or months, they meet up on the opposite side of the earth. They both kept careful logs of the days that passed, but somehow, they find that one says it is the first day of the week and the other the second day. If they both complete their circumnavigation back to their point of origin, they will then find that they are actually two days off from each other and one day off from the folks who never left the country.

In reality, this is not an experiment because it has actually happened. This same problem would also occur with migrating people. Even if the migration happens over years, the day will still become one day off after reaching a sufficient distance, even though the days have been tracked religiously. This has happened many times with different peoples and cultures, so who is to say which day of the week should be kept in any location?

These experiments show that the days of the week are not grounded in anything real as they are currently kept. They are an abstract concept that is impossible to prove, especially over long periods of time with traveling inhabitants.

Yet there is an alternate way of calculating the Sabbath that relies completely on nature, and which, curiously enough, is written about historically. The idea is called the *lunar Sabbath*, and gets its name, as you might expect, from looking at the moon.

The basic idea is that the visible portion of the lunar cycle is broken up into four seven-day sections, with the new moon (the non-visible portion of the cycle) being a different kind of day that is outside of the weekly cycle. The first seven days would go from the earliest crescent to the waxing half-moon, which would be visible in the sky directly overhead as the sun sets. The second seven days would take you to the full moon, which would be just coming over the horizon at sunset, and directly overhead at midnight. The third is a waning half-moon visible directly overhead as the sun is rising and just setting when the sun is directly overhead at noon. The fourth is the last waning crescent which is only visible just before sunrise. These work as time markers and are evenly laid out at right angles in the sky, like hands of the clock marking 3, 6, 9, and 12 o'clock. Because of the 29½-day cycle of the moon, roughly every other month there will be a second new moon day added at the end before the month starts over.

Date-wise, every month will look like this: The new moon day will be the first day of the month. The waxing quarter moon will be seven days later on the eighth day, the full moon on the fifteenth, the waning quarter on the twenty-second, and the last visible crescent on the twenty-ninth.

These dates just so happen to line up handsomely with the dates for the largest festivals of the appointed times: Unleavened Bread and the Feast of Tabernacles both start on the fifteenth of their months, and Tabernacles actually ends with another day called simply "the Eighth Day" that takes place on the twenty-second. These days are to be kept as Holy Convocations with no servile work to be done, just as the Sabbath is. This calendar takes the opposite stance of the Zadok calendar, stating that the holy days *should* fall on Sabbath days instead of making sure to avoid them.

There is actually evidence that this was the original way that the Hebrews kept the Sabbath. The traditional view, that the Jews have kept consistent track of a continuous seven-day cycle since the creation does not hold water. First, where is the record that has supposedly been kept and maintained since creation week, or even since the giving of the law? I hear about the meticulous record-keeping of the Jews but have never heard of anyone who has seen this record or knows where it is. The Jews were not even a people at the creation, and after the law there is still no record of the continuous cycle until much, much later. Second, and perhaps more importantly, the Jews own reference books that we *can* look at claim that they originally kept a lunar Sabbath! Here are just a couple of statements.

> Shabbat originally arose from the lunar cycle, containing four weeks ending in Sabbath, plus one or two additional unreckoned days per month[14].

---

[14] Landman, Isaac, and Simon Cohen. *The Universal Jewish Encyclopedia: An Authoritative and Popular Presentation of Jews and Judaism Since the Earliest Times.* 1943, p. 482–483.

Appointed Times & the Meaning of Life

> The Sabbath, as marking the end of the week, reveals its lunar origin; the phases of the moon having taught the shepherds, whose weal or wo depended so largely upon the benevolence or malevolence of the night season, to divide the period elapsing between two new moons into four equal groups (weeks), the last day of each—in imitation of the moon's coming to rest, as it were—becoming the day of rest. Indications are not wanting that at first the New Moon festival was not counted among the seven days of the week (see Week); but after 7x4 (=28) days had elapsed, one or two days were intercalated as New Moon days, whereupon a new cycle of four weeks began, so that the Sabbath was a movable festival. Later the week and the Sabbath became fixed; and this gradually resulted in taking away from the New Moon festival its popular importance. The New Moon is still, and the Sabbath originally was, dependent upon the lunar cycle[15].

There are also many references in other historical sources that admit the same thing.

> The mode of reckoning among the Israelites was originally doubtless the same as that of the Babylonians, by dividing the first 28 days of each month into four weeks terminating respectively on the 7th, 14th, 21st, and 28th day, and by making the first week of the new month always begin with the new moon. This intimate connection, however, between the week and the month was soon dissolved[16].

> A continuous seven-day cycle that runs throughout history paying no attention whatsoever to the moon and its phases is a distinctly Jewish invention. Moreover, the dissociation of the seven-day week from nature has been one of the most significant contributions of Judaism to civilization. Like the invention of the mechanical clock some 1,500 years later, it facilitates the establishment of what Lewis Mumford identified as "mechanical

---

[15] Hirsch, Emil G. *The Jewish Encyclopedia, Volume 5*. 1906, p. 376

[16] Marti, Karl, D. D. *Encyclopedia Biblica, Volume IV*. 1903, p. 5290

periodicity," thus essentially increasing the distance between human beings and nature. Quasi [lunar] weeks and [continuous] weeks actually represent two fundamentally distinct modes of temporal organization of human life, the former involving partial adaptation to nature, and the latter stressing total emancipation from it. The invention of the continuous week was therefore one of the most significant breakthroughs in human beings' attempts to break away from being prisoners of nature and create a social world of their own[17].

It does seem, then, that nature could have been the original timekeeper for the week. This system seems confusing to modern day thinkers because the Sabbath seems to be "floating". And if we overlay it on our own Gregorian calendar, yes, it is. But of course, originally, the lights in the sky were the only system being used. So, when Yahweh sanctified the seventh day, He had no reference to Saturday. It was simply the seventh day of existence on the earth, and it likely coincided with the waxing quarter moon. The moon would have been created on day four lit up as a waxing crescent.

There is evidence in the creation week for the "unreckoned" new moon day as well. Genesis 1:1–2, "In the beginning God created the heavens and the earth. The earth was without form, and void; and darkness was on the face of the deep. And the Spirit of God was hovering over the face of the waters." This is before day one of the creation week, and we see that the earth was already there; it was just *dark*. A day was not called a day until light came into existence on day one, and that seems the only qualification for calling it such. We have discussed how in both Hebrew and English the word *day* can refer to either a twenty-four-hour period or to the daylight portion of it. It should be worth noting, then, that it is the light that defines a day. A day without light cannot be a day. So, it seems that the new moon days were meant as a memorial to this portion of the creation,

---

[17] Zerubavel, Eviatar. *The Seven Day Circle: the History and Meaning of the Week*, The Free Press, 1985, p. 11

before day one, as the seventh day was a memorial to God's rest from the six days of work that preceded it.

Our human nature seems to innately understand even intervals. When a number is round, such as 100 or 250, that number is somehow easier for our minds to "rest" on, so that when we are faced with 98 or 253, we want to round them up or down to the more restful figure. When our early forefathers looked at the sky, they would have felt the same thing when the moon was directly overhead at a right angle with the setting sun; it would just seem like an even interval, and restful to their minds.

Today we have been trained to think in repeating cycles, but since those cycles have no basis in nature, it is obvious that they are learned only through training. Genesis tells us plainly to look at the creation, specifically the lights in the sky, to tell time, not to a contrivance of man.

Those who start looking into this system, however, will also start to find things to argue with, myself included. I actually discarded the idea immediately the first time I heard of it from somebody else because it occurred to me that the count to Pentecost could not work with a lunar Sabbath count. When I started thinking about it again later on my own, however, I decided to actually research what those who keep it say. What I found involved so much rethinking of everything that I held true that I wasn't sure whether to take it seriously, or not. But going on the notion of Proverbs 18:13, "He who answers a matter before he hears it, it is folly and a shame to him," I decided to dive in.

The problem made by using the lunar count is that adding in a day or two of new moon days keeps the count of "seven Sabbaths" from equaling forty-nine days, as Leviticus 23 says it should. The lunar count would have to equal fifty-two days in most years.

This seems like a killer until we look at how Leviticus 23:15–16 is translated. Most versions give something like the NKJV here.

> And you shall count for yourselves from the day after the Sabbath, from the day that you brought the sheaf of the wave offering: seven Sabbaths shall be completed. Count fifty days to the day after the seventh Sabbath; then you shall offer a new grain offering to Yahweh.

The Lunar Sabbatarians say that is a mistranslation, opting for translations like the Interlinear or Literal Version (LITV) that state the counts of seven weeks and fifty days as two separate items instead of two ways of stating the same thing.

> And you shall number to you from the next day after the sabbath, from the day you bring in the sheaf of the wave offering; they shall be seven complete sabbaths; the next day after the seventh sabbath, you shall number fifty days; and you shall bring near a new food offering to Jehovah;

Very different! There are arguments that go way deeper into the Hebrew grammar than I'm willing to go here. But if that is true, it changes some things and creates its own problems. Adding them together puts the date for Pentecost in early summer instead of mid-spring. But there is actually evidence that this could be the case!

One piece of evidence that is used for an early summer Pentecost is found in Acts 20:16 where Paul states that he would like to be in Jerusalem, if possible, by Pentecost. Chapters 20–21 give a chronology of his journey from the time of Unleavened Bread (20:6) until his arrival in Jerusalem. Adding up the days he travelled and tarried, and researching the distances he had to travel, it becomes apparent that it would have been a physical impossibility for Paul to make it to Jerusalem in the time allotted using the traditional fifty-day count. Of course, the account does not state that he actually made it in time, but it does appear to be some sort of festival season when he arrived, with many foreigners around Jerusalem.

As further evidence that early summer is actually the correct time, they look at the plagues of hail in Exodus 9:31–32 when "the flax and the barley were struck, for the barley was in the head and the flax was in bud. But the wheat and the spelt were not struck, for they are late crops." Agriculturally, wheat can be either planted in the winter or in the spring. A winter planting will lie dormant most of the winter but will come up earlier and ripen earlier than spring-planted wheat. The early wheat would have been up at the same time as the barley, even though it would ripen later, and so would have been damaged along with the barley and flax. The spring wheat, however, would have come up much later and been spared the damage, which is apparently what happened.

Of course this was Egypt, so there is no guarantee that Israel would have used the same planting methods, as it has different climate zones from Egypt. Currently, however, Israel is quite capable of growing both plantings well. Either way, it is quite possible that the later planting is what they used at the time, or that they sowed both.

The winter planting, which is the same as the barley, gives a harvest time that is compatible with the traditional view of Pentecost starting roughly seven weeks later than the barley harvest starts. Spring planting delays the wheat, so that it is harvested in the summer, beginning roughly another fifty days later. This is very interesting to me, because it actually justifies both dates, as well as the reasoning for having two counts, separated by two different methods of counting.

Also interesting is the fact that in the Old Testament, the festival is exclusively called the Feast of Weeks, whereas in the New it is called Pentecost, which literally means five-ten, or fifty, which is not a translation of the Hebrew into Greek at all, but a new term that was not used until New Covenant times. Pentecost might actually be a dual celebration then, with the first part called the Feast of Weeks, representing the Old Covenant harvest, and the second part being Pentecost, instituted for the first time under the New Covenant, when Pentecost had "fully" come, as was stated in Acts 2.

Part 3: The Sky-Clock

It may sound like I am trying to convince you that this is the one correct calendar to use, but that is not the case. I am defending it as an intellectually honest attempt at looking to Yahweh's creation as He said to do, knowing that most people tend to write it off before looking at it. I do still have a few reservations about it, and you will see in my conclusion why I don't actually think there even is a correct way to find God's true calendar today.

THE STARS

At the start of the chapter, I quoted Genesis from the Literal Version, where it said, "and the small luminary and the stars to rule the night." Other translations, such as the King James and New King James, state that, "the lesser light to rule the night. He made the stars also." So, it is unclear whether the stars are to share in the "ruling" of the night. Obviously, they do shine then, so whatever duty they have takes place at night. But what is that duty?

The sun told us about the cycle of a day and year, the moon told of the month and possibly the week. Genesis says that the duties of the luminaries would be, "for signs and for seasons, and for days and years." We haven't seen how the sun or moon would take care of seasons yet (except possibly in the Zadok calendar), so by default, that leaves the stars!

This, for a great number, if not most people, is the luminary category we are least familiar with. It is certainly the one I feel least prepared to talk about. Ancient people, without the use of electric lights, spent far more of their time looking at and studying the stars and constellations than we do today. Today, most people will be lucky if they can locate more than a couple of constellations on any given night. But that does not excuse us, so I will do my best here to speak of the stars.

If the stars are speaking about seasons (appointed times or feast days), then we need to know how they do so. The sun and moon are each single points that pass through the vast sky each day and night.

The stars act as the backdrop over which they travel. This backdrop is spinning around the North Star, so that the stars return to almost, but not quite, the same place every night. They will shift by about one degree per night, so that in the course of a year, they have moved through the entire sky and back to almost, but not quite, the same position as the previous year, in turn causing the constellations to move through the sky at a rate that will take 25,772 years to cycle completely through.

These motions are the gears of the clock that move the sun, moon, and wanderers (planets) through the sky in a constantly changing and *almost* recurring pattern. This *almost* is important because it allows each year to be different from the previous one. The "seasons" will always be there as promised to Noah in Genesis 8:22, but the subtle changes of the cycle allow for "signs" to show up from time to time, such as the aligning of certain stars and planets, or an eclipse. And it also throws everything off over large amounts of time!

This being God's Creation, the sky can also be unpredictable, with stars, comets, and other lights occasionally showing up out of nowhere, such as the star that showed the wise men the location of the newborn Messiah.

The predictable cycles are what we are most concerned with, however, for calculating seasons. When we see the moon sitting in a certain constellation, it should tell us something. When it is in that position while the sun is in a certain constellation (inferred by the position of the stars as seen just after the sun goes down or just before it comes up), it will tell us even more. For example, every spring, at the start of the month of Abib, the sun will be in Aries (using tropical astrology) and so will the moon (at new moon, they will always be very close together). Aries is always considered the first sign in astrology for this reason. Fifteen days later, at the beginning of the Feast of Unleavened Bread, the moon will be passing through the constellation of Virgo. The picture of the constellation of Virgo

Part 3: The Sky-Clock

has almost always been rendered with a sheaf of grain in the hand of the virgin, symbolizing the time of year. Leviticus 23 tells us that there must be a first fruit of barley offered during the Feast of Unleavened Bread on the wave-sheaf day. Virgo is telling us that the timing will be correct to find the first ripening barley.

Many Christians will be thinking that they are not supposed to be involved in things like astrology, but there is a big difference between using the stars to tell times and seasons and using them to predict behaviors or foretell "fortunes." Maybe the term *astronomy* is more comfortable than astrology. But it is astrology that has always been more concerned with attaching meaning to the relative positions of the celestial bodies to each other, while astronomy is more of a mechanical study of what is there and understanding the math behind it.

The Bible certainly attaches meaning to these things, so astrology does seem the more appropriate term to use. Attaching meaning to the stars and constellations would have been a natural thing to do based on the life cycles of seed time and harvest, when the ancients noted patterns of repetition in the sky that followed the patterns of repetition on the ground. It was not coincidence that they lined up year after year. The Bible itself mentions the various constellations and the zodiac itself. The book of Job calls it Mazzaroth.

What the Bible explicitly says not to do with the stars is divination, which is an abomination. What the adversary has done is to conflate divination with the calculations of the seasons. Christians have done the right thing in refusing to be involved in divination, but in doing so have fallen into the adversary's trap of throwing out the baby with the bath water and in the process have lost much knowledge.

We have forgotten how to look at the sky, and in many cases, due to light pollution (or other pollution) we cannot see the stars even if we want to. I am also not saying that all of the constellations of the modern zodiac contain accurate symbolism for the cycles that

Appointed Times & the Meaning of Life

our Father laid out. They have likely been corrupted by Greek and Roman, Egyptian, and Arabian mythologies. Some have tried to uncover older biblical foundations of the constellations, but it is a difficult undertaking to do so, with very little historical record. Some constellations, however, such as Virgo, seem to have remained remarkably similar throughout millennia, and throughout many cultures.

Another problem we run into if we actually start studying the sky, instead of just looking at the textbooks, is that the constellations are not where they are supposed to be! At the first new moon after the spring equinox, my computer app will say that the sun is in Aries, but if I go look at which stars the sun is actually passing in front of, it will be in the constellation Pisces. Why? The most commonly used form of astrology in western nations is known as tropical astrology, which is based on the position of the stars as they were seen about two thousand years ago. At that time the sky was divided into twelve equal sectors, each representing one "sign," and every year the sectors would not move, even though the constellations inside of them slowly did. It did not take into account the precession of the equinoxes as I described above, that they do not return exactly to the same place every year.

Another form of astrology, known as Sidereal astrology, does account for this yearly change. In the last two thousand years, the signs have actually moved almost a whole sign over, so that where Tropical shows the year beginning with Aries, Sidereal will show the sun in Pisces when the year starts because that is actually where the sun is at that time. Sidereal astrology also divides the sky into twelve equal thirty-degree sectors though, and what that means is that in reality, neither tropical nor sidereal astrology will account for exactly which constellation the sun and moon will be found in at a given time! You see, the constellations do not happen to all take up an even thirty degrees of the sky. Some are quite large, like Virgo, and some quite small, like Scorpio.

For instance, during the thirty or so days that sidereal astrology calls Scorpio, six days the sun will actually be in Libra, six will be in Scorpio and eighteen of them will be in Ophiuchus, which is usually not even considered a zodiacal sign in either form of astrology!

There are a small number of astrologers who use the actual visible constellations, referred to as *astronomical astrology*. Using the actual placement of the sun and moon in relation to the stars makes sense, since it was the actual lights that were given for signs and seasons, not an artificial division of space.

Regardless of how the sky is divided up by the twelve constellations, however, doing so creates a situation where the zodiac cannot relate consistently to the months, as they do in our current twelve-month calendars. Lunar months create the need to add a thirteenth month roughly every third year, which is different than the twelve equal divisions of astrology. But was it always that way?

A month calculated by the moon today is about 29.5 days long. But in Genesis it appears that it was an even thirty days when we look at the flood narrative of Genesis 7:11–24. The flood started on the seventeenth day of the second month and the ark rested on Ararat 150 days later on the seventeenth day of the seventh month. This is exactly five months, which divided into 150 days equals an even thirty days for each month. Because of this, some have speculated that there used to be a perfect 360-day year divided by twelve perfect thirty day lunar months at creation, and that it got out of whack somewhere, possibly with the flood, Joshua's long day in Joshua 10:12–14, with the suns shadow turning backwards for Hezekiah in 2 Kings 20:8–11, or in some other unrecorded event on earth. But we just cannot know this.

When things are very close to being perfect, we have a tendency to think that they used to be or should be perfect. But the Bible gives no indication that this is true, and our idea of perfection can be different from God's.

Appointed Times & the Meaning of Life

There are extra-biblical texts that give explicit information on the length of months and years. Both the book of Jubilees and the book of 1 Enoch speak of the year being a regular 364 days, divided by an even 52 seven-day weeks and twelve months, eight of them 30 days and four of them (every third month to start each season) had 31 days, so that the head of each season is given a special day outside of the month itself. Either way, 29.5 or 30 with every third month 31 days, this can never match the five consecutive 30-day months spoken of in Genesis 7, nor can it line up with the vastly different sizes of the constellations as we know them, such as a six-day solar transit through Scorpio.

If the stars were to be consistent with both the seasons and the months, year after year, it seems that the ancient Mazzaroth must have used different star clusters to make its constellations, ones that would have created an equal twelve divisions in the sky, but that would also be making the assumption that the lengths of the months were consistent and had no need to intercalate a thirteenth month.

But in the end, there are very few details about the divisions and meaning of the stars that we can know for certain today. The Bible itself does not command these divisions, and the stars themselves do not give any indication as to where one constellation should end and another start. And if the moon is already counting the months, is there really a need for the stars to do the same? Likely the division and any attached meaning of constellations was added later by people looking to attach that meaning, based on the cycles of life. Yet, the sun and moon traversing the same stars at the same time each year is certainly a visible fact, and for that to be used as a sign for knowing when next year's repetition will occur is only natural. So, for now, I'll leave it at that.

Conclusion?

It should be obvious by now that there are too many unknowns and inconsistencies to make any solid guess at what the sky-clock looked like at creation or at the giving of the law. We only have what we have right now, and though it is similar, our current sky does not seem to match the sky of the Bible 100 percent. What are we to do with that?

I talked about the appointed times being a good thing to keep; something that we can glean meaning from about the plan of salvation and more, but if we cannot keep them accurately, should we just give up and call it all off? I say no. If you are led to think about these things, then the Holy Spirit is moving you, and the Spirit does not move you to do things that are evil. Yahweh only created things that were "good." The seasons (Moedim, or appointed times) were created in the first chapter of the Bible, not at mount Sinai. During the Exodus, Yahweh expounded on how to keep these days, on their meaning and sacrifices. But He never said He was creating a new thing; He just commanded that they celebrate something that had already been created.

Israel was never good at keeping commandments, however. They would keep them for short periods, then forget for decades or centuries. Then someone like Nehemiah would come along and realize that they screwed up and would put Israel back on track keeping the feasts. Then Israel would start making an attempt to keep them, but their hearts would be in the wrong place, they would turn them into something they were not supposed to be, and Yahweh would not be pleased. He says to Israel,

> "What are the multitude of your sacrifices to me?", says Yahweh. "I have had enough of the burnt offerings of rams, and the fat of fed animals. I don't delight in the blood of bulls, or of lambs, or of male goats. When you come to appear before me, who has required this at your hand, to trample my courts? Bring no more vain offerings. Incense is an abomination to me; new moons, Sabbaths, and convocations: I can't stand evil assemblies. My soul hates your New Moons and your appointed feasts. They are a burden to me. I am weary of bearing them (Isaiah 1:11–14 WEB).

Appointed Times & the Meaning of Life

> I hate, I despise your feast days; and I will not delight in your solemn assemblies. Though you offer Me burnt offerings and your grain offerings, I will not be pleased; nor will I regard the peace offerings of your fat animals (Amos 5:21–22).

In fact, He was so displeased with what these appointed times and associated sacrifices had become to Israel that He did something remarkable. He took them away. Hosea 2 is speaking about the shame of Israel's harlotries. In verse 11 Yahweh says,

> I will also cause all her joy to cease, her feast days, her new moons, and her sabbaths, and all her solemn feasts (LITV).

He causes her to cease her feast days, new moons, and Sabbaths! He takes them away! We are left to wonder, though, how and when did He do that?

Hosea was a prophet during "the days of Uriah, Jotham, Ahaz, and Hezekiah, kings of Judah" (Hosea 1:1). Previously, I mentioned that some think that when Yahweh moved the shadow backwards for Hezekiah it could have had permanent consequences with the gears of the sky-clock. So, the timing with Hezekiah seems right, and although it is only speculation, a ten degree change in the position of the sun seems like it could be enough to account for significant changes to the solar/lunar cycles.

Of course, it still could have been some later event that changed things. We do still see Yeshua and the disciples keeping the feast days in the New Covenant period without a word of correction about the days the Jews were keeping being incorrect. However, some passages could be taken as inference that Jesus was keeping the days differently from others. In John 7:6–10, when the Feast of Tabernacles was nearing, He tells His brothers,

> Then Jesus said to them, "My time has not yet come, but your time is always ready. The world cannot hate you, but it hates Me because I testify of it that its works are evil. You go up to this feast.

Part 3: The Sky-Clock

I am not yet going up to this feast, for My time has not yet fully come." When He had said these things to them, He remained in Galilee. But when His brothers had gone up, then He also went up to the feast, not openly, but as it were in secret.

Maybe He just wanted to go incognito, which was apparently the case, but why would He go late and state that His time had not yet come? We also see the Passover/Feast of Unleavened Bread referred to at the time of the Crucifixion as "a feast of the Jews," (John 5:1 and 6:4) as if they were no longer the feasts of Yahweh, or perhaps were timed differently than the feasts of Yahweh. I'm just bringing out possibilities here, as we cannot really know for sure.

Yet another possibility is that it was the church itself that took away the feast days and the Sabbaths. There is much historical evidence to the Sabbath being changed by Constantine in the third century, later to be enshrined by the Catholic church wanting to separate itself from Judaism by doing away with all things Jewish.

In those early centuries, the church had quickly turned into a powerful governing body whose dictates would be followed by all believers, with dire consequences for those who did not adhere. Certainly, for about 1500 years, there is very little evidence of Christian churches keeping the Sabbath or feast days. This would allow for the possibility of the sky-clock being still unchanged, if not for the evidence that we can see with our eyes that it differs from the descriptions given during the time of Noah.

The main point here is that God did state that He would take the feasts away from Israel, and then for much of the last two thousand years, very few believers in Messiah have kept them.

It is possible that there were isolated individuals or congregations that kept the Sabbath through this time, but the earliest organized group I have found in my research is the Seventh Day Baptist movement, which had its founding in London in 1650, and in the USA in 1671, and remains active today.

Appointed Times & the Meaning of Life

In the mid nineteenth century, individuals and small groups who were part of the Millerite movement (famous for their setting the date of the second advent of Christ on October 22, 1844, and the ensuing "Great Disappointment") started promoting keeping the Sabbath as well. A number of church organizations formed from the Millerites over the next century, including the Church of God (Seventh Day), Seventh Day Adventist, and Worldwide Church of God. Worldwide (which started as the Radio Church of God) was the first to espouse Holy Day keeping in addition to the Sabbath.

In more recent decades, there have been many new churches and fellowships formed in movements known as "Hebrew Roots" and "Messianic Judaism" and others that are not aligned with any particular movement but still espouse the keeping of Sabbath and feast days. Almost all of these groups and movements disagree at some level on the timing and function of the holy days, and some on the timing of the Sabbath. Yet they continue to grow, with many even within mainstream Christianity starting to question pagan holidays and wonder about the authority behind Sunday worship.

The questions then are: Why is there such a resurgence in keeping God's calendar now? And why is there such universal disagreement on how to do it? The former, I believe, is the movement of Holy Spirit guiding His people in these last days to find His truth. The Bible talks of the millennial reign, especially in the book of Ezekiel, and apparently during that time, there will again be temple worship, holy days, and sacrifices. My personal belief is that we are seeing the birth pains that will deliver us into this millennial reign, and that God is raising up people with the understanding to restore proper worship at that time. The latter question is what I have been attempting to answer here: If the Spirit is moving people to find and keep these days, then why does He not reveal the proper way to do so?

If we are indeed living in the times just before the millennial reign, then there is one good, functional reason that we would not be able to keep the calendar in the same way as they did in the Bible. Ezekiel's third temple period, which I believe is the millennial reign, speaks of the appointed times that will be kept, and they are different than the ones of Leviticus 23:

> Thus says the Lord Yahweh: "In the first month, on the first day of the month, you shall take a young bull without blemish and cleanse the sanctuary. The priest shall take some of the blood of the sin offering and put it on the doorposts of the temple, on the four corners of the ledge of the altar, and on the gateposts of the gate of the inner court. And so you shall do on the seventh day of the month for everyone who has sinned unintentionally or in ignorance. Thus you shall make atonement for the temple. "In the first month, on the fourteenth day of the month, you shall observe the Passover, a feast of seven days; unleavened bread shall be eaten. And on that day the prince shall prepare for himself and for all the people of the land a bull for a sin offering. On the seven days of the feast he shall prepare a burnt offering to Yahweh, seven bulls and seven rams without blemish, daily for seven days, and a kid of the goats daily for a sin offering. And he shall prepare a grain offering of one ephah for each bull and one ephah for each ram, together with a hin of oil for each ephah. "In the seventh month, on the fifteenth day of the month, at the feast, he shall do likewise for seven days, according to the sin offering, the burnt offering, the grain offering, and the oil" (Ezekiel 45:18–25).

We see the first and seventh days of the first month being days of atonement that were either not commanded in Leviticus or were moved from its single day in the seventh month previously. Passover and Unleavened Bread seem the same, but then there is no mention of the Feast of Weeks/Pentecost, or of the day of Trumpets. The Feast of Tabernacles is then kept consistently with Leviticus, except that the Eighth day is left out. There is a lot to think about with the reasons for the changes. But the fact is, they are presented as being kept very differently in what could actually be the near future. Should we worry about getting the timing right for when they used to be kept when they will be changing shortly anyway? God could be putting the idea of the holy days back into the hearts of His people, but waiting to reveal how it will actually be done until later. A lot has been fulfilled in the plan of salvation since the holy days were initially implemented, so there will likely be a different emphasis during the third temple/millennium period.

There is likely another reason for our lack of understanding at this time as well, and it is perhaps far more important to our current walk.

As I mentioned earlier, keeping these days is not a salvational issue, although some churches, such as Worldwide Church of God and some of its offshoots, have taught that it is. There are many, like myself, who have a history with these churches and have become fed-up with the constant judgment or have been kicked out of church based on questioning official doctrines, such as whether the new moon should be a sighted first crescent or a conjunction. In the same manner as the Catholic church, there is a view that doctrine can only be decided on at a corporate level, and individuals are not qualified to study or understand such matters.

I have been involved in these disputes and know the hurt that is caused by them. I have seen people disfellowshipped and had their name dragged through the mud and I have been one of them. The behavior is very un-Christlike, yet books could be written on the many abuses of power that have taken place just from the stories I have heard, which are but a small percentage of those that have actually taken place.

For those reading this who have no background in any of these churches, it may seem crazy for people to fight over such things. But what I see is a logical outcome for a group of people who saw a lack of biblical truth in mainstream Christianity and set out to correct it. "Truth" became the be-all end-all of the gospel, and in the process, much of what other mainstream denominations did have right was left out—namely loving your neighbor as yourself and a reliance on the Holy Spirit.

Shortly after Herbert W. Armstrong, the founder of Worldwide Church of God, died, the new leadership started throwing out his teachings, starting first with the rightly questionable cult-like ones so that they could start focusing on the love, forgiveness and mercy of Jesus (all good), but continued straight until the holy days and the Sabbath were thrown out and Christmas and Easter were brought back in.

This caused members to either join an offshoot splinter group that maintained "the truth" or go back into mainstream Christianity. It epitomized the idea that we can only have truth *or* the spirit of love. Having both seemed like an impossibility.

John 4:23–24 tells us, "But the hour is coming, and now is, when the true worshipers will worship the Father in spirit and truth; for the Father is seeking such to worship Him. God is Spirit, and those who worship Him must worship in spirit and truth." Truth is necessary, but it cannot come at the expense of the Spirit! The focus has been one-sided for too long. Mainstream Christianity has indeed ignored much biblical truth, but those who tried to remedy that situation swung the pendulum wide on the opposite end.

> And He Himself gave some to be apostles, some prophets, some evangelists, and some pastors and teachers, for the equipping of the saints for the work of ministry, for the edifying of the body of Christ, till we all come to the unity of the faith and of the knowledge of the Son of God, to a perfect man, to the measure of the stature of the fullness of Christ (Ephesians 4:11–13).

What does this say? It is saying that the purpose of apostles, prophets, evangelists, pastors and teachers in the body of Christ is to edify each other *"till"* (or until) we can come to the unity of the faith (read spirit) and knowledge (read truth). We are not to divide ourselves because we see our beliefs as right and others' as wrong. Dividing cannot lead to unity! Unity is a process, and we are not expected to have all doctrine correct to be part of the body. That unity will come as a result of our focus of edifying each other in love through the Spirit of faith, and the knowledge of truth.

The reason that Yahweh took away the feast days from Israel was because their hearts were not right with Him. They were not worshipping in spirit and truth. We cannot expect it to come back to us now when we are still suffering from the same problem! Until we have this focus correct and are not denying either side of the coin, the fullness of the truth of God's sky-clock will not come into focus. It may take another miracle realignment of the celestial bodies, or it may take revelation from God that is currently being withheld or both. But it will come, for He truly desires a body that will worship Him in "the measure of the stature of the fullness of Christ."

The hope lies in the individuals and small groups that refuse to organize into corporate structures with bylaws and top-down leadership because this is the only way for open, non-judgmental discussion to take place. If people are afraid to change their understanding, how can there be growth? No denomination or individual has it all correct. Some will be given knowledge in certain areas, and some will be gifted the spirit in certain areas. But all will be expected to share and teach what they have been given, and to do so in love, patience, and humility.

10
Music of the Calendar

After all of that exhaustive, or perhaps just exhausting, discussion on the calendar, I think it is time to take a gander at a far more "upbeat" side of the calendar.

I often think that God's language must be music, and when I look at the patterns that make up music, it is confirmed. This language is featured prominently in the sky-clock and the Sabbath in particular. Take a look at the following information, then decide if it could all just be coincidence.

The calendar is made up of several rhythms: Seed time and harvest, seven days in a week and twelve months in a year, seven of which contain the Holy Day Festival year and five months which do not.

Music is based on rhythm as the backbone, with every composition having an intro and a finale (end). A melody is made up of seven notes in a scale out of twelve notes from the full chromatic offering, leaving five notes that do not make up the individual scale.

Furthermore, the calendar has a Jubilee cycle of seven times seven years, with the following year, the fiftieth being the year of release. The count to the Feast of Weeks is the same. Our ears generally recognize seven octaves as being musical. We can hear

Appointed Times & the Meaning of Life

higher and lower frequencies, but they are generally not seen as useful in music. Seven notes in a scale times seven octaves works out to fifty notes when we count "one more" to end on the octave (octave literally meaning the "eighth note"). If you play through the notes of the scale and do not end with repeating this eighth note, it will sound incomplete. This is roughly the range of a piano.

These same seven octaves are also the length that it takes to get through the *circle of fifths*. For non-music people, this means that if you take the fifth note in a given scale, then use that note as the starting point to count your next fifth, and continue doing this twelve times, you will eventually make it through all twelve notes of the scale and back to the starting note, only seven octaves higher.

Certainly, there are other musical scales in use in various cultures throughout the world. There are scales made up of five notes (pentatonic, such as used in Japanese court music), six notes (hexatonic, as popularized by Claude Debussy), and fully chromatic scales (making use of all twelve notes). Any number of notes have been used as a scale, with varying spaces between each note. They each have a name and a cultural context where they have been used.

In the same manner, there have been many calendars used throughout time and culture. As mentioned earlier, the Romans held an eight-day market week for centuries, but there are many others as well. The ancient southern Chinese used a twelve-day week which was further divided into three day and six-day market cycles. Three-day market weeks were also used in ancient Columbia and New Guinea. Five-day weeks were used in ancient Meso-America and Indochina, and ten-day weeks in ancient Peru. The four-day market week is still popular in many parts of Africa. The Baha'i faith breaks up their 361-day year into nineteen 19-day weeks.[18] And there are plenty of others.

---

[18] Zerubavel, Eviatar. *The Seven Day Circle: The History and Meaning of the Week*. University of Chicago Press, 1989. Pages 45–47

Yet for some reason, both the seven-day week/twelve-month calendar and the seven-note scale/twelve-note chromatic offering have come to dominate world thought. Why? Could there be a correlation between them? We've seen in nature where the calendar divisions are found, with twelve lunar cycles per solar cycle (year) and four seven-day divisions of each lunar cycle. Is there a similar reason for dividing up music? The answer lies in harmony.

INTERVALS AND HARMONY

The discussion of harmony could get into a very lengthy study, and certainly many books have been written about it, but the interesting thing is that, like the scales themselves, there are many different systems that have been used. At its simplest level, harmony is the counterpart to the melody—a related set of notes different from those in the melody that mirror them in a way as to add beauty and complexity.

But what makes one note sound beautiful and another *off*? It is all a matter of the note's frequency—the number of vibrations per second that make it up (hertz). If you double any note's frequency, it will become an octave of that note. In between those two frequencies are all of the other notes, but how to divide them up is far from a settled matter.

Today we use a system that would have seemed sacrilegious to anyone prior to the twentieth century called *equal temperament* where the notes are simply divided up into twelve equal sections. This makes every key work in exactly the same fashion, which is *almost, but not quite,* in tune. In previous times, however, the concern was to find harmonies that were rich and satisfying, which equal temperament is certainly not, at least to trained ears.

The problem with harmony is that no matter how you divide up the notes, you create problems. Our ears are satisfied when they hear frequencies which are simple mathematical ratios of other notes, such as 3/2 and 4/3. We can take a note such as A=27hz and find the fifth which is a 1.5 times higher frequency (a 3/2 ratio), which would be E=40.5hz. Then we can take that number and add another fifth, which would be B=60.75hz. If we do this twelve times, we will be back to A, seven octaves higher than we started. This is the circle of fifths in music theory.

The problem is that we end up at A=3,503.15, but the octave (if we kept doubling 27, seven times) should actually be A=3,456, about 47.15hz below where the circle of fifths took us. We are left with a conundrum. Do we allow the octave to be off and dissonant, or do we change the intervals in between to force a perfect octave? Pretty much universally, people have opted to keep the octave perfect, but they have had many differing solutions for the intervening notes.

During the times when most of our beloved classical music was written, from the sixteenth to nineteenth centuries, the intervals between notes was different depending on which key the music was played in, which is why the key was so important, and why you see names like "Canon in D" or "Sonata in E-flat Major." Each key had its own unique character, and if you wanted to change keys for another piece, you would need to re-tune your instrument. If your instrument was a piano or harpsichord, this was a major ordeal.

Equal temperament was a compromise to avoid this constant change. There have been other attempts at correcting equal temperament to more pleasing intervals, such as the "scale of twelve fifths" by Maria Renold in the 1960s[19], which uses actual fifths for most notes, but gets them back on track by reducing two of the intervals in every octave. It is a much more satisfactory sound to listen to, but in reality, is too complicated to catch on universally. And at this point, there are many who, having grown up hearing only equal temperament, actually prefer it when they are exposed to more perfect tuning methods.

---

[19] Reynolds, Maria. *Intervals, Scales, Tones, and the Concert Pitch C=128*. Temple Lodge Publishing, 1985

Part 3: The Sky-Clock

The point of all this is to show the similarities we have in the musical system and the calendrical system. Neither works out with the even divisions our worldly brains would like to see because God's perfection is not perfect in our eyes. The year is very much like the octave—an obvious place to start and end a repeating cycle that almost everyone can agree upon. The lunar month is very much like the division of the octave into twelve notes; some years require a thirteenth month to keep the seasons aligning with the year, and there are actually some temperament systems (such as "just" intonation) that have thirteen notes—making the augmented 4th and diminished 5th different notes—whereas they are the same note in others. The seven-day week and the seven-month holy day calendar is very much like the seven-note scale; when you cycle through both repeated times, you do not end up quite where you think you should, leaving an excess of days or partial notes that need to be accounted for so that we can start our years and octaves over in the same place we left off. They are both cycles within cycles that *almost, but don't quite* line up with each other.

Classical composers often use this idea of slight imperfection to makes a symphony beautiful. There is an opening that introduces the main themes, but as the movements are developed, they change slightly, never repeating exactly what came before. It is a spiral as opposed to a circle. Modern music has succumbed to the laziness of circles and generally uses riffs or phrases that are simply repeated over and over, making simplistic and predictable songs. While there is a certain satisfaction that comes from this predictability, the staying power of the music is nothing compared with the classical music of prior centuries.

God's calendar uses the classical approach of spiraling time rather than circular time, and it is the imperfections in the calendar that lead to its beauty. Every year is slightly different. There are seasons every year, just as He promised that seed time and harvest would never end, but at the same time no two years are alike. Some are warmer or colder, drier or wetter, stormier or calmer, so that, "to everything there is a season, a time for every purpose under heaven," as Ecclesiastes 3:1 tells us.

11

Appointed Times and the Meaning of Life

"Speak to the children of Israel, and say to them: 'The feasts of the LORD, which you shall proclaim to be holy convocations, these are My feasts'" (Leviticus 23:2).

After we have decided that the days we have been keeping (Christmas and Easter, and more obvious ones like Halloween and Valentines, which you can research on your own) are opposed to the Bible and should not be kept, we are left with a void. Does God not want us to enjoy ourselves? Is there no reason for celebration left?

Somehow, we forget that God actually commanded His people to celebrate three times per year. Many Christians refer to them as the "Jewish" feasts, but they are not Jewish. Yahweh says, "These are *My* feasts." He did not give them to the Jews, but to all of Israel, to anyone called by His name. We are told by other Christians that we are "Judaizing" if we keep these things, yet we have already seen where that term came from in the quotes from Constantine who could not stand Christians having any similarity to Jews. It is not putting us back into bondage to keep these feasts or any of the law unless we tie our salvation into our keeping them. Even after Jesus died and was resurrected, John told us over and over that if we love Him, we will keep His commandments.

At least most Christians can look at the Ten Commandments and see value in keeping them (aside, perhaps, from the fourth). With the holy days, however, many don't find any value because they cannot see the meaning behind them. But the fact is that they are full of meaning that is quite pertinent to us today! They tell the entire story of our salvation and of the very meaning of life using the harvest seasons as the symbols found in creation to do so, and they show us where in the story we are today. Why would we not want to know this?

Because I've already talked about the difficulties and infighting that happen trying to pinpoint *when* to keep these times, I'm going to focus mainly on their meaning here, which is far more important.

It turns out that these appointed times were also not a new thing with Moses but were based on spiritual concepts that have been around from the beginning.

THE SABBATH

> Speak to the children of Israel, and tell them, "The set feasts of Yahweh, which you shall proclaim to be holy convocations, even these are my set feasts. 'Six days shall work be done, but on the seventh day is a Sabbath of solemn rest, a holy convocation; you shall do no kind of work. It is a Sabbath to Yahweh in all your dwellings. These are the set feasts of Yahweh, even holy convocations, which you shall proclaim in their appointed season'" (Leviticus 23:2–4 WEB).

I am going to talk much more about the Sabbath in the next section, Part 4, under the fourth commandment. But for here I feel obliged to mention it because it is mentioned as part of the appointed times. Verse 3 in the middle of the above quote is all that is said about it in Leviticus 23, which is the chapter that lays out all of these times in detail.

The Sabbath is mentioned there not only in the context of the week, but also as a sort of overarching pattern for the appointed times that are about to be discussed, because, except for Passover, they are all Sabbaths as well. The Sabbath is mentioned here as a type of overarching pattern of rest and Holiness that is required for all of the appointed times. The verse about the Sabbath is sandwiched in between two verses introducing "the feasts of Yahweh," which should be proclaimed at their appointed times. There surely must be a connection there.

PASSOVER

> In the first month, on the fourteenth day of the month in the evening, is Yahweh's Passover (Leviticus 23:5 WEB).

Verse 5 is all that Leviticus 23 has to say about the Passover. The instructions for it were given in Exodus 12. I won't bother quoting the entire chapter here, but please read it if you are not familiar with it. It is both the story of the original Passover in Egypt and the instructions on keeping it henceforth as a memorial of that day. The synopsis is that after nine previous plagues, Pharaoh had not yet let Israel go to the wilderness to worship Yahweh their Elohim, so it was time for number ten—death of the firstborn. Yahweh was going to kill all the firstborn in the land, whether of man or livestock, but as a sign that Yahweh differentiates between His people and Egypt, He told Israel to take a lamb without blemish and place it in their house for four days, after which they would kill it and eat it. Before eating it, they would take its blood and paint their doorway with it, so that when the death angel came at night, it would see the blood and pass over their house.

It is widely understood among Christians that this was foreshadowing the blood of Yeshua on the cross, causing death to pass over our sins. He was the Passover lamb that was slain. I'd like to take this a bit further, and it may get graphic or disturbing, so bear with me or skip to the section on Unleavened Bread.

During the Passover service of 2021, as I was eating the bread and drinking the wine, I was overcome with the realization of what I was doing. It was both very disturbing and humbling, and it shed new light on the profoundness of what Yeshua did for us.

That year I was learning a lot about the Satanic cult that runs the world—how widespread and intensely sick it really is. I'd learned about the mind-control programming, sacrifice, rape, ritual torture, murder and cannibalization of children, and how this is still done today at high levels of our society: in government, big business and religion. This used to seem like twisted fantasy or only the stuff of horror movies, but I now know that fiction is probably tame compared to reality.

If you would like to learn more about what I'm referring to, research MK Ultra, Monarch programming, Satanic Ritual Abuse (SRA), and the testimonies of Cathy O'Brien[20], Nathan Reynolds[21], Kay Tolman[22], J. R. Sweet[23], Mary Lou Lake[24], and the teachings of

---

[20] Read either of her books:

O'Brien, Cathy, & Phillips, Mark. *Trance Formation of America*. Reality Marketing Incorporated, 1995.

O'Brien, Cathy, & Phillips, Mark. *Access denied: For Reasons of National Security*, 2004

[21] Reynolds, Nathan. *Snatched from the Flames: One Man's Journey to Uncover the Family Secrets Buried in His Blood-Stained Past*, 2018

Or his website: https://snatchedfromtheflames.com/

[22] Revelation Gateway ministries—https://www.rgmconnect.com/

[23] https://mormonmonarch.com/

[24] Lake, Mary Lou. *What Witches Don't Want Christians to Know–Expanded Edition*. Biblical Life Publishing, 2014.

Part 3: The Sky-Clock

Dan Duval[25] and Gina Phillips[26], who have dedicated their careers to working with SRA survivors. These things are real and far more prevalent than you realize. Those who have been involved estimate at least six to ten percent of the U.S. population are affected by intentional mind-control programming and/or Satanic Ritual Abuse. It's not a matter of whether you might know somebody who has been affected, but how many you know.

History teaches about ancient civilizations who sacrificed children and drank human blood, but we tend to think that we are beyond that in modern times. The truth is that these things have existed since the earliest times and have never gone away but have only been hidden from the eyes of the uninitiated.

This is why God destroyed all humanity and started over with Noah, why He confused the tongues at the Tower of Babel, why He always warned Israel not to learn the ways of the nations around them, and why we are told that the times of the end will be like those of the days of Noah. Israel was well aware of the practices of their neighbors who sacrificed their children to Molech. They were aware of their propensity for drinking blood—blood that can become a strong drug when taken from the body of one (especially a child) being tortured, as it becomes infused with adrenaline (research Adrenochrome if you have never heard of this). The Roman rulers during Christ's day were likely taking part in such rituals. When Yahweh gave the law, He specified that Israel should never drink blood, even of animals, for this very reason: The life is in the blood, and there is power in that life, for good and for evil.

There is a pattern throughout the Bible of God teaching His ways using the examples of worldly ways that the people would understand but changing those things to make them His own. Originally God's creation required no codified rule book. But as the

---

[25] https://danduval.com/, https://www.bridemovement.com/

[26] https://www.gina-phillips.com/

nations around developed legal systems, then used them to rule over Israel, God created His own, so that Israel could see what a true and just legal system would look like, even though it could only be a shadow of God's reality, which was already visible in the creation.

Originally God set up Israel to have no king, but as the nations all around had one, Israel wanted their own, so God brought forth David to show the nature of a king who is after His own heart. The nations all had temples to their gods, so Yahweh designed His own temple, patterned after the human body, the temple He had created previously on day six. And the nations all had sacrifices to their gods which involved ritual murder, rape, and drinking of human and animal blood. These were used to appease their gods.

Yahweh created His own sacrifices, not to appease an angry god, but to atone for sin and foreshadow the sacrifice of the very God they were sacrificing to. They did not realize the shadow at the time, that the sacrifices they offered and took part in symbolized their hand in killing their future Savior!

And this brings me back to the Passover, the sacrifice that it all foreshadowed. Even those disciples who spent so much time with Yeshua did not understand the sacrifice He was about to make.

What they *did* understand was the sacrificial systems of the nations around them. They were not unaware of ritual sacrifice of children and eating their bodies and drinking their blood. So, when Yeshua suddenly told them that the bread was His body and the wine was His blood, and that they must eat and drink it, this must have hit them as a shock. Never in the Torah was it explained this way. Not only was their Messiah about to be sacrificed, but they were to eat His body and drink His blood! This was the behavior of the worst of the pagan nations!

There is no lower, more disgusting behavior, and our Messiah was telling them and us as well, to take part in it! Only instead of the sacrifice appeasing a god, it was God Himself giving His own lifeblood to and for sinners. This is what hit me as I internalized His body and blood this Passover. My own behavior has caused me to kill my Savior in the worst possible manner, cannibalizing His physical being. But here is the amazing part of it, where God shows us how His way differs from the world's.

When the nations make a sacrifice of the firstborn, they are doing so to appease their god to gain power and greatness and liken themselves to the god. They will inevitably fail because their gods are either not real, so there is no greatness or power to be gained, or they are demonic in nature, meaning they are only there to deceive, not to keep promises.

But when we eat the symbols of Christ's body and blood, the result is humility and forgiveness, which, because His blood is pure in all ways, actually does make us like Him, gaining the power over death itself unto eternal life. The most disgusting act we can do to our God is transformed into the greatest act of love imaginable, absolute forgiveness for our part in that sacrifice and victory over the adversary who made the sacrifice necessary. Yeshua's life is surely in His blood, and the nature of that life shows absolute mercy to us. It cleanses us and grows His own godly nature in our hearts!

Of course, I've known of the cleansing nature of the Passover symbols before, but the depth and absolute extremeness of it has evaded me. Satan is and always has been the god of the nations and of the world and his ways have not changed. He wants nothing less than to see us depraved to the extent of sacrificing children. Yeshua's choice of language at the Passover was intentional. We are to view ourselves as having sunk to that level, because our sins say that we have, but His perfect nature is able to overcome it because of His lifeblood that we have internalized.

UNLEAVENED BREAD

On the fifteenth day of the same month is the feast of unleavened bread to Yahweh. Seven days you shall eat unleavened bread. In the first day you shall have a holy convocation. You shall do no regular work. But you shall offer an offering made by fire to Yahweh seven days. In the seventh day is a holy convocation: you shall do no regular work.'" Yahweh spoke to Moses, saying, "Speak to the children of Israel, and tell them, 'When you have come into the land which I give to you, and shall reap its harvest, then you shall bring the sheaf of the first fruits of your harvest to the priest: and he shall wave the sheaf before Yahweh, to be accepted for you. On the next day after the Sabbath the priest shall wave it. On the day when you wave the sheaf, you shall offer a male lamb without defect a year old for a burnt offering to Yahweh. The meal offering with it shall be two tenths of an ephah of fine flour mingled with oil, an offering made by fire to Yahweh for a pleasant aroma; and the drink offering with it shall be of wine, the fourth part of a hin. You must not eat bread, or roasted grain, or fresh grain, until this same day, until you have brought the offering of your God. This is a statute forever throughout your generations in all your dwellings (Leviticus 23:6–14 WEB).

The Passover leads straight into the Feast of Unleavened Bread. Some even refer to the entire Feast of Unleavened Bread as Passover (I'm not going to get into the arguments for or against right now). After Israel was passed-over, they immediately left Egypt, escaping their bondage but also leaving behind everything else they knew and held dear, both good and bad. It was a time of humbling and testing.

The main symbolism from the creation that the Bible uses for this time of year is the barley, made into unleavened bread. Barley is used because it is starting to ripen at this time, and is in fact critical to even starting the year. If it was not going to be ripe, the year could not be started because it was commanded to offer the first fruit of the barley as a wave offering during this feast, just two weeks into the year.

The group I used to be a part of was known for traveling to Israel every year to inspect the barley prior to the start of the year to see if a thirteenth month would be needed for the barley to ripen properly, but I never personally went there. Even though I do not hold to the necessity of this practice anymore, there was a lot of good information I learned from the way God has designed the barley, and why it was chosen to be used by Him to designate the first harvest festival.

As barley matures, the weight of the head will cause it to start to droop, giving the effect of the stalk bowing down, which speaks to its being known as the "humble" grain. Wheat, usually seen as the superior grain, will remain erect, or some might say "stiff-necked." So, when Yahweh repeatedly calls Israel stiff-necked, He is speaking to their pride in wanting to act as though they were in a higher class than they were. God wanted them to be humble, especially at this stage of their journey.

Leavening also speaks to humility and pride. It has been said by many teachers that leaven equals sin, and I was taught this myself. My teacher was adamant that it had to be so and went so far as to disfellowship people for questioning that doctrine. Yet the Bible never actually says leaven is sin, nor does it support the idea. The Feast of Unleavened Bread in Exodus 12 and 13 speaks of taking leaven out of our homes so that we will not eat of it during that week, with the consequence of being cut off from God's people. Yeshua also said to beware of the leaven of the Pharisees (Matthew 16:6). Thinking of leaven as sin in both of these contexts seems to make sense.

But if we look at Matthew 13:33, "The kingdom of heaven is like leaven, which a woman took and hid in three measures of meal till it was all leavened," it would seem strange to liken the kingdom of heaven to sin. In Leviticus 23:17 there was also a wave offering offered at the Feast of Weeks (Pentecost) that was two loaves baked with leaven. Why would anything with sin be commanded to offer to Yahweh? It becomes obvious that leaven cannot equal sin in scripture. Yet I have seen people do great contortions with their interpretations of Matthew and Leviticus to try to make them fit with their preconceptions of leaven. It should not be necessary to do such mental gymnastics. But how are we then to reconcile all of these passages consistently?

All we need to do is look at the nature of leaven to find an answer that fits in all of these contexts. Leaven makes bread rise, making the loaf loftier than it would otherwise be. That's it. It does not make the bread go bad or give it any sinful nature. If we take that thought and then ponder the difference in contexts for when leaven is used in a negative vs. a positive way, something starts to take shape. When we leaven ourselves, it is always a negative thing. When leaven refers to God or heavenly things, it is positive. The solution is this: We are not to raise ourselves up, making us more than we are, because that is pride and arrogance. Yet if we raise up God/Yahweh, that is giving Him glory! It is all in the context.

The kingdom of heaven in Matthew is all about glory and raising others (the lump) up. If we are raised up by God, what grace He has shown! It is His glory to do so! But we are never to attempt to lift ourselves up. Pride was the sin that caused Satan to fall from heaven and is the basis for all other sin that man contends with. That is the theme for the Feast of Unleavened Bread—humility in, pride out.

The way we are to do so is by leaving pride behind and starting over, ingesting only the unleavened bread of humility. This is a theme that started long before the Exodus, during the story of Noah. During Noah's time, sin got so bad that it covered the earth so that "every intent of the thoughts of his heart was only evil continually." God decided to start over, leaving everything behind except Noah's family, seven pairs of clean animals and two pairs of all other animals. Noah packed up these essentials into a box called an ark and left the prideful world behind, bringing only what was absolutely necessary to start over. The world was flooded, raining for forty days and nights, destroying evil and leaving Noah's family in the ark, wandering on the water for many days until they could start their humbled life over in a new cleansed land.

During the exodus, the pattern was remarkably similar. Egypt's pride was overflowing to the point that Israel was told to leave it behind and start over on their own. They left, crossing the Red Sea on dry land, while the river closed on the evil enemy, flooding and destroying them. The Israelites were then given the law, the essentials of which were written on stone and put into a box called an ark, so that they could start over their new life with these simple laws. They then wandered for many days, forty years actually, learning humility through their trials before they could start over in a new land.

These are the lessons we are to learn during this time. What do we need to leave behind? (Answer: pride) What is essential for starting over? (Answer: the same commandments but written on the heart—the box or ark in the holy of holies of the tabernacle of our bodies). How do we do so? (Answer: pass through the water of baptism, flooding out and destroying our old evil selves, leaving a humbled and cleansed version of ourselves to start over anew.)

The other thing to remember with all of these festivals is that they are harvest festivals. We need to think of ourselves as the fruit which God will one day harvest to everlasting life. During the Feast of Unleavened Bread, the thing the barley needed to ripen for was so that it could be offered as a wave offering of the firstfruits. At Passover we had a sacrificial lamb offered, then a few days later there was a wave-sheaf offering of the firstfruits of barley. In the New Testament, we see the same thing when Christ, our Passover Lamb was killed and three days later was resurrected as the first of the firstfruits:

> But now Christ is risen from the dead, and has become the firstfruits of those who have fallen asleep. For since by man came death, by Man also came the resurrection of the dead. For as in Adam all die, even so in Christ all shall be made alive. But each one in his own order: Christ the firstfruits, afterward those who are Christ's at His coming. Then comes the end, when He delivers the kingdom to God the Father, when He puts an end to all rule

and all authority and power. For He must reign till He has put all enemies under His feet. The last enemy that will be destroyed is death. For "He has put all things under His feet" (1 Corinthians 15:20–27).

This is an outline of the harvest festivals of Yahweh. The first of these was Jesus Christ Himself, pictured as the wave-sheaf offering during the Feast of Unleavened Bread. His resurrection was the first ever unto eternal life. As such, He took preeminence as the Head of the body, just as Noah was the head of his family on the ark. The humility we are modeling our lives after during this feast is the humility of Christ, in that He died for us while we were yet sinners, so that we might have eternal life as well.

Barley was the first crop to ripen in the year, and the wave-sheaf was the first of that harvest. During the barley inspections our group did in Israel every year, they discovered that there was a strain of barley that would show up in the wild fields here and there that had reddish streaks on it. It was called "red strain" barley. This strain always matured faster than all of the barley around it. It is a fascinating testimony in nature to Jesus, who was also streaked with red blood and was the wave-sheaf of the firstfruits.

The barley would continue to be harvested for the next seven weeks until the Feast of Weeks. These harvests speak to the order of our salvation and resurrection to new life. We will not all come to the knowledge of our Savior at the same time. Some will do so in our lifetime, and some will not have a chance until after they die in this world. We'll talk about each harvest as we come to it.

FEAST OF WEEKS/PENTECOST

> And you shall number to you from the next day after the sabbath, from the day you bring in the sheaf of the wave offering; they shall be seven complete sabbaths; the next day after the seventh sabbath, you shall number fifty days; and you shall bring near a new food offering to Jehovah; you shall bring in bread out of your

> dwellings for a wave offering, two loaves; they shall be of two tenth ephah of flour; they shall be baked with leaven; firstfruits to Jehovah And besides the bread, you shall offer seven lambs, without blemish, sons of a year, and one bull, a son of the herd, and two rams; they are a burnt offering to Jehovah, with their food offering and their drink offerings, a fire offering of soothing fragrance to Jehovah. And you shall offer one he-goat for a sin offering, and two lambs, sons of a year, for a sacrifice of peace offerings. And the priest shall wave them, besides the bread of the firstfruits, a wave offering before Jehovah, besides the two lambs; they are holy to Jehovah for the priest. And you shall make a proclamation on this same day; it is a holy gathering to you. You shall do no work of service. It is a never ending statute in all your dwellings throughout your generations (Leviticus 23:15–21 LITV).

Leviticus 23 tells us to start the count to the Feast of Weeks from the day that the wave sheaf was brought in during the week of Unleavened Bread. When the count is reached, we are given the new symbolism.

> you shall bring in bread out of your dwellings for a wave offering, two loaves; they shall be of two tenth ephah of flour; they shall be baked with leaven; firstfruits to Jehovah (Leviticus 23:17 LITV).

Here we see the leavened wave loaves that we mentioned in the last section. Why are they specified to be baked with leaven? They were to be offered to Yahweh as a fitting symbol of His glory. Whereas the unleavened bread was for our own consumption, the leavened loaves are waved to Yahweh for His consumption, His glory. Humble ourselves; raise up Yahweh.

When we come to the New Covenant Pentecost, we see something that is seemingly unrelated to these loaves. Fire comes down and lights on the tongues of three thousand followers of Yeshua!

> And in the fulfilling of the day of Pentecost, they were all with one mind in the same place. And suddenly a sound came out of the

heaven, as being borne along by a violent wind! And it filled all the house where they were sitting. And tongues as of fire appeared to them, being distributed, and it sat on each one of them. And they were all filled of the Holy Spirit, and began to speak in other languages, as the Spirit gave ability to them to speak (Acts 2:1–4).

What is that about? It is fire that doesn't burn up what it is on, and we have seen this kind of fire before. It showed up first in the burning bush that appeared to Moses, then in the tabernacle above the mercy seat. Isaiah 43:2 says of it:

> When you pass through the waters, I will be with you; and through the rivers, they shall not overflow you. **When you walk through the fire, you shall not be burned, nor shall the flame scorch you.**

This is also exactly what happened with Shadrach, Meshach and Abednego. When fire does not consume what it is burning, it is always representative of the Holy Spirit. When it is a consuming fire, it is sometimes of the Holy Spirit as well, or sometimes just regular fire. When the Holy Spirit fire lands on something, it is there to burn impurities. It is the refiner's fire that will test the purity of metal. The dross is burnt off, and the pure metal is left. When it lands on something that is already pure or Holy, it will not consume it, but if it contains impurities, it will.

At the Passover, we were made holy. Our sins were forgiven by the blood of our Passover Lamb. During the Feast of Unleavened Bread, we learned how to stay holy through humbling ourselves. Then, at the Feast of Weeks, we raised up holiness to Yahweh with the leavened loaves, giving Him glory. Now, under the New Covenant, God sends His glory back to us in the form of the refiner's fire and it finds His people pure, so it does not consume them.

But something else important happened during the New Testament Pentecost as well. The residence of the Holy Spirit was transferred from the tabernacle that had been hauled around the land of Israel and the subsequent temples built to house it, to the human body, which the tabernacle had always represented. The flame of fire and the pillar of cloud had lived in the holy of holies of the tabernacle. This is where the mercy seat was, and as we learned earlier, the mercy seat was Yahweh's lungs, because that is where He spoke from. From that Pentecost on, however, Yahweh/Yeshua was telling us that He will live directly in us. He will speak through the lungs of His people because we are now, quite literally, the Body of Christ.

This was "a new grain offering to Yahweh." Something new happened. The harvest of the humble barley had ended and made way for the new harvest of the wheat, the glorified grain. He has glorified His people and brought them firmly into the new covenant.

This new covenant is a marriage contract just like the old one. He originally married His people Israel, who later divided themselves into two kingdoms, becoming the sisters of Israel and Judah, and both were married to Yahweh. Then both went around as harlots, prostituting themselves to other gods. Yahweh eventually divorced Israel but stayed married to Judah (Jeremiah 2–4) until He came in the flesh and then died. The two acceptable ways the Bible outlines to break the marriage contract are if your spouse commits adultery (Matthew 5:32) and through death (Romans 7:2). Yahweh/Yeshua used both methods. After His death He was free to marry another, which He did. He married *us*. This is why the church is thereafter referred to as His bride or wife.

> Husbands, love your wives, just as Christ also loved the church and gave Himself for her, that He might sanctify and cleanse her with the washing of water by the word, that He might present her to Himself a glorious church, not having spot or wrinkle or any such thing, but that she should be holy and without blemish. So husbands ought to love their own wives as their own bodies; he who loves his wife loves himself. For no one ever hated his own flesh, but nourishes and cherishes it, just as the Lord does the

church. For we are members of His body, of His flesh and of His bones. "For this reason a man shall leave his father and mother and be joined to his wife, and the two shall become one flesh." This is a great mystery, but I speak concerning Christ and the church (Ephesians 5:25–32).

This passage even brings the idea back to the very creation of woman in the first place. The reason Eve was created was because, "for Adam there was not found a *helper* comparable to him" (Genesis 2:20). This word *helper* is found again in reference to the Holy Spirit that Jesus promised to send:

But the Helper, the Holy Spirit, whom the Father will send in My name, He will teach you all things, and bring to your remembrance all things that I said to you (John 14:26).

This is the one who arrived on Pentecost in Acts 2. Peter, filled with the Spirit, explained to the crowd what was happening, quoting from Joel 2:28–32:

And it shall come to pass afterward that I will pour out My Spirit on all flesh; your sons and your daughters shall prophesy, your old men shall dream dreams, your young men shall see visions. And also on My menservants and on My maidservants I will pour out My Spirit in those days. And I will show wonders in the heavens and in the earth: Blood and fire and pillars of smoke. The sun shall be turned into darkness, and the moon into blood, before the coming of the great and awesome day of the LORD. And it shall come to pass that whoever calls on the name of the LORD shall be saved.

The Holy Spirit was being sent, but these were end-time words that Peter was claiming were being fulfilled before their eyes. Did the sun also turn to darkness and the moon to blood? Those things are also predicted for the end in the book of Revelation. Are we still in the same time period Peter spoke of? It seems that two thousand years is a long time for humanity to still be going through it.

Part 3: The Sky-Clock

During the life of the apostles there seems to have been an expectation that the second coming of Christ was imminent. He had come to earth, died, and would come again to receive His bride. If Yeshua led His disciples to believe that His absence would be very short, then why have we had to wait for so long for Him to return again? There is a biblical pattern that may shed some light.

During the exodus, there was an expectation that they would be entering the promised land in short order. Moses had been told to tell Pharoah that they were simply going on a three-day journey to worship their God. But we have learned that that was a time of testing the Israelites faith. They failed that test and were delayed by forty years, until that entire generation had passed away.

Today, if we look at the biblical feast days as rehearsals for the large-scale plan of our salvation, we again see that after Pentecost comes the return of Christ at the Feast of Trumpets, which is a prelude to entering the promised land of the Feast of Tabernacles and the Eighth Day. But there is a long gap between Pentecost and Trumpets. There is a separation between spring holy days and fall holy days. Lunar Sabbatarians would put Pentecost in early summer, but regardless, there is still a considerable time until the fall festivals. It would seem fitting that there would be a long period of time until Christ's return.

It may have actually been possible for His return to be during that first generation, but that once again the faith of the new believers suffered. I don't really know that, but, if we look at the period of time from then until now, we have about two thousand years and many (myself included) are again thinking that His return must be soon. The count of seven sabbaths and fifty days of Pentecost are intricately linked to the jubilee cycle of 50 years spoken of in Leviticus 25:8-22. It just so happens that two thousand years works out to exactly forty jubilee cycles of fifty years, matching the forty-year pattern of wandering in the desert during the Exodus and linking its symbolism to the jubilee.

His bride has been wandering in the wilderness all of this time but now has the promised land in sight and is about ready to cross over the Jordan River!

HOLINESS

With the Holy Spirit being such a large part of this holy day, this seems like a fitting place to look at what it means to be holy in the first place, and where we can find holiness in the creation.

The definition of holiness is something that is set apart. Strong's and most other lexicons tell us the same thing. But what is something holy set apart *from*? Can we find the answer in nature? If all truth can be found in the creation, where do we find holiness? This question came to me as a result of meditating on Romans 1:20—that His invisible attributes are clearly seen in the creation, even His eternal power and Godhead. But at the time, I had also been thinking and studying about faith as the underlying necessity for miracles. We should also be thinking here about the necessity of faith for entering the promised land.

Faith is something we all think we have, yet it is also elusive. We all ask for things "in Jesus' name" and often don't see results. James has the answer to this,

> But let him ask in faith, with no doubting, for he who doubts is like a wave of the sea driven and tossed by the wind. For let not that man suppose that he will receive anything from the Lord; he is a double minded man, unstable in all his ways.

Easier said than done, but we cannot have faith and doubt simultaneously, because faith will no longer be faith but mere "belief."

I put belief in quotes because it is a word that is often used but gives the wrong impression to the English speaker. In the Old Testament, belief is usually translated from *aman*, Strong's H539, "to stand firm as a support" from the root word meaning "firm, sure or kind (as in a species)." Other words that are of the same root are *aman*, Stong's H542, "a Craftsman: One who is firm in his talents," *emeth*, Strong's H571, "Truth: what is firm," *amen*, Strong's H543, "An affirmation of firmness and support," and *emun* and *emunah*, Strong's H529 and H530, "Firmness, Faith." (Definitions from *Ancient Hebrew Lexicon*.) Aman and its derivatives are words that do not allow for the possibility of untruth or weakness. Our word *belief* however, has a connotation of thinking something is true even if it may not actually be so. It is possible to "be-lie-ve" a lie. However, if a Hebrew were to *aman* something, it is a firm thing, planted on a firm, immovable, foundation—truth itself. It is more akin to our word *knowing*. To know something, in contrast to belief, is certain. Like aman, knowing does not leave room for error. If we know wrongly, we do not know at all but have a mistaken belief instead.

Faith is what we do with the knowledge that we have. It is the works that are a requirement to show our knowledge. I do not believe in God; I know God and I have faith in God; I *aman* God. So, I will use the word *faith* or *know* instead. Although these still may not be perfect translations, they are closer to the firmness that aman requires.

Through faith, based in true knowing, not belief, we can move mountains, heal the sick, and perform miracles, all of which are things that occur outside of natural processes. So how do we see miracles occurring in nature when the definition of a miracle is something that occurs outside of nature? If they were part of what we see as "natural" or obeyed the physical laws that we can all comprehend, then they would cease to be miraculous.

This is when I started thinking about holiness (*qodesh*—Strong's H6944), which is defined as being set-apart. Those who are holy have been set apart from something. But what? Could that something be nature—the creation? I believe so, or rather I know so. If I have been given the Holy Spirit, that Spirit exists outside of the natural processes that dictate the things of the earth. We are granted the Holy Spirit when we are accepted into the body of Yeshua, the

Christ, the one who overcame nature in His lifetime by performing miracles everywhere He went and especially by His resurrection from the dead, which granted us the access to become members of His body.

This makes sense when we think of Yeshua as being the Creator of the world before being born into the world as flesh (John 1). The Creator and the created cannot be the same. The Creator is always greater than the creation, so must exist outside of it. Said another way, the Creator is set apart from the creation—holy. He can work miracles because He is outside of and greater than the creation—able to manipulate or change it at will.

When I make a sculpture out of bronze, I am that sculpture's creator. I am set-apart from the sculpture because our natures are different. After the sculpture is completed, it will have no ability to change anything on its own because it is a lifeless chunk of metal; that is its nature. But I, as its creator, have tools—grinders, saws, welders, etc.—to destroy it, change it, and repair it, all at my own will. This is also why a sculpture is an idol and can never be a God; the relationship goes in the wrong direction, in effect making myself into a god, which is offensive to the true Creator! I am supposed to be the image and Him the Creator.

When we receive the Holy Spirit, having been accepted into the body of Yeshua, we are now able to work outside of the natural processes, too! If we aman, that is know (not believe) that we can, and if we ask in accordance with the will of Yahweh, then we can. It is His will "that [not] any should perish but that all should come to repentance," 2 Peter 3:9, and "that whoever believes in [has faith in, or knows] Him should not perish, but should have eternal life" (John 3:15). This eternal life is a direct result of being set apart into the life of the Creator, no longer being subject only to the life of created nature, which will die in corruption.

We then find holiness in nature only in that being set apart from the nature of the creation brings us into the spiritual nature of the

Creator Himself. Not only have we found the "eternal power and Godhead" by looking at and meditating on the created things of Romans 1:20, but we have found some profound truths about our eternal life and the Holy Spirit! When we look at the Biblical things that are described as holy we can think about them a bit differently now. Leviticus 10:3, "By those who come near me I must be regarded as holy; And before all the people I must be glorified." Why must He be regarded as holy? Because He is set apart from the very nature of our existence, being the One who created it. Why is the holy place of the tabernacle called holy? Because it is set aside for the Creator to reside in. Supernatural communication takes place there! Holiness is the supernatural. Super meaning above = above nature. Set apart from it.

Let us meditate on this holiness that we have been given on this holy day of Pentecost, the Feast of Weeks, and let us *know* the truth and power that it contains, that Yahweh may be glorified!

MEMORIAL OF TERUAH

> Yahweh spoke to Moses, saying, "Speak to the children of Israel, saying, 'In the seventh month, on the first day of the month, shall be a solemn rest to you, a memorial of blowing of trumpets, a holy convocation. You shall do no regular work; and you shall offer an offering made by fire to Yahweh'" (Leviticus 23:23–25 WEB).

This appointed time brings us into the season of the fall feasts. Jews call it the new year (Rosh Hashanah), and in many ways that is not wrong. It is a time of starting over, of rebirth, if you will. It is also a time prophecy points to as unfulfilled. The events it pictures are still in the future, even though it may well be the case that we are on the very threshold of that future.

But first things first: What is this day about? We'll get there by following the use of *trumpets* throughout Scripture. To start we should define the phrase "blowing of trumpets" from Leviticus 23:24. In Hebrew it is one word, *Teruah* (Strong's H8643), meaning:

1) Alarm, signal, sound of tempest, shout, shout or blast of war or alarm or joy
  1a) alarm of war, war-cry, battle-cry
  1b) blast (for march)
  1c) shout of joy (with religious impulse)
  1d) shout of joy (in general)

This definition, from the *Brown-Driver-Briggs Lexicon*, does not even mention a trumpet. The *Ancient Hebrew Lexicon* definition also does not mention a trumpet, although *The Strong's Concordance* does add "especially clangor of trumpets, as an alarum." Looking at these definitions, we see them pointing toward the sounds and reasons for trumpets to blow instead of just the act of blowing them, as well as the fact that an actual trumpet may not even be necessary! Teruah is used thirty-six times in the Bible, and translated variously as shouting (eighteen times), alarm (six times), rejoicing/joy (four times), a sounding/loud noise (three times), blowing (two times), and once incorrectly as jubilee. Only twice is it referred to as a trumpet, both times in reference to the feast of trumpets. But from all of the other uses, it is clear that *Teruah* does not refer to the object itself.

There are three other words that are also often translated as trumpet that are helpful to look at. The first, *yobel* (Strong's H3104), also does not refer to an instrument. It is usually transliterated as *Jubilee*. It refers to the *blast* of the trumpet, not the instrument itself. It is the sound that the ram's horn trumpet makes in Leviticus 25 for the fiftieth year in the Jubilee cycle, the year of release. It is a blast which sets the captives free and gives land back to the poor and oppressed. It is the blast of Exodus 19:13 that called Israel to the mountain of God to hear Him speak the Ten Commandments, and it is the blast that knocked down the walls of Jericho in Joshua 6.

Another word for trumpet is *shofar* (Strong's H7782), which refers specifically to a ram's horn. It is the most common trumpet in biblical usage, with seventy-two references. All of the above yobel blasts were made with a shofar, yet the shofar can also make the sounds described by teruah.

The last word is *chatsatserah* (Strong's H2689), which is referred to twenty-nine times in the Bible. They are the trumpets made of hammered silver, used solely by the temple/tabernacle priests (although the priests could also use a shofar). Their crafting and use is described in Numbers 10:1–10:

> And Jehovah spoke to Moses, saying, Make two trumpets of silver for yourself. You shall make them of hammered work, and they shall be to you for the calling of the congregation, and for causing the camps to pull up stakes. And when they blow with them, all the congregation shall gather themselves to you at the door of the tabernacle of the congregation. And if they blow with one, then the rulers, the heads of the thousands of Israel, shall assemble to you. And when you blow an alarm, the camps that lie on the east side shall then pull up stakes. And when you blow an alarm the second time, the camps that lie on the south side shall pull up stakes; they shall blow an alarm for their journeys. But when the assembly is gathered, you shall blow, but you shall not sound an alarm. And the sons of Aaron, the priests, shall blow with the trumpets. And they shall be to you for a never ending statute throughout your generations. And when you go into battle in your land against the foe distressing you, then you shall blow with the trumpets, and you shall be remembered before Jehovah your God. And you shall be saved from your enemies. And in the day of your gladness, and in your appointed times, and in your new moons, you shall blow the trumpets over your burnt offerings, and over the sacrifices of your peace offerings. And they shall be to you for a memorial before your God. I am Jehovah your God (LITV).

This shows a number of uses given for *chatsatserah*: for calling the congregation or leaders to assemble, for sounding the alarm to pull up stakes and move, to be remembered by God when going to war, and as a memorial in the days of gladness, for the appointed times and new moons. Other scriptures will reveal shofar being used for these same purposes, so the specific instrument used is unimportant. But all of the uses are important to the Memorial of Teruah.

One thing to note is that the shout of a human voice can and is naturally used for all of the same purposes as well. It can come as a sound of surprise or fear (alarm), as a call to others at a distance to come near (assembly), as a battle cry when going into war, a sound of gladness and victory (joy), and to announce a new moon or festival. Some people actually refer to this memorial as the day of shouting, which may be a more accurate translation judging simply by the number of times that most translations choose that word over a trumpet blast. Shouting is the method that God chose in His creation for these duties. A trumpet is simply an extension of the human voice, performing the same function but louder, and using the same air from our lungs.

Timing-wise, the day takes place at the new moon of the seventh month, a day in which they were also commanded to have a holy convocation, a sacred assembly. The last passage states that when the trumpet is sounded for assembly, it is not to be sounded as an alarm. The alarm was for movement of troops so that they would be ready for battle, but it was not the battle itself—more of a state of heightened alert. Then, when the battle was certain, they were to blow the trumpet again, and Yahweh would remember them and save them from their enemies.

This battle is an important theme biblically. It is usually referred to as "the day of the LORD [Yahweh]." The day when Yahweh comes back to take vengeance on the earth. It is prophesied in the Old Testament in Isaiah, Jeremiah, Lamentations, Ezekiel, Joel, Amos, Obadiah, Zephaniah, Zechariah, and Malachi.

Joel 2 is a prime example of a prophecy of the Memorial of Teruah, in which is mentioned the blowing of the trumpet, calling of the assembly, war, destruction, and God's mercy and ensuing joy:

> Blow the trumpet in Zion and sound an alarm in My holy mountain! Let all the inhabitants of the land tremble; for the day

Part 3: The Sky-Clock

of the LORD is coming, for it is at hand: A day of darkness and gloominess, a day of clouds and thick darkness, like the morning clouds spread over the mountains. A people come, great and strong, the like of whom has never been; nor will there ever be any such after them, even for many successive generations.

A fire devours before them, and behind them a flame burns; the land is like the Garden of Eden before them, and behind them a desolate wilderness; surely nothing shall escape them. Their appearance is like the appearance of horses; and like swift steeds, so they run. With a noise like chariots over mountaintops they leap, like the noise of a flaming fire that devours the stubble, like a strong people set in battle array.

Before them the people writhe in pain; all faces are drained of color. They run like mighty men, they climb the wall like men of war; every one marches in formation, and they do not break ranks. They do not push one another; every one marches in his own column. Though they lunge between the weapons, they are not cut down. They run to and fro in the city, they run on the wall; they climb into the houses, they enter at the windows like a thief.

The earth quakes before them, the heavens tremble; the sun and moon grow dark, and the stars diminish their brightness. The LORD gives voice before His army, for His camp is very great; for strong is the One who executes His word. For the day of the LORD is great and very terrible; who can endure it?

"Now, therefore," says the LORD, "Turn to Me with all your heart, with fasting, with weeping, and with mourning." So rend your heart, and not your garments; return to the LORD your God, for He is gracious and merciful, slow to anger, and of great kindness; and He relents from doing harm. Who knows if He will turn and relent, and leave a blessing behind Him—a grain offering and a drink offering For the LORD your God?

Blow the trumpet in Zion, consecrate a fast, call a sacred assembly; gather the people, sanctify the congregation, assemble the elders, gather the children and nursing babes; let the bridegroom go out from his chamber, and the bride from her dressing room. Let the priests, who minister to the LORD, weep between the porch and the altar; let them say, "Spare Your people, O LORD, and do not give Your heritage to reproach, that the nations should rule over them. Why should they say among the peoples, 'Where is their God?'"

Then the LORD will be zealous for His land, and pity His people. The LORD will answer and say to His people, "Behold, I will send you grain and new wine and oil, and you will be satisfied by them; I will no longer make you a reproach among the nations" (Joel 2:1–19).

If you read through all of the mentions of the day of the LORD given in the books listed above, it sounds like a horrific day. It is a terrible time to live through, a time of death and destruction, doom and gloom. Yet the context is prophecy. These verses were written to warn people of the coming of this day so that they could repent, turn to Yahweh, *and be saved from it!* Zephaniah 2:3 says:

Seek Yahweh, all you humble of the land, who have kept his ordinances. Seek righteousness. Seek humility. It may be that you will be hidden in the day of Yahweh's anger. (WEB)

If we have repented, "Then you will be remembered before Yahweh your God, and you will be saved from your enemies" (Numbers 10:9, WEB).

We can't forget that one of the reasons given to blow the trumpet was in the day of their gladness. That day is lumped in with all of the other trumpeting for a reason! It was the end result of the assembling, alarms, movement of troops, war, repentance, and calling on Yahweh.

When we bring this into the new covenant, we see the following about the use of trumpets:

Part 3: The Sky-Clock

> But I do not want you to be ignorant, brethren, concerning those who have fallen asleep, lest you sorrow as others who have no hope. For if we believe that Jesus died and rose again, even so God will bring with Him those who sleep in Jesus. For this we say to you by the word of the Lord, that we who are alive and remain until the coming of the Lord will by no means precede those who are asleep. For the Lord Himself will descend from heaven with a shout, with the voice of an archangel, and with the trumpet of God. And the dead in Christ will rise first. Then we who are alive and remain shall be caught up together with them in the clouds to meet the Lord in the air. And thus we shall always be with the Lord. Therefore comfort one another with these words (1 Thessalonians 4:13–18).

This is a clear focus on the joy and positive aspects of the Memorial of Teruah. Just after this statement, however, Paul confirms that he has been talking about the day of the Lord, and that yes, there is disaster, too, but only for those who are "in darkness:"

> But concerning the times and the seasons, brethren, you have no need that I should write to you. For you yourselves know perfectly that the day of the Lord so comes as a thief in the night. For when they say, "Peace and safety!" then sudden destruction comes upon them, as labor pains upon a pregnant woman. And they shall not escape. But you, brethren, are not in darkness, so that this Day should overtake you as a thief. You are all sons of light and sons of the day. We are not of the night nor of darkness. Therefore let us not sleep, as others do, but let us watch and be sober (1 Thessalonians 5:1–6).

He mentions that this is "concerning the times and the seasons." He is acknowledging that the day of the Lord is indeed an appointed time, or holy day. He also uses the analogy of "labor pains upon a pregnant woman" to describe the destruction that comes on the unrighteous who lie about "peace and safety." This is important, because it brings in the natural world that is visible for us to see for ourselves.

Appointed Times & the Meaning of Life

What happens when a woman goes into labor? She goes through much pain, calling out in her agony, the shout of Teruah, and then she gives birth! It is difficult but worth it for the gift that is received on the other end.

In Revelation, we get more of the picture filled in, in the final fulfillment of this day. Starting in chapter 8 we start reading about the seven trumpets sounding, each one bringing in a new wave of destruction, just as the contractions of labor pains come in waves, until the seventh trumpet in chapter 11 verse 15, when we read, "The kingdoms of this world have become the kingdoms of our Lord and of His Christ, and He shall reign forever and ever!"

Skipping to verse 19, "Then the temple of God was opened in heaven, and the ark of His covenant was seen in His temple." This is all exactly the pattern that was laid out in Joshua 6, when the Israelites marched around Jericho once every day for six days blowing trumpets until the seventh day when they marched around seven times. On that final lap, Joshua gave the command to "Shout! [rua, the root word of Teruah], for Yahweh has given you the city!" The walls fell down, so that the ark of the covenant that the priests carried could be seen in the city.

Then the story continues in Revelation 12:1–6:

> Now a great sign appeared in heaven: a woman clothed with the sun, with the moon under her feet, and on her head a garland of twelve stars. Then being with child, she cried out in labor and in pain to give birth.
>
> And another sign appeared in heaven: behold, a great, fiery red dragon having seven heads and ten horns, and seven diadems on his heads. His tail drew a third of the stars of heaven and threw them to the earth. And the dragon stood before the woman who was ready to give birth to devour her Child as soon as it was born. She bore a male Child who was to rule all nations with a rod of iron. And her Child was caught up to God and His throne. Then the woman fled into the wilderness, where she has a place prepared

Part 3: The Sky-Clock

by God, that they should feed her there one thousand two hundred and sixty days.

Again, we see the trumpet followed by birth pangs and a birth. It looks like this birth is significant, even reminiscent of the birth of Yeshua Himself, and it happens directly after the seventh trumpet.

It is worth noting that at the beginning of the seventh month, both the sun and the moon are in the constellation of Virgo, the virgin, with the moon passing by her feet a couple days after the conjunction. The constellation Serpens lies right next to Virgo, its head directly under her feet. The serpent is being held by Ophiuchus, whose identity is debated, often simply called a snake charmer. Perhaps he has charmed Serpens, enabling the child to be swept away to God before the serpent could devour Him. Serpens is divided into two parts, one on each side of Ophiuchus. The head side is made up of seven main stars (brighter than magnitude five), perhaps indicating seven heads.

These are things that we have forgotten over the centuries how to read, but it does appear that, at least at one time, the stars proclaimed, even shouted, the story of our salvation to all mankind, and it is not unlikely that some of those voices are still there to be heard.

In Matthew 24:29–31, Jesus also described much of the same imagery around this day.

> "Immediately after the tribulation of those days the sun will be darkened, and the moon will not give its light; the stars will fall from heaven, and the powers of the heavens will be shaken. Then the sign of the Son of Man will appear in heaven, and then all the tribes of the earth will mourn, and they will see the Son of Man coming on the clouds of heaven with power and great glory. And He will send His angels with a great sound of a trumpet, and they will gather together His elect from the four winds, from one end of heaven to the other."

This really ties together a lot of the things we've read in the other verses. The sign of the Son of Man appears in heaven, like it did in Revelation. Then there is mourning from the unrighteous as they see Him arrive, the death and destruction that has been long prophesied. Then as He arrives, the angels blast the trumpet and gather the elect, just as 1 Thessalonians said about the dead in Christ and those who are alive and remain, meeting the Lord in the air.

We should be seeing by now that this day is about the very return of Jesus, Yeshua, the Messiah that we have all been waiting for! It is written in the stars using imagery from His first appearance to identify Him (a male child born of a woman—the Son of Man). Except that this time the woman represents His elect, and she is given wings of an eagle to flee from Satan, meeting Christ in the air on the way to the "wilderness," the place prepared for her by God, where she will stay protected for 3½ years before returning to earth to rule with Christ. But that starts to get into the next appointed time.

It may seem strange that it is Christ's elect, His virgin bride, who is pictured giving birth to Jesus. Does a bride give birth to her husband? But what is being stated by that picture is the term *Son of Man* that Matthew uses. It pictures His birth from a human mother, which happened during His first coming physically, but will happen this time spiritually.

During the time He has been gone, it has been the duty of the church, His bride, to act and speak in His stead. She has been the mouthpiece of Jesus, and it was given to her to walk as He walked. She was told by Jesus before He left that she would work miracles and even perform greater things than He did. We can look around and wonder if that has ever come true, but more and more I am confident that she has done those things, and that most of those stories have simply been suppressed or forgotten.

Now in these last days, however, many of those testimonies have been getting out. I have heard many wonderful stories of great miracles and selfless acts of love where she has literally given her life for the good news of Jesus. It is these acts of love and faith by a bride who has complete trust in her Husband, whom she has never seen in the flesh, which prepare the way for Him to return to the earth again to receive her. He could not come back without her, and that is the meaning of the sign of the Son of Man being birthed by the virgin that will precede His return.

It should be stated that I find it unlikely that the bride spoken of here will include all or even most of those who consider themselves Christian. There seems to be a level of exceptionalism among those called the "elect" or "bride." She is the virtuous wife described in Proverbs 31:10–31. Verses 10–11 and 30–31 state,

> Who can find a virtuous wife? For her worth is far above rubies. The heart of her husband safely trusts her.
>
> "Many daughters have done well, but you excel them all." Charm is deceitful and beauty is passing, but a woman who fears Yahweh, she shall be praised.

Christ's bride having a special place in His kingdom certainly does not preclude others from entering, however, because salvation is not an all or nothing endeavor. Jesus often speaks of the least and greatest in the kingdom, and He also lays out what it takes to be the greatest, and that is a life of sacrifice and service with an attitude of humility.

I state this mostly because of the doctrine that many call "the rapture." They look at the same verses we are talking about and see Jesus' bride caught up into the air to meet Christ, and assume that it will be all Christians, and further, that it will get them out of the coming tribulation. But neither statement will be true. The former because of what I just explained. Jesus' bride has sacrificed everything to be who she is, and because of her humility, she probably doesn't even realize it. The reality is that very few will reach that state of exceptionalism. Read Matthew 25:31–46.

The latter actually has a partial truth in that she will apparently be removed for 3½ years of tribulation. But there will also be plenty of tribulation before that time. She will not have gotten to be who she is without being tested in tribulation. She has not shied away from it but has had loving and proclaiming Jesus as her number one priority no matter the cost to her or her family's comfort or safety. She will have given up everything for Him.

Remember, too, that there are seasonal harvests for those entering into the kingdom:

> For as in Adam all die, even so in Christ all shall be made alive. But each one in his own order: Christ the firstfruits, afterward those who are Christ's at His coming. Then comes the end, when He delivers the kingdom to God the Father, when He puts an end to all rule and all authority and power (1 Corinthians 15:22–24).

At the Memorial of Teruah it is the timing of Christ to return to harvest his bride.

ATONEMENT

> Yahweh spoke to Moses, saying, "However on the tenth day of this seventh month is the day of atonement: it shall be a holy convocation to you, and you shall afflict yourselves; and you shall offer an offering made by fire to Yahweh. You shall do no kind of work in that same day; for it is a day of atonement, to make atonement for you before Yahweh your God. For whoever it is who shall not deny himself in that same day; shall be cut off from his people. Whoever it is who does any kind of work in that same day, that person I will destroy from among his people. You shall do no kind of work: it is a statute forever throughout your generations in all your dwellings. It shall be a Sabbath of solemn rest for you, and you shall deny yourselves. In the ninth day of the month at evening, from evening to evening, you shall keep your Sabbath" (Leviticus 23:26–32 WEB).

The Memorial of Teruah will leave a big mess. Death and destruction will reign as Yeshua comes back and unleashes the fullness of His wrath on the ungodly. Atonement is about the cleanup.

This is a pattern that goes back to the garden of Eden. The story of the fall of Adam and Eve is actually a microcosm of the plan of salvation. After they sinned, God cursed them, but we need to look at that curse not simply as punishment, but as God immediately implementing a pathway back to Him. Eve was told that her pregnancy and childbearing would be through much pain, but it did not stop her from bearing children. Somehow Paul, in his first letter to Timothy, took the curse to mean that she would be *saved* through childbearing.

> And Adam was not deceived, but the woman being deceived, fell into transgression. Nevertheless **she will be saved in childbearing** if they continue in faith, love, and holiness, with self-control (1 Timothy 2:14–15).

Paul saw that the curse was also the way back. She would simply have lessons to learn from the new trials she brought on herself. Man would also have lessons to learn through the sweat of his brow in bringing food to his table. That extra pain and work would make apparent to them the path forward, because in both cases, it was their fruit that would show them when they did well. Healthy, well brought-up children, the fruit of her womb, would show the woman that she did well, just as would the fruit of the field to the man.

In both of their cases, sacrifice would be involved to have success. Any responsible woman to this day will tell you of the sacrifice involved in bearing and raising children. Any responsible man will tell you of the sacrifice involved in putting healthy food on the table for his family. To bring this idea home to Adam and Eve, God also made the first animal sacrifice to clothe them, literally covering them from their sins.

There was sin, then a curse showing the path forward, then a covering to make things well again. This is exactly what we see in these fall holy days. Sin, which has been with us since the fall, will be avenged at the Memorial of Trumpets, then atonement will be made to cover over the destruction caused from that deliverance. Sin, then curse/wrath, then atonement/covering.

Thinking through the curse reveals something else to me as well. With sin came death, but with death comes the need to clean up dead things. I believe that this was where the nature of many of the animals was changed. It is prophesied in Isaiah 11 and 65 that in the future, lions and lambs will get along, children will be able to play with vipers and lions will eat straw like oxen do. If they will one day behave like that, then it makes sense that they were once like that in the past as well.

The serpent got his own curse in Genesis 3:14:

> So the LORD God said to the serpent: "Because you have done this, You are cursed more than all cattle, And more than every beast of the field; On your belly you shall go, And you shall eat dust All the days of your life.

The word for cattle can refer to any animal, not just cows as we tend to think of it. The serpent was cursed "more than" the other cattle and beasts. This sounds like other animals were cursed as well, just not as heavily. When we look at the animals that are considered clean and unclean, it starts to make sense that the nature of clean animals was not changed as much as that of unclean. The unclean beasts are largely ones that killed or scavenged dead things for the bulk of their food, whereas clean ones tend to rely on grass and vegetation.

If the unclean ones had their natures changed from the curse, there must have been a good reason for it. Were they just being punished, or did their curse also serve a function in God's plan? I believe that they were changed in order to act as clean-up crew for the death that wasn't supposed to be part of the picture originally.

We can see birds especially, but also other beasts performing this function in Exodus 40:19, 1 Samuel 17:44, Psalms 79:2, and Revelation 19:21. Of course we can also see animals eating dead things by going outside and watching vultures on roadkill or seeing predators hunting prey. Even insects and worms, also described as unclean, help with decomposition, which is an essential part of the clean-up.

Leviticus 16 is the most complete description of any holy day service, except for maybe Passover in Exodus 12. But it seems to come from out of the blue when most people read it because, as with much of the Bible, it doesn't directly explain its meaning. There is a sacrifice of a bull to cleanse the priest so that he can enter the holy of holies, a censer full of burning coals that the priest must bring in to avoid dying, and then two goat kids, one of which is killed for Yahweh and another which has the sins of Israel confessed over it before it is let go in the wilderness, and lots of blood is sprinkled over the mercy seat. What is going on?

We need to go back to the beginning of the chapter to gain context. Verse 1 states, "Now Yahweh spoke to Moses after the death of the two sons of Aaron, when they offered profane fire before Yahweh, and died."

It was back in chapter ten that Aaron's sons had done this, pretty much immediately after the tabernacle had been consecrated. Leviticus 10:1–3 says,

> Nadab and Abihu, the sons of Aaron, each took his censer, and put fire in it, and laid incense on it, and offered strange fire before Yahweh, which he had not commanded them.
>
> Fire came out from before Yahweh, and devoured them, and they died before Yahweh.
>
> Then Moses said to Aaron, "This is what Yahweh spoke of, saying, 'I will show myself holy to those who come near me, and before all the people I will be glorified.'" Aaron held his peace. (WEB)

This is followed by six chapters of new regulations about how to designate what is clean and what is unclean so that this sort of thing will not happen again. In those chapters, we learn about clean and unclean foods (chapter 11), the uncleanness after childbirth (chapter 12), dealing with the uncleanness of leprosy (chapter 13–14), and unclean bodily discharges (chapter 15).

Yahweh was pounding into them the connection between cleanness and holiness, and that both were required to be in the presence of God. Nadab and Abihu had not understood, thinking they could take things lightly, so God used them as an example before elaborating on the topic.

This is where we find things when we finally get to chapter 16 about the atonement ceremony. I'll avoid printing the entire chapter here, but please read it if you are not already familiar with it. Yahweh was acknowledging that even after being given all of the regulations, there would still be sin and uncleanness that needed to be atoned for. There would be a mess to clean up, and it would be the job of the high priest every year on the tenth day of the seventh month to do so.

The chapter goes over the necessary sacrifices and procedures for making atonement. The main sacrifices are a bull, a ram, and two kids, although one is not actually killed. How did these bulls and goats atone for sin?

The bull was a symbol of power. We get our modern English word *bull* from the Hebrew Baal, which is often used in the Bible as a pagan deity. Literally, however, it just means Lord, and because of the bull's association with power, the Baals, or Lords, used a bull to represent their gods, which they referred to as Baal. Yahweh showed His superiority to the Baals and overcame them many times, typified in Elijah's test with the prophets of Baal in 1 Kings 18, where they each asked their god to send fire on the sacrifice of a bull. Yahweh showed up in power and glory, even licking up the twelve water pots worth of water that drowned the sacrifice. Elijah's burnt offering was accepted and the Baals were defeated.

The bull of Leviticus 16 was specifically for cleansing Aaron, the High Priest, so that he would be clean coming into the Holy of Holies. He would have to bring in some of the bull's blood to sprinkle on the mercy seat. Yeshua is also our High Priest and Lord (Baal), and here it will help to again think about the tabernacle as our bodies. He was sacrificed to bring the life that was in His blood into our bodies—into our hearts, the holy of holies. The blood of Him who overcame all other false gods is brought in and sprinkled and mingled with ours, cleansing us and making us pure like Him.

Next there is a ram to be sacrificed as a burnt offering. The ram also represents Yeshua. It is the same ram that got caught in a thicket, freeing Isaac from being sacrificed by Abraham on the mountain in Genesis 22. It is a reminder that His sacrifice freed us, the offspring of Isaac, from certain death.

The high priest also brings in a censer full of burning coals and sweet incense beaten fine to the Holy of Holies, "that the cloud of the incense may cover the mercy seat that is on the Testimony, lest he die." The smoke of the incense is prayer. In this case it is Aaron's prayer for mercy as he enters, because he is not yet perfectly clean before he can sprinkle the blood. Seeing Yeshua as high priest, He is praying for us, just as He prayed in the upper room at the Passover for His disciples. These prayers are to mingle with the cloud of the Holy Spirit, which is already present there, becoming one with our thoughts and prayers.

Then there are the two kids of the goats. There is a choice to be made between them. They both look the same but will have very different functions: "One lot for Yahweh and the other lot for the scapegoat." The Hebrew word for scapegoat is Strong's H5799 *azazel*, meaning goat of removal. The one for Yahweh would be sacrificed as a sin offering for the people of Israel, with the blood sprinkled on and before the mercy seat, and the azazel goat would have the sins of Israel confessed over it before it is taken to a wilderness devoid of inhabitants and let go.

Lots are cast to see which goat is which. The lot for Yahweh again represents Yeshua, Jesus, as did the bull and ram. However, each animal represented a different aspect of Yeshua. The bull was His power, announcing His right to rule as high priest. The ram was His substitution for us, dying the death that we deserved. The goat was the forgiveness of our sins, allowing us to enter into His body, cleansed and perfected.

The lot for the azazel goat represents the adversary, who is the one on which the sins actually belong:

> Aaron shall lay both his hands on the head of the live goat, confess over it all the iniquities of the children of Israel, and all their transgressions, concerning all their sins, putting them on the head of the goat, and shall send it away into the wilderness by the hand of a suitable man. The goat shall bear on itself all their iniquities to an uninhabited land; and he shall release the goat in the wilderness (Leviticus 16:21–22).

Why let this goat live? If it really represents Satan, shouldn't it be the one to be killed? We need to step back a bit to see clearer. First, let's realize this goat is already in custody. There is no part of the service involving catching or subduing the goat. It is already awaiting its trail. The two goats are Jesus and Barabbas from Matthew 27:15–23. Both are in custody. One is guilty and one innocent. One will be killed and one released. But it was the guilty who was released and the innocent who was killed.

Revelation 20:1–3 reveals the final application that the service foreshadows:

> Then I saw an angel coming down from heaven, having the key to the bottomless pit and a great chain in his hand. He laid hold of the dragon, that serpent of old, who is the Devil and Satan, and bound him for a thousand years; and he cast him into the bottomless pit, and shut him up, and set a seal on him, so that he

should deceive the nations no more till the thousand years were finished. But after these things he must be released for a little while.

We can see the "hand of a suitable man" being an angel holding a certain key. The uninhabited land and wilderness are the bottomless pit, which the key can open up. This is not the final defeat of Satan, for he, in his dragon form, had already been permanently defeated back in Revelation 12.

> And war broke out in heaven: Michael and his angels fought with the dragon; and the dragon and his angels fought, but they did not prevail, nor was a place found for them in heaven any longer. So the great dragon was cast out, that serpent of old, called the Devil and Satan, who deceives the whole world; he was cast to the earth, and his angels were cast out with him. Then I heard a loud voice saying in heaven, "Now salvation, and strength, and the kingdom of our God, and the power of His Christ have come, for the accuser of our brethren, who accused them before our God day and night, has been cast down. And they overcame him by the blood of the Lamb and by the word of their testimony, and they did not love their lives to the death.

Satan the devil was delivered into the hand of Michael the archangel. He was taken into custody on earth, no longer able to travel to heaven. Notice that he is called "the accuser of our brethren." At atonement, those accusations are put back on his own head. And the brethren overcame him by the blood of the lamb, the sacrifice of the other goat, and by their testimony, and because they were willing to lay down their lives to do so.

Revelation shows us that God still has a use for Satan after the thousand-year reign is completed, to deceive the nations for a short time because that generation will have never been tested. That will be covered in the last appointed time.

Having a thousand years to be without Satan's influence and accusations sounds like an amazing time to be part of! But one thing we need to keep in mind today is that we already have the blood of the sacrificial goat representing Yeshua living in our hearts. That has already taken place, which means that we have already cast our lot with Him. We have the power to banish Satan *now!* He cannot touch us if we do not invite him back in. If we tell him to get behind us, or resist him, he is forced to flee because the guilt is already on his head, so his accusations cannot stick. He is banished from us now if we claim the lot of Yeshua, Jesus Christ, accepting His blood in the heart of the tabernacle of our body. The two goats cannot exist in the same location.

We have cleaned up the mess of our hearts and are ready for what the next appointed time brings us.

THE FEAST OF TABERNACLES

> And Jehovah spoke to Moses, saying, Speak to the sons of Israel, saying, In the fifteenth day of this seventh month shall be a Feast of Booths seven days to Jehovah. On the first day shall be a holy gathering; you shall do no work of service. Seven days you shall bring a fire offering to Jehovah; on the eighth day you shall have a holy gathering; and you shall bring the fire offering to Jehovah; it is a solemn assembly; you shall do no work of service.
>
> Also, in the fifteenth day of the seventh month, when you gather the increase of the land, you shall keep the feast of Jehovah seven days; on the first day a sabbath, and on the eighth day a sabbath. And you shall take to yourselves on the first day the fruit of majestic trees, palm branches, and boughs of oak trees, and willows of the valley, and shall rejoice before Jehovah your God seven days. And you shall keep a feast to Jehovah, seven days in a year, a never ending statute throughout your generations; in the seventh month you shall keep it. You shall live in booths seven days; all who are native in Israel shall live in booths, so that your generations shall know that I caused the sons of Israel to live in booths, when I brought them out of the land of Egypt; I *am* Jehovah your God. And Moses proclaimed the appointed feasts

of Jehovah to the sons of Israel (Leviticus 23:33-36 and 39-44 LITV).

This is the feast that all the others have been leading up to. It is the thousand-year reign when Israel finally enters into the promised land. The language in the above description actually brings us all the way back into Eden, using branches, boughs, and fruit of all different trees, symbolizing the Tree of Life. Israel was to make temporary dwellings from the boughs and branches of the trees mentioned. But those trees were not just for building materials or else they could have used any basic lumber tree. They were beautiful, leafy, and fruit-filled trees, and both trees that are specified have amazing healing properties.

The palm tree mentioned specifically refers to the date palm, which is a tree Bedouins in the Middle East actually call "the tree of life" because of its vast array of useful properties. We all know about the sweet, dried fruits, but there is much more to this super-tree. The fruit of the date, even with its extremely high sugar content, yields a much lower glycemic index than the cane sugar it often replaces. But its medicinal properties make its value far higher.

Among the Bedouin, the unripe green fruit and flowers are well known as fertility and conception aids, stimulating the function of the ovaries and the testes, as well as strengthening the health of pregnant and nursing mothers. Dates have been used for colds, fevers, chest infections, asthma, intestinal problems, and externally to counteract poisonous bites. The date trunk is used to treat diarrhea and genitourinary ailments. The roots have been used for toothaches, and the date seeds can be ground into a paste to treat malaria and skin allergies and roasted to brew "Arabic coffee," which is good for gout.

The leaves can be eaten fresh or cooked as a nutrition-rich vegetable when picked young and tender. The fibrous parts of the leaf are used to make rope and brooms. Both the trunk and leaf stalk are extremely strong and are often used as building materials, such as for the temporary dwellings of the Feast of Tabernacles, but also for permanent structures.[27]

The list for the willow is at least as long as the date, with most of its healing properties coming from the inner bark and leaves. One of its main uses, going back millennia, has been easing pain. It can treat joint and back pain and the associated sciatica (I wish I had researched this years ago!), toothaches, headaches, and migraines. It is both antioxidant and anti-inflammatory, lessening the risk of cancer and reducing fever. It eases menstruation and gastrointestinal discomfort and can reduce blood clotting, maintaining heart health.

It is even good for the skin, helping with conditions ranging from acne to psoriasis and warts. The wood, small branches and parts of the bark are well known for making excellent baskets and other wood products. Being one of the fastest growing trees known, it is also a quite renewable resource![28]

This season is also a harvest festival. We started in the spring with the barley harvest, then either late spring or summer for the wheat harvest. Now in the fall it is the in-gathering of bounty of all of the fruits: grapes, figs, pomegranates, dates, olives, and more.

Yahweh wants Israel surrounded by the beauty and bounty of His creation during this time. Satan will have been chained in the bottomless pit during atonement, making this a time of peace, prosperity, and healing, like no other era the world has experienced since the garden of Eden. Humans will have a chance to see what their potential is for life on earth. I honestly don't think we can begin to imagine what life will be like then.

---

[27] Awal, R. (2023, April 15). *Uses and Benefits of Date Palm That Will Surprise You.* Remedy Grove. Retrieved November 8, 2024, from: https://remedygrove.com/traditional/The-Various-Uses-of-Date-Palm-Tree

[28] Sylvia, & Sylvia. (2017, December 4). *Willow facts and health benefits.* Health Benefits | Health Benefits of Foods and Drinks. https://www.healthbenefitstimes.com/willow/

Part 3: The Sky-Clock

Yeshua will be there with His bride, teaching the nations the wisdom that had been kept from them through the scheming of the adversary. With Satan locked up, they will be more than willing to comprehend and implement what they learn.

I personally believe (but don't *know*, so could be wrong) that humans will live for close to 1,000 years again, as they did at the beginning of Genesis. Whatever post-flood conditions changed to lower man's lifespan would be reversed as men would learn to live as Yahweh always intended. In Genesis 6:3 Yahweh said, "My Spirit shall not strive with man forever, for he is indeed flesh; yet his days shall be one hundred and twenty years." Without Satan around, perhaps God's spirit will not need to strive with man.

The only reason I can think of for Satan to be loosed at the end of this time is to test the nations because they will have not had any testing for the last thousand years. So, it makes sense to me that the millennial reign will involve only one generation, even though that generation will continually grow larger, as they will be being fruitful and multiplying. If many generations had come and gone by the time Satan is loosed, most would die never having been tested. Surely God can decide to never test some if He wishes, but would it be consistent with how He has raised the rest of His children? He has spent the last 6,000 years training up those that He can trust to be in His kingdom, and that training has involved discipline in the face of temptation. Without Satan around, there is no temptation. Adam and Eve would not have eaten the fruit. However, this is just speculation, as the Bible is silent on the topic.

What is not speculation is that one thousand years is still a finite time span, which is why the tabernacles, both the ones built for this holy day and the tabernacles of our bodies, are temporary dwellings. Even though this week-long feast and the 1000 years it represents are the culmination of all of the appointed times, they are only the culmination of the physical aspect of God's plan. There is still a spiritual aspect that will be permanent, and that is the significance of the Eighth Day of the feast.

THE EIGHTH DAY

Revelation 22:1–2 reveals a reality that is similar to the symbolism given to Israel for the first part of the feast, but it is obviously referring to a final spiritual reality after the great white throne judgment, when the New Jerusalem has descended from heaven.

> And he showed me a pure river of water of life, clear as crystal, proceeding from the throne of God and of the Lamb. In the middle of its street, and on either side of the river, was the tree of life, which bore twelve fruits, each tree yielding its fruit every month. The leaves of the tree were for the healing of the nations.

We will finally be able to eat freely from the Tree of Life and drink from the Water of Life and all nations will be healed.

It is a time of starting over, which is why it is represented by the eighth day. If the seventh day is the end of the week, then the eighth is actually the first, a new beginning. Revelation 21:1–4 is an incredibly beautiful description of this new beginning. It is everything we all have ever hoped for and is perhaps my favorite passage in the Bible.

> Now I saw a new heaven and a new earth, for the first heaven and the first earth had passed away. Also there was no more sea. Then I, John, saw the holy city, New Jerusalem, coming down out of heaven from God, prepared as a bride adorned for her husband. And I heard a loud voice from heaven saying, "Behold, the tabernacle of God is with men, and He will dwell with them, and they shall be His people. God Himself will be with them and be their God. And God will wipe away every tear from their eyes; there shall be no more death, nor sorrow, nor crying. There shall be no more pain, for the former things have passed away.

That pretty much sums up everything better than I can ever do.

All of God's covenants with man will have their fulfillment here. The covenant with Adam: The tree of good and evil will be gone and the tree of life will be made available again. Adam's curse will be reversed, and the ground will willingly bring forth good fruit again, and Adam's seed will have crushed the enemy's head.

The covenant with Noah: The promise of the rainbow will no longer be needed because death will have been defeated once and for all (Revelation 20:14).

The covenant with Abraham: His descendants have already been multiplied to be quite numerous, but it could be argued that they are not yet as the sand of the sea. During the thousand-year reign, however, this number could grow exponentially if one human life can span that entire time, as I proposed a little bit ago.

To be conservative, let's say that most of the eight billion currently on earth die in the events pictured by the Memorial of Trumpets, so that there are only 1 million people left on earth to inherit the thousand-year reign. If each married couple averages twelve children, which is not so many for living so long, and they don't start having children until they are 117 years old (the average of the pre-flood generations), then in nine generations (roughly 1,000 years), if nobody died, there would be about 840 billion people. That's over one hundred times the current population starting with an extremely conservative number. If we start with more than a million people, with shorter generations, or with more children per family, we will see numbers in the trillions!

The covenant with Moses: This was the big one, the Law. If Israel obeyed, they would be blessed and if they didn't, they would be cursed. Even though our salvation does not depend on the Law anymore, the blessings and curses are still largely in effect. But after the thousand years, they will not be necessary at all, for unrighteousness and uncleanness will have been banished from existence.

The covenant with David: David was told that he would always have someone from his line to sit on the throne. This one will remain in effect forever because Jesus will rule for eternity from the New Jerusalem.

And finally, the new covenant:

> "Behold, the days come," says Yahweh, "that I will make a new covenant with the house of Israel, and with the house of Judah: not according to the covenant that I made with their fathers in the day that I took them by the hand to bring them out of the land of Egypt; which covenant of mine they broke, although I was a husband to them," says Yahweh. "But this is the covenant that I will make with the house of Israel after those days," says Yahweh: I will put my law in their inward parts, and I will write it in their heart. I will be their God, and they shall be my people. They will no longer each teach his neighbor, and every man teach his brother, saying, 'Know Yahweh;' for they will all know me, from their least to their greatest," says Yahweh: "for I will forgive their iniquity, and I will remember their sin no more" (Jeremiah 31:31–34 WEB).

People debate whether this refers to Christians during the church age (where we are now) or after the millennium, because it seems that we do not currently have the law in our hearts from the least of us to the greatest. Some say that if we have the Holy Spirit in us, then we do have His law in our hearts and that it is only referring to believers, not the least and greatest of all humanity. Regardless of whether it is already true for believers or not, by the time of the millennium it will certainly be true, and be true of all who exist, fulfilling the ultimate goal of the new covenant, that our sins will be remembered no more. The passages from Jeremiah 31 and Revelation 21 both make reference to Yahweh/Yeshua being our God and us being His people.

I cannot wait for that time!

PART FOUR
The Ten Ordered Matters

12

The Original Contract

A couple of nights ago I awoke from a dream and knew I had to get up to write it down, and that it would have to go into the book. The problem is the book is already at the editor's and I promised I wouldn't send over any more changes. So, this next section about the dream and the resulting conversation with Jesus will be unedited, at least by a professional, written as I wrote it down at 3:30am.

I was shown contracts. The first contract was shown as a great column of words. They were white, written in a vast black space. Another column of words appeared and obscured the view of the first, also white on black. I was asked, "Which contract is in force?" I thought about it and responded that the one which I obey is in force.

He said, "Correct, but that which stood originally has preeminence. The newer contract brings into bondage, but because it appears to be in front, obscuring the view of the other, it is easier to follow and is the one that the world follows and prefers us to follow. If we bring that new contract into court, any court on earth or heaven, its ruling will stand. But if we decide to claim the original contract, bringing it into any court on earth or in heaven, it will also stand. If we bring the original, but someone else brings the newer against us, the new cannot stand against the original and we will be vindicated by the original."

I woke up and thought about these things but could not be sure how to apply them. I thought of some of the concepts I've heard others talk about, like property rights and taxes. If I claim the original law of the land, can I uphold my right to not pay taxes on my land? I prayed and asked Jesus to clarify the application and examples that He showed me, so that I don't add my human thinking into it.

He answered and said that the two contracts are the law that was written into the creation, which was written by the finger of God Himself, and the law given to Moses at Sinai. Jesus came and removed that newer law from our view so that it could no longer obscure the original. This is the "new" covenant, that we can have open eyes to see, as things were meant to be originally. This is why Jesus is a priest after the order of Melchizedek, as the book of Hebrews explained. The "new" covenant is simply reverting back to the original, removing that which was obscuring our view of it, so that we can have eyes to see and ears to hear.

The Mosaic contract was given to a people who were disobedient already, who would or could not read the original contract any longer. It was not a wrong or evil contract, but rules that could point one back to the original eventually, a temporary stopgap.

When we are little children, we naturally do not know how to obey our parents' wishes, even if we might want to. When we consistently do that which opposes their will for us, they start to make rules to clarify their will. "In our house, we ask permission before going outside to play," so that Mom and Dad will know where we are and can regulate if it is good timing for that. But at a certain age it is expected that the rules are no longer necessary, because the reason behind them is understood. For a 40-year-old to continue to have to ask a parent for permission to go outside would be bondage. Jesus gave us the maturity to see and understand that which before was obscured by the pillar of the law. We can understand the original, which gives us the freedom of adulthood in the household of God.

The Ten Commandments are part, indeed the core, of the original, as they were all around before Moses, and when they were finally written, "the writing was the writing of God engraved on the tablets," (Exodus 32:16). This is important, because all of the later law was written by the hand of Moses and put *beside* the ark of the covenant, not inside of it, where the Ten Commandments were (Deuteronomy 31:24–26). Those parts that were not inside were the temporary contract put in place as explanation of the original eternal contract written into the creation. They are the ones later removed so we could again see the original clearly, as we, through Christ, became able to reach spiritual maturity in understanding.

Please realize that this removal is very different from saying that the law is no longer pertinent in any way. The original contract is still in effect, and the one that was removed was based wholly on that original! It was simply written specifically to ancient Israel, relating the eternal contract to the issues that they were facing at that time.

Some of those laws will not make sense in an eternal context for all cultures at all times. But some will make sense, and we can even see them being kept before the law of Moses was given. Just because they were not part of the Ten Commandments does not mean they bear no importance.

Noah knew which animals were clean and unclean, as he was told to bring seven pairs of clean and only two pairs of unclean animals on board the ark. This was long before Moses was born, and I believe he was able to read those instructions in the creation itself. Because of this, I tend to think it is still worth keeping the dietary laws of clean and unclean foods, but I will also not judge anyone who sees it differently.

The main point is that the contract put in place by Moses was removed not so that we can have freedom to break the law, but so

Part 4: The Ten Ordered Matters

that we can have the freedom to apply it appropriately to our own situations today, as mature adults in the body of Christ.

I believe this seeming dichotomy between the removal of the law and its remaining significance was what Paul struggled so hard to try to explain in his letters, and that people had and still have such a hard time comprehending. Most of the book of Romans is dedicated to it, as well as Galatians 3–5 and Hebrews 7 (if Paul actually wrote Hebrews, as some theorize).

It is also what Jesus was meaning when He said, "Do not think that I came to destroy the Law or the Prophets. I did not come to destroy but to fulfill," in Matthew 5:17. He showed us through example what it looked like to fulfill the law, which, to pretty much everybody, looked very different than their picture of the law of Moses.

Now back to our originally scheduled introduction!

I've talked about the Ten Commandments being the heart of our spiritual bodies, so it makes sense to look deeper into them to see where we can find them in the natural world, and what new insights we can glean by doing so. But first, I'd like to just give a quick look at the term *ten commandments*.

The term is only used in Exodus 34:28, not when the commandments were actually given in Exodus 20 or Deuteronomy 5. It says, "So he was there with the LORD forty days and forty nights; he neither ate bread nor drank water. And He wrote on the tablets the **words** of the covenant, the Ten **Commandments**." The word for *words* and for *Commandments* in that verse is the same word, Strong's H1697, *dabar*. Between the *Strong's Concordance* and *Brown-Driver-Briggs* definitions, it can mean a word, matter, speech, utterance, saying or thing, with commandment being a possible stretch with certain combinations of other words. The *Ancient Hebrew Lexicon* says of *dabar*: "a careful arrangement of words," with the root word meaning, "an arrangement or placement of something creating order." God was carefully creating order in these commandments, just as He created order with the creation itself in Genesis 1.

My point is not to say that these aren't commandments, but mere suggestions or proverbs, because internally in the ten He does refer to them as commandments; He just uses a different word. In Exodus 20, He says at the end of the second "ordered matter," "showing mercy to thousands, to those who love Me and keep My **commandments**." That word is Strong's H4687, *mitsvah,* which according to all sources, means simply "a command," with the root word, *tsavah,* meaning, "to command, charge, give orders, lay charge, give charge to, order." But there is that word, *order* again. Does it not make sense that the reason somebody "gives orders" is to create order? Both meanings of our word *order* come from the same place. In Deuteronomy 5, there are three more uses of the word 'Commanded'—twice in the command to keep the Sabbath and once about honoring your father and mother. In both of these cases, the root word *tsavah* is used.

Ordering is very important to our Father. Not in the sense of ordering around or barking orders, but putting in order, organizing in a way to make sense of something complex. He has given charge to His people to keep the Sabbath and honor their father and mother but has done so in order to keep order. The Sabbath command is a direct reference to the ordering that was done at creation when He set the Sabbath aside as a holy day of rest. There were six days of work, then a day of rest: The days were ordered.

"Honor your father and mother, as Yahweh your God has commanded you, that your days may be well with you in the land which Yahweh your God is giving you." This is setting in order the direction that honor is to flow. Honor your parents, as your family is a picture of the heavenly family, and our Father in heaven is worthy of all honor. Every new generation sees the children trying to change the order so that the children receive the honor, and parents are ruled by their children, but God says it was not created to be so.

Part 4: The Ten Ordered Matters

From here on you will hear me refer to the commandments by either the word *command(-ments)* or *ordered matters*, depending on which feels better at the time. Both are correct, and I hope that this expands the way we think about them.

So, let's look at these ordered matters one by one to see how the natural world confirms them and shows them to us in its own created order. We'll also go a lot of other places, so hold on!

Oh, but first, one more quick thought. Exodus records that God wrote the Ten Commandments with His own finger. How many fingers does God have? Since we are made in His image, I would assume He has ten, five per hand. It just so happens to match the number of commandments that He gave us, written on two tablets, five on each.

One: No Other Gods Above

I am Yahweh your God, who brought you out of the land of Egypt, out of the house of bondage. You shall have no other gods before me (Exodus 20:1–3 WEB).

Another way to translate the word *before* in this ordered matter is *above*, as in, "You shall have no other gods *above* me." See Strong's H5920. There is only one God "above" all others. Even if you believe in the existence of other gods, they can all only have power over a limited area of influence, for instance, a god of the water or of the mountain, etc.

The Bible does speak of other gods and does not necessarily deny their existence: angels, both fallen and good; cherubim and seraphim; nephilim and demons; mighty ones of old and "spiritual forces of wickedness in the heavenly places" (Ephesians 6:12). There is definitely a whole spiritual realm with spiritual beings of various kinds. Real or imaginary is not the point here. The point is that only one can have preeminence. There is only one Creator of all heaven and earth. If other gods are real, then the one Creator created them, too. This is an obvious fact of nature, that one being must have created all there is. This ordered matter orders all created beings. It puts them in their correct positions, and the one Creator is above all others.

When we look at nature, we can marvel at the life that it sustains. We can understand that we cannot live without the fresh water that flows through the rivers and falls out of the sky. But do we worship the water? No! But why? Because there is something *above* it, more important than it, that created it. How about the sun? It is above us and is also essential for sustaining life. Many cultures throughout history have indeed decided to worship the sun for this reason. There is perhaps nothing else visible to us that is more important to our survival, and it appears to be above all the earth. But on its own, can it create life? No, it cannot. So, it must be a created thing itself, and if it is created, there is something above it. To worship it would be out of order.

We can understand all of this simply by looking at the natural world and understanding that all things that have been created must have a Creator that is greater than them.

Much more will be said about this command in the next section, as the first and second matters are closely related.

14

Two: Images – Gateway to Deception

> You shall not make for yourself a carved image—any likeness of anything that is in heaven above, or that is in the earth beneath, or that is in the water under the earth; you shall not bow down to them nor serve them. For I, the LORD your God, am a jealous God, visiting the iniquity of the fathers upon the children to the third and fourth generations of those who hate Me, but showing mercy to thousands, to those who love Me and keep My commandments (Exodus 20:4–6).

Images are not always bad. All of nature is full of images. The sun, moon, and stars are all images that speak of their Creator. Humans are images too, made in the image of God. It is all about worshipping images *or* the Creator. God created all things to point to Him so that we are without excuse. That is the whole thing! Worship nothing else but Yahweh Elohim! Find Him in all of His creation and let it be to *His* glory, not the glory of the thing!

This topic is all encompassing, and as such this will be, by far, the longest chapter of the Ten Ordered Matters. All ten can easily be boiled down to image worship or idolatry in their essence. It is the story of the Bible in a nutshell and explains why the world is in the state it is in today. It is also the one that is the most personally important to me.

When humans create images, we get into trouble, because we think we are doing something worthy of attention. I should know because I was trained as an image maker. I went to college and got a degree in sculpture. I made images of people, animals, and objects. They got attention and as a result, so did I. As an artist, that is the whole point, to get attention. Because the more attention the sculpture/image gets, the more sales I can get, and the bigger my ego can grow. Being an artist, however, is not a profession that is easy to make a living at because there are never enough people giving enough attention, so at some point the job becomes self-promotion as much or more than just making images.

I have to convince people that the sculptures are more than they are. They cannot just be a well-designed or beautiful object, they must also be a deep thought about the world around us, especially a deep thought about some topic that is at the forefront of modern political ideology because that is what public commissions are about! They are not going to simply choose a piece that looks cool on the wall of the public building. No! It must also speak of diversity and inclusion, sustainability, or whatever political idea is popular at the moment. Then there it will sit on the wall or pedestal for generations to look at and give attention to, at least until the next ideology makes it unpopular.

Here is the problem. When attention goes too far, there is another word we can use for it—worship. Worship is simply to give attention to something in an extreme sense. In ancient times this was done by prostrating yourself, bowing low to something to show your status in comparison to the thing being worshipped. Today, we in the west do not bow much, but that does not mean we don't worship anything. We can show our worship of something simply by the time we spend or desire to spend with it. Not that everything we spend time with is being worshipped, but it is a danger.

Two: Images – Gateway to Deception

What is the point in giving someone or something attention? I can give attention to another person in order to lift them up, to encourage them or help them out. I am doing something for them, not for myself. That attention is not worship, but edification. I can also hang out with someone because I want them to like me. I want to show them how cool I am and worthy of their attention. Or maybe I want them to buy my sculpture. The motive is selfish and if I am successful, I have lifted myself up above them because I am so cool. This makes them lower, and that means they worship me. That ends up being the entire point to my making sculpture. It needs to be so good that people worship not just it, but me. Often-times those viewing my art have no idea who I am. Maybe it's in a gallery or somewhere in public, but they don't personally know me or even who I am. The hope, then, is that they will ask around or see my signature and try to seek me out.

In this way, being an artist is very much like being a little creator-god. We put things out into the world that will garner attention, but with the hope that the attention doesn't just stop at the thing but somehow gets back to us. We want the attention for ourselves. The true God is no different. He has created the entire world we live in. He filled it with beautiful and amazing things worthy of our attention. When we see those amazing things and don't ever find His signature on them, but just keep giving attention to the thing, God is sad because the attention is misplaced.

This is what most of humanity has done since the beginning of creation. People have looked up at the sun and seen the amazing things that it does—how it warms us and gives us light and makes our plants grow. We have looked at it and thought how nothing can survive without it and decided it is worthy of our attention and stopped there. We never stopped to search for the signature of its Creator.

People have done this with all sorts of things besides the sun as well: the moon, the stars, the ocean, rain, rivers, mountains, animals, trees, kings, and other people. Every one of these things was made by the same Creator and bears His signature. Every one of them is indeed worthy of our attention. But the reason they are worthy of our attention is because they show a different aspect of the Creator Himself. They point to Him. Genesis 1 actually says humans were created in His image! I believe all of these other things are either created in the image of other things in God's realm or point to different aspects of God. Either way, they are physical images of spiritual things: All are created by the one Creator with the hope of us finding Him.

Then it sounds simple, these first two ordered matters: Worship God alone and nothing else. And it is…except when it's not.

First, remember one thing: We have an enemy whom the Bible describes as "the deceiver of the whole world" (Revelation 12:9 WEB), and "the father of lies" (John 8:44 WEB). He is very good at what he does and will stop at nothing to keep us from understanding God's truth. He is so good in fact, that we are told that during the end times even the very elect would be deceived if it were possible (that is, if Christ Himself were not in some way keeping the deception from them). So let us not be ashamed or surprised to find out that many things we currently hold as true are nothing but lies. In fact, we should be surprised if that *isn't* the case.

The method the adversary uses to create much of the deception is through images—idolatry, if you will. The second ordered matter in Exodus 20:4–6 is more pertinent to today than most think.

> You shall not make for yourself a carved image—any likeness of anything that is in heaven above, or that is in the earth beneath, or that is in the water under the earth; you shall not bow down to them nor serve them. For I, the LORD your God, am a jealous God, visiting the iniquity of the fathers upon the children to the third and fourth generations of those who hate Me, but showing mercy to thousands, to those who love Me and keep My commandments.

Two: Images – Gateway to Deception

This is a commandment that most of us think we've got a pretty firm grasp on. There aren't too many of us bowing down to sculptures or paintings. But let's take a closer look at the meaning behind the words and statements in it and try to put it in a contemporary context to get a better idea of what this commandment is really saying.

There are seven questions that need to be answered for a full understanding:

1. What is a carved or graven image?
2. What is a likeness?
3. What does "bow down to them" mean or imply?
4. What does "serve them" mean or imply?
5. Why is God jealous and does this contradict the tenth commandment?
6. Why visit iniquity to the third and fourth generations?
7. Why only kindness to thousands and not to everybody?

Our time here will be spent on the first four questions. Number 5 will be dealt with in the tenth commandment, and 6 and 7 will have to be for another time. I bring them up because they are important questions to think about.

"Carved image" or "graven image" is Strong's H6459, *pecel*, meaning "an idol, carved or graven image." It comes from the root word *pacal*, Strong's H6458, "to cut, hew, hew into shape. To carve, whether of wood or stone."

"Likeness" is Strong's H8544 – *temunah*, meaning "something portioned (i.e. fashioned) out, as a shape, i.e. (indefinitely) phantom, or (specifically) embodiment, or (figuratively) manifestation (of favor): - image, likeness, similitude." Its root word is Strong's H4327 – *miyn*, meaning, "to portion out; a sort, i.e. species: - kind."

So, we are not to make any carved or hewn images or objects that are fashioned to embody or manifest anything on the earth, under the waters, or in heaven. Then it says not to bow down to or serve them, which is a separate statement from the one about making them. Don't make them. Don't worship them. It does not say not to make them only if you are going to worship them. It says don't do either one.

The obvious question is "Why?" We tend to think of them as one statement because we can't imagine all images today, including photography, drawing, sculpture, video, digital processes, painting, etc., being banned by the Bible. Are we really not supposed to make any of these things? If I was to make my decision based solely on reading the commandment, I'd have to answer yes.

But then we read elsewhere about God telling the Israelites to make images of cherubim (a likeness of something in heaven) to place on the ark of the covenant, and almond flowers (a likeness of something on earth) to decorate the lampstand. Isn't that contradictory? Are we then forced to conclude that the context refers to the worshipping aspect as being the main point after all, and not the making? Even though both of these objects were used in the tabernacle/temple, which was a place of worship, they were not worshipped themselves. Is there anywhere else that can shed light on the subject to see if we are missing something?

Just a little further down in Exodus 20, in verse 25, we hear something else about the concept of hewing stone, "And if you make Me an altar of stone, you shall not build it of hewn stone; for if you use your tool on it, you have profaned it." Joshua followed through on that command when he built an altar after the destruction of Ai:

> Now Joshua built an altar to the LORD God of Israel in Mount Ebal, as Moses the servant of the LORD had commanded the children of Israel, as it is written in the Book of the Law of Moses: "an altar of whole stones over which no man has wielded an iron tool." And they offered on it burnt offerings to the LORD, and sacrificed peace offerings (Joshua 8:30–31).

Two: Images – Gateway to Deception

Solomon, although he didn't keep it perfectly, made an effort to show he understood the principle when building the temple:

> And the house, when it was in building, was built of stone made ready before it was brought thither: so that there was neither hammer nor axe [nor] any tool of iron heard in the house, while it was in building (1 Kings 6:7).

The stone was hewn, but he made the effort not to do it in front of God's face, to keep the building holy.

God wants to be worshipped in purity. Not hewing the stone is an acknowledgment that He is the Creator. To put our mark on the stones of the altar would be to change His creation to suit our needs. Put this in spiritual terms: Who is the rock of our salvation, the chief corner stone? Can we put our own thoughts of what we think He should be on Him in any way? No! We look only to His word, because He *is* the Word! We do not add to or take away from it! Once we change Him, we are no longer worshipping Him but an idol, a false god. The point being that there is another aspect to what makes a graven image. If it is graven (or cut, carved, or hewn), it has been changed or altered from the way God created it.

Let me pause here for a minute to explain why this is important to me. Most of those reading this would never change the Father or the Son intentionally, and I do believe that that is the most important spiritual aspect of this commandment. But it is still a physical command as well, and we know that keeping the commandments in their physical aspect is the best way to learn their spiritual nature.

Now, my worldly background is as an artist, specifically a sculptor, but ever since studying art in college, I've had a sense of unease about making art, enjoying the process but not caring much for the result. I would have never been an art collector, even if I had money, even before I came to know God in any real sense. I could never really understand why I liked to make art but at the same time didn't really like art. This is not to say that I didn't have favorite artists or other works that I appreciated or even envied. I just didn't see the point to making art, as it seemed a selfish pursuit even if I really enjoyed making it myself.

I especially enjoyed studying and sculpting the human figure but never cared much for most figurative sculpture. After coming to know my Creator, my feelings of unease with art, especially that of the human figure, intensified, although I didn't at all understand it. I often pondered whether I was making idols, although I knew that my sculptures were never made or purchased for worship specifically.

At one point, a few years after college and shortly after getting married, just as I was starting to study the Bible in a serious way, I was hired to do a portrait bust in bronze for a rather vain fellow who would ask me to give him a bit more hair than his receding hairline showed and "Couldn't you smooth over that scar," that I thought was a skin crease that needed to be there.

The portrait and casting turned out very well in the end, looking very much like him, but he was not happy with it because I still must not have made him look so much better than he actually did. When it was done, I was naive enough to let him take the sculpture with him while he went to get cash to make the final payment, and of course I never saw him again.

I learned a hard business lesson, but I also started to learn something about what makes an idol. That was in 1998, and it was the last human sculpture I did.

I only sensed what it was about then. I could not put it into words for another twenty years. But what I now know that I was sensing then was a connection between a person's vanity and their need to change reality to cater to it. It made me think about portraits of famous people and memorials made to them. How much of reality was edited in order to increase their glory? I realized that very seldom is a portrait done simply to remember what a person looked like. Portraits were made to remember what they did, using a very

Two: Images – Gateway to Deception

controlled story. The sculpture or painting itself would of course be suppressing any unwanted features, and/or made from the person's best side and cast in pleasing light, but it would also be put in a setting that either literally or figuratively told of the heroic deeds of the individual (or the money they gave to the cause), and put great emphasis on a few desired traits or qualities. The full truth of who the person was would not be told.

It is human nature to only want our good side to be shown to the public. It is godly nature to admit our sins and faults. (Obviously God has no faults, but it is the godly nature that allows us to see our faults, and thus our need for forgiveness). I saw that the idea behind every public piece of portraiture that I could think of had as its main idea giving glory and honor to that person. But there is only one who is worthy of all glory and honor!

So, this gets me back to where I was before I paused. If we are giving glory and honor to a person through changing the reality of who they were by editing, or putting our mark/tools on them, then we have turned them into an idol!

I've referred so far to portraiture, which to me at twenty-six years old seemed the most obvious example of what I should not be doing because it is easy to envision worshipping another person. However, most of us today, at least in the western world, have a hard time envisioning animals or objects as things to worship, which is why I turned my sculptural focus to wildlife.

My career started taking off after I did so, garnering recognition first in galleries, then in a major purchase from the Maryhill Museum of Art. *Percent for the Arts* commissions (a program in most states that earmarks at least one percent of construction costs for any publicly funded building to go toward artwork in that building) started coming in as well, from places such as the University of Oregon, the City of Eugene, and the Woodland Park Zoo in Seattle.

Part 4: The Ten Ordered Matters

I was offered a teaching position at Lane Community College and then received a private commission to make five life-sized hammerhead sharks in bronze for a private aquarium on the Red Sea in Saudi Arabia before I took a full-time job as the Assistant Coordinator at the Craft Center at the University of Oregon.

But did wildlife art also need to be looked at as image making? After all, the commandment did say not to make a likeness of *anything* in the earth, not just people. That question was harder for me to answer for a long time.

In theory, for both human portraiture and animals, if we could just not add our "mark" to the piece, or change its reality, then we wouldn't be giving glory and honor to the subject instead of the Creator. If we could make the piece true to the spirit of what God made, we should be okay. But is that even possible? Wouldn't "our mark" be inevitable to leave on the piece? Isn't that what makes art, art?

When I was in college studying the human body in figure studies class, we worked from a live human model. At the end of each session, we lined up the pieces for critique and it was a remarkable thing to notice that every sculpture looked not only like the model, but also like the sculptor! It was a phenomenon that was most pronounced in the beginner's work but never went away even with the most advanced students. Our familiarity with our own bodies was impossible to completely override when looking at a different body type from our own. This to me shows the impossibility of not putting our own mark on anything we make (and the same for God's mark on His own creation).

So, what is the answer? Is it acceptable to the Creator for us to make any sort of image? Before I answer I'm going to move on to what worshipping is—or as the commandment puts it, bowing down to and serving the idol. I think then that things will make a little more sense.

"Bow down" is Strong's H7812:

Two: Images – Gateway to Deception

> shâchâh, shaw-khaw'; a primitive root; to depress, i.e. prostrate (especially reflexive, in homage to royalty or God):—bow (self) down, crouch, fall down (flat), humbly beseech, do (make) obeisance, do reverence, make to stoop, worship.

The sense is that of showing deep respect through making ourselves lower than that of the thing which is bowed to, thus raising it up and giving it glory. We are acknowledging the thing's relative greatness and truth and submitting to it.

"Serve" is Strong's H5647:

> 'âbad, aw-bad'; a primitive root; to work (in any sense); by implication, to serve, till, (causatively) enslave, etc.:—× be, keep in bondage, be bondmen, bond-service, compel, do, dress, ear, execute, husbandman, keep, labour(-ing man, bring to pass, (cause to, make to) serve(-ing, self), (be, become) servant(-s), do (use) service, till(-er), transgress (from margin), (set a) work, be wrought, worshipper.

To serve, then, is to work for something, serving it either through our own choice because we are compelled through its truth, or because we are compelled through our bondage to it, unable to free ourselves. Either way, we are taking action to maintain our service. It is how we live our lives in response to our submission (bowing down) to something.

An idol or image does not have to represent the whole truth, but only part of it. When the Israelites made the golden calf, they knew that the sculpture itself did not create them, but they thought of it as a representative of the one who did, just as the foreign idols represented the deities they were fashioned after. To them, they were not necessarily creating a new God, but justified in their minds that they would be worshipping the same Yahweh that was traveling with them in the pillar of cloud and fire, only the calf was much easier on their eyes, something they could comprehend without fear.

Psalm 106:19–20 says, "They made a calf in Horeb, and worshipped the molded image. Thus they changed their glory into the image of an ox that eats grass." They both added to and took away characteristics from the true God that they were supposedly representing, so that by looking upon it and acknowledging its truth (that it actually represented God), they changed the reality to suit their needs.

And there is the real reason idols have always been made – to suit our needs. The ruling classes have usually been the ones to create them (although not always), and the people accepted that they were given as the truth. That truth led the people to live in certain ways, usually to give of themselves to the leaders, who in some way had referenced themselves to the gods that the idols were pointing to. Sometimes, as in the case of the golden calf, the people create the god themselves, also to serve their own needs, thinking it will make their lives easier in some way.

At least we don't fall for those idols now, right? Or do we? None of us would say we bow down to or serve an idol. But if we look at what is behind bowing down and serving, we might need to think again. Is there anything that we show submission to by acknowledging its truth besides the Bible or the creation—especially anything that could possibly be seen as an idol or image?

Images in modern times certainly make me think of television, movies, the internet, and print media. But certainly, we know the difference between truth and fiction on the screen and in books, and certainly we don't "submit" ourselves to what they tell us, right? What would submitting ourselves to it even look like? Serving? Serving involves giving our time and making decisions based on what we are told.

Do we do that with television or other image media? I'm convinced that we do, and we do it with very dangerous consequences. We have unwittingly taken many lies to be the truth—lies about God and the world He created for us. Lies that have caused many to fall away from His ways and teachings, and that will cause even many of us who are still holding on to His Word to fall away in

Two: Images – Gateway to Deception

the future. The lies have been made very real to us because we have not learned how to identify images and idols in modern times.

Even the best of us occasionally watches TV or videos. Many realize that most of the programming is worthless garbage but will still say things like "I only watch the news," or "I just have my couple shows that I watch in the evening to relax," or maybe, "I only watch when my team is playing." All of these "onlys" still count. We still get fed with the ads and a picture of the world that the adversary wants us to believe. I don't want this to become a study on the evils of television because I'm sure we've all heard it. But there are two aspects of it that most don't quite get yet.

One of them is how much fiction is put into the "news" and the other is how much truth is put into the "fiction." The end result is a world view that is completely distorted and removed from God's truth. And we *all* fall into it. The deception has been very, very great for many years and we've submitted to it like a frog in a gradually boiling pot of water. And it isn't just television. It has been a combination of news (printed, television, radio, internet), school textbooks, a 100 percent fabricated pop culture, and a new religion called "science."

Many Bible-believing Christians understand this to a certain extent. We know that evolution has been propped up as a great, unquestionable truth when it is an outright lie. But there are others—many others—and they all rely heavily on images of all sorts in their deception. There are some specific examples that I badly want to go into that typify the spirit of deception that is upon us all today, but the Holy Spirit tells me I should not, but instead to continue talking about my personal story. I will honor the Spirit's advice, but first let me just add a few general warnings and advice.

There are plenty of people out who have gone deep into the many deceptions and conspiracies that have been foisted on the public, and if the spirit moves you to look into them, then do so without fear of what the world calls you. Remember that Proverbs

18:13 tells us "If one rejects a matter before he hears, it *is* folly and shame to him" (LITV). Understand that the term *conspiracy theory* was coined by the CIA after the Kennedy assassination to make people who searched beyond the official narrative look crazy. It worked amazingly well and has since been applied to many other topics that the conspirators do not want you to look into. The enemy knows that people tend to put the approval of men before that of God.

Of course, a spirit of discernment is essential as well since there are at least as many false theories as ones that contain truth, and many more that contain kernels of truth among the weeds.

Pray always and focus only on what edifies you and brings you into closer relationship with Jesus Christ. Not everybody needs to know all truth, and indeed nobody can, which is why the spirit is telling me to shut my mouth here. So, this is simply advice for if and when you are moved to actually start looking, once you realize the world might not be the place you thought it was. If you are never moved to do so, there is no issue with that either, as long as you do not mock those who do.

And with those warnings and advice out of the way, I'll move on with my story. I will still give one (Spirit approved) example of the deception afterwards.

LESSONS FROM BANJOS

This section will seem like a digression from the topic at hand of idolatry but bear with me and it will eventually meander back.

As I struggled with whether I needed to give up art, I went back and forth, knowing deep inside that I needed to stop, but also knowing that I could never convince anyone else that it was wrong to make images, especially in light of biblical commands to make them in certain situations.

I have always wished I was the sort of person who could just have a conviction and immediately act on it. I tend to be slow and uncertain, weighing all options for far too long before making

Two: Images – Gateway to Deception

changes. Yet God knows me and is very patient, so that by the time I do make a decision, I fully understand why. From the time I made my last figurative artwork until I stopped making any sculpture at all was at least twelve years.

There was never really a defined point where I said to myself, *I'm giving it all up*. I just gradually stopped pursuing it. I had a decent job that paid the bills at that point and didn't need the extra income. Commissions started getting in the way of family time anyway, making me busier than I wanted, so I just stopped applying, willingly letting the sculpture career slide away.

Because I didn't make a hard choice to stop, small requests still found their way in which I obliged, especially repairs on old commissions. But I tried not to worry so much about those.

I worried more about my job, because it was still in the field of art. I found myself trying not to make art, yet I was organizing classes and studios for others to make it, which seemed rather contradictory. The job was also stressful for a variety of other reasons, and eventually I knew I needed to leave. The problem was that I didn't have anything else lined up yet.

I didn't know what to do, so I fasted and prayed. I went for twelve days with only water, asking God what to do next (among other things I felt the need to be praying for). Toward the end of this time, I had a dream that I interpreted as needing to quit my job and work for myself.

In retrospect, I'm not sure I got that interpretation completely correct, looking at the stress I put my family under by my decision. Even though I had been fasting, I still had my own desires in my heart.

I started planning on making musical instruments, specifically banjos. If you haven't figured it out yet, I can be an extremely selfish person! Sanae tried to convince me that it was a bad idea, but I was sure that this was from God. It would be great: I would be working from home, I could help her out more and relieve her stress, not add to it!

Lesson #1—Not all dreams are from God. Or maybe we just do not always receive the gift of immediate interpretation. If God truly wants us to know, He will let us know the interpretation with certainty, but often it requires time before it is revealed.

My son has shown a gift for music since he was in the womb, when he would respond to music whenever we put it on. At this point he was five years old and really lit up whenever we played fast banjo music on the stereo. I had built some guitars shortly after graduating from college, so I figured that banjos couldn't be that hard to make and he could learn to play as he grew up. He was already playing drums and piano.

Since I couldn't find anyone else in the area who built them, I thought maybe I could find a niche. It didn't matter much to me that I didn't know how to play a banjo, or even a guitar for that matter. I gave notice at my job and started designing a unique banjo I could market.

I had thought a lot about the nature of art-making and whether making instruments would still be art. Looking at the biblical examples, I came to the conclusion that the pieces of art in the tabernacle were not stand-alone pieces or art for art's sake. They were decoration, beautification of something else. Almond designs were on the lampstand. Pomegranates and cherubim were on the curtains. I could still use my artistic skill to make functional objects and make them beautiful.

I soon discovered that I had greatly underestimated the difficulty of making a banjo from scratch. When most people say they have made a banjo, what they mean is that they bought a bunch of prefabricated parts and assembled them. The more skilled ones will turn the pot (body) on a lathe and shape their own neck. I felt I had to make even the metal parts from scratch (except for the tuners) and also redesign every traditional aspect from the ground up.

Two: Images – Gateway to Deception

It took me over six months of frustration after frustration to finish my first one. The first big frustration I had was learning how to turn on a lathe, which I had never done even though I was experienced with most other woodworking tools.

My first piece was not just for practice but was supposed to be for the back of the banjo, called the resonator, which is basically a 16" diameter round dish with shallow sides. The wood I chose was a piece of burl wood, which I later learned can be very difficult to work with.

One of the guitars I had made previously had back and sides hand-carved from a large piece of burl and it had worked great, never warping or moving on me. I guess I had been lucky. This resonator warped and changed constantly. Then, after it seemed to calm down, it started getting too thin and revealing voids. I tried to get creative, carving out the voids and thin parts and filling them with inlaid designs. But then it started moving more, causing the inlays to pop out. I kept working it, adding more inlay until it seemed kind of reasonable and even looked good in my own estimation.

Then I showed it to Sanae, and she did not like it. At that point, my patience left, and I went back into the garage where I had been working and kicked a thick steel plate that was propped against the wall as hard as I could. The steel won the battle and broke my foot in multiple places. I was rewarded with meeting my next frustration with crutches and a "boot" on my foot.

That next, and probably biggest frustration was with something I felt compelled to redesign that is inherent in every five-string banjo because one string is shorter than the others. Being a different length means that when capoing (putting a barre on a fret to play in a higher key), the fifth string needs to be capo'd at a different fret than the other four. The common solution is to hammer little model railroad spikes into the fretboard on the most used frets so the string can be pushed under the head of the spike. It works for people but seemed like a rather crude solution to me. There were other after-market systems that were bulky and invasive, too, but no banjo company had ever really come up with an elegant way to accommodate the issue. So, I set out to do it.

My brainchild was to create a system of magnetic pop-up buttons that could be raised up when in use, then pulled flush with the fretboard afterwards. I ran into problem after problem. First, I used magnets that were too big and caused the steel string itself to react to the magnets, causing weird frequencies. Next, they were too close to the edge of the neck and broke through the side when I shaped the neck. Then when I glued the fretboard on, the glue seeped into the holes where the buttons were supposed to move freely. The more I adapted my design, the more the solution thwarted me.

I was convinced that the only way I could make a name for myself as a serious banjo maker while starting as a nobody with zero ties to the bluegrass music world was to be so radically better than everyone else that people would be forced to notice. My fifth string capo was the key to making that happen. But at this point, with my broken foot, no income for months, a dysfunctional banjo neck, and an increasingly bitter wife, I was desperate.

I started praying about what to do and immediately knew I had to give up on the fifth string capo. I needed to humble myself and admit defeat. Just make beautiful banjos and let that be enough! I told you I can be selfish, but I can also be very stubborn. I was so far into the capo design and felt so close getting it right that I couldn't give up completely. I told God that if He would let me finish this first neck in good working order, I would not make any more with that capo design. God, in His mercy, let me finish it, and it worked as I had hoped.

I finally had one finished banjo to show to the world. Then, by what was undoubtedly a miracle, I was able to have a private showing of my banjo with Béla Fleck, the best banjo player who has ever existed, after a concert. He was very gracious, but also quite honest. He thought it looked cool but sounded awful (although he used

Two: Images – Gateway to Deception

kinder words than that), and he was almost completely uninterested in the capo design. Then he gave me good feedback on how to improve things for my next one. I took his advice to heart.

Because it was unique, and because the timing just happened to be perfect, I was also able to get that banjo into The Museum of Making Music in San Diego, where they were putting together a big show on the history and future of the banjo. It wasn't a sale, but it was a big resume booster.

Lesson #2—God is faithful to keep His Word.

The next banjo took about three months, and I didn't keep up my end of the bargain with God. The capo system worked well enough that I just *had* to work to perfect it. I convinced myself that because I changed the capo design a little bit, it might be okay, and maybe God didn't really mind. When it actually worked well, I figured He must have approved. I also completely redesigned the rest of the banjo, based a lot on what Béla Fleck had told me. It was very different and sounded much better.

I wasn't able to sell that one either. Finally, though, through networking on a popular banjo forum, I got some interest, and by being willing to greatly underprice myself to get started, I got a commission to do another one. My goal was to make one in under one month, but I just couldn't get there. That third one still took at least three months, in large part because I felt I had to put a capo system on it, which was extremely painstaking to make.

The design of the banjo itself was completely customized to the buyer's wishes. But the capo system didn't work right. Glue had gotten into a few of the buttons, causing them to stick. I thought I had fixed them when I sent the banjo out, but the problem came back and they never worked for the buyer. He got such a good deal that he was not worried about it, because otherwise the banjo looked good and played well, but I felt awful that I had sent out a faulty product and started to realize I had been trying to cheat God.

Lesson #3—If you make a bargain with God, hold up your end of the deal! Better yet, don't make a bargain with God! I was still trying to change God into what I wanted Him to be, to put this in Idolatry terms.

At this point, it was closing in on a year since I had quit my job, and I had earned enough to pay about 2 weeks of bills. Our savings were going quickly away, and my wife was extremely stressed and rightly angry with my decision.

Lesson #4—Listen to your wife! At the very least, take her worries seriously! This is how to fulfill Ephesians 5:25, "Husbands, love your wives, just as Christ also loved the church and gave Himself for her."

I finally decided to ditch the capo system completely. Model railroad spikes actually worked very well and were far easier to install. And then I finally started getting a few real orders.

The money was still going out much faster than it was coming in, however, and I could no longer live in the hope that things would suddenly get better. I could neither work fast enough to produce them at the prices I could demand nor charge enough to cover my time. I started looking for another day job.

All of the lessons I learned from the banjo business were pointing toward one singular lesson, and it turns out that it was the same one I still hadn't fully comprehended from making art.

Lesson #5—The idols were not the stuff I was making; they were me.

I had put away the art as a way to rid myself of idolatry, then picked up another business that put me right back into it because I still had to promote myself constantly in order to make a living. The promises I made to my wife of helping out around the house more and taking away her stress never materialized because I was so panicked about not making any money that I felt I had to work all hours in the shop. And I was still selfish and stubborn.

Two: Images – Gateway to Deception

God started giving me not-so-subtle hints that I needed to stop the self-promotion when my website was hacked to the point of being unusable. Twice. After it happened the first time, I started from scratch redesigning the website. Then it happened again, only through such a series of events that my URL itself was taken away. If I wanted it back, I would have to pay thousands of dollars and there was nothing I could do about it.

I took the hint and gave up promoting myself (easy enough to do now with no website to point people to), and then a couple more orders came in. Those were probably the best two banjos I've made, although very different from each other, and they paid closest to a real wage (OK, maybe half of what my time was worth, but I was already working at another day job by then, so things were looking better.)

So that's where I am with idolatry and art. I don't believe that art or image-making is inherently bad and always equals idolatry. I still have no issues with making decorative art, unless it involves self-promotion. As for stand-alone art pieces, I understand that I personally cannot make them without it being idolatry because of who I am and my relationship with God. At this point I have given it up and consider it a free-will offering to God. He does ask us what we are willing to give up to follow Him.

I still have plans for making instruments, but I do zero promotion. I am now more interested in them for my own playing, which I've started doing more of, finding much joy in playing praise music during fellowship and by myself.

It's now been over ten years since I got the new day job. I'm a fire service technician, servicing fire extinguishers, backflow assemblies, and fire sprinkler systems, none of which has anything to do with art. Most would see it as a big step down from my cush administrative job at the university that I quit previously. Certainly, the pay and benefits were a big step down. But I have been far happier and less stressed there, as has Sanae. Partially because of the job itself, which has been a direct blessing from God, but also because of the years of humbling lessons that God has taught me through struggling to undo the tangled web of idolatry.

MEDICINE

There is one more thing I skipped over in my story earlier because it fit so much better here as a segue to this section. When I was breaking my twelve-day fast, I had the smallest bite of food and a small sip of juice, just to let my stomach know it was time to start up again.

I went to bed and woke up in the middle of the night with the worst headache I have ever experienced. I eventually gave up trying to sleep and got out of bed. I started journaling to pass the time, but the pain was so severe, all I could think about was when I could get to the doctor. I didn't want an emergency room trip, nor did I want to wake up Sanae and panic her, so I toughed it out until the doctor's office opened. When I called, the earliest they could get me in was 11:00, so I waited some more, without any relief.

When I finally arrived, the doctor looked in my ears and declared I had an ear infection and started writing up a prescription for antibiotics. I could not believe it was a simple ear infection, but I had never had one before, so I assumed that he must be right, and I gained a new respect for those kids who were always getting ear infections!

I asked the doctor what would happen if I didn't take the antibiotics. Because I had been fasting for so long, I thought they might not be safe in my condition. He said, "Worst case, you'll get meningitis and die, but most likely your ear drums would rupture before that happens, which would release the pressure and then you would heal naturally."

I went home to discuss my options with Sanae before I picked up the prescription, and not five minutes after getting home, both of

Two: Images – Gateway to Deception

my eardrums ruptured. I lay down as liquid came out of both ears and the intense pressure gradually subsided.

For the next week or so, I had a foggy sensation as the ruptured eardrums healed. But after the hearing was returning to normal, I noticed a different kind of fogginess replacing it. I couldn't balance! I noticed it while trying to push a wheelbarrow and couldn't keep it upright. Then I couldn't even walk in a straight line, stumbling like a drunkard. Bicycling to work was dangerous (although I still did it) and even driving was hard.

I spent the next month being referred to specialist after specialist who gave me test after test, none of which ever found out what had really happened. In the end, they called it "idiopathic bilateral vestibulopathy," which the doctor told me was just a fancy way of saying, "something unknown affecting both of my inner ears." The doctor's assumption was that the vestibular nerves that send signals from the cochlea (which regulates our balance) to the brain were fried. He tried to confirm it by ordering an MRI, but they botched it, scanning the wrong part of my brain. With or without the scan, though, it was permanent and irreversible.

My own research later discovered that I most likely had bacterial meningitis, which could easily have killed me, and is one of the most painful things a person can go through. Permanent loss of balance is a known side of effect of survivors. To compensate, I rely almost completely on my vision for my balance. However, I was also born legally blind in my left eye and have been told my whole life by doctors that it means I cannot see in three dimensions. Somehow, I was still able to play soccer and basketball all the way through high school, and excelled at sculpture, the three-dimensional art. And somehow, in spite of my new disability, I have been able to function at a remarkably high level, although it did take time for my brain to make the adjustment.

We are truly fearfully and wonderfully made, and God has installed back-up plans in our bodies to compensate when things go wrong, much like the plan He put in place when sin entered the world.

One effect of not getting a signal from the vestibular nerve, which to me is worse than the lack of balance, is what is called oscillopsia. When a normal person walks or moves around, the motion is effectively canceled out by the brain, much like image stabilization does in modern cameras. But my brain no longer does that. Every up and down, every bump and vibration is noticed, making focusing on things very difficult. When I need to read something, it is imperative for me to keep my head perfectly still and my eyes focused. Moving my head in either direction throws me way off.

It has been a constant reminder for me to stay laser focused on God at all times. Moving to the right or left will get me off of the narrow path.

This all happened right as I was quitting my job and starting the new banjo business. Most of the testing took place after I was done working but still had one last month of health insurance. My last appointment was the day before my insurance ran out. I was glad that I didn't have to pay for any of it because in the end they did nothing for me but tell me what I already knew. My actual diagnosis I figured out by myself. I had been questioning the medical system for some time before this, but now I really started to wonder. Let me be clear that I am not blaming the medical system for my condition. In this case it was simply completely ineffective in either diagnosing or treating.

But there are many cases where it is to blame as well.

Blind belief has been a term used against religion for a long time, yet the Bible never tells us to believe anything blindly, but to "test the spirits" whether they can be relied on or not. The same people who say that faith is blind are the ones who will believe anything that

Two: Images – Gateway to Deception

anyone with letters like Ph.D. or MD after their name says, without understanding it at all.

Some have dubbed this blind belief in science as "scientism," but I simply call it idolatry because that is what the Bible calls it, and there are many more examples of it in modern life. One is medicine, our modern "healthcare." It is a field where we have been led to put complete faith in scientists and doctors for all areas of our health, with the end result often being the destruction of the very health we entrusted them with.

Do you know what the leading cause of death is in the U. S.? It's not cancer or heart disease. It's the American medical system itself! In a very in-depth study by a group of five doctors titled "Death by Medicine," the argument is laid out in very clear numbers, using the government's own statistics, that our medical system is responsible for more harm than good, killing, by very conservative estimates, well over 700,000 people every year[29]. By the way, this report came out before the Covid pandemic and its "vaccines" were created, which would make those numbers much, much higher still.

There is much to be said about the destructiveness of the medical system regarding vaccinations, prescription drugs, manufactured diseases, and more, and they are topics that you would do well to research on your own if you haven't already.

Cancer can be both prevented and cured in many, if not most cases through diet, fasting and other safe but "unapproved" therapies, yet corrupt organizations like the American Cancer Society and the American Medical Association convince us we need to spend absurd amounts of money on drugs and unnecessary procedures just to "manage" the cancer, and then they fundraise nonstop to search for the cure that they make sure they never find.

It is amazing, after becoming aware of these things, that we still feel that health insurance is something we are willing to pay so much

---

[29] http://www.lifeextension.com/Magazine/2004/3/awsi_death/Page-01

for! It is my opinion that relying solely or even heavily on this system is most certainly putting other gods before Yahweh, creating idols to them and worshipping them.

I will link one very well written short article summing up these things and linking them to idolatry. It is called, appropriately enough, "Medicine—Idolatry in the Twenty First Century," by Brian Shilhavy.[30] I love his definition of idolatry:

> The heart of idolatry is looking to sources outside of God for our basic needs and desires in life. The idols that are erected flow out of our experiences in life, and the idol is an attempt to explain life apart from the Creator.

Evolution is a perfect example of attempting to explain life in this way. One of the tricks the deceiver uses in getting people to believe in evolution is with large numbers that people cannot comprehend. The timelines are so vast that our brains shut down when faced with them and we are forced to conclude that the scientists who came up with their theories must be smarter than we are.

Einstein's theory of relativity has been a critical tool in creating the irrationally long timelines that evolution requires. The absurdity that the theory of relativity presents simply makes us step back because we don't have the knowledge to counterattack it. Yet there have been a few who have and have done so with success.

In his book, *Starlight and Time, Solving the Puzzle of Distant Starlight in a Young Universe*, D. Russell Humphrey, Ph.D. shows how Einstein's own formulas can just as easily, and more convincingly, arrive at a universe that is less than 10,000 years old. The only thing that needs to happen to make the theory of relativity arrive at a young earth is changing the starting assumption. Einstein took the position that since there is no God, the earth must not have any special

---

[30] https://created4health.org/medicine-idolatry-in-the-twenty-first-century/

Two: Images – Gateway to Deception

position among the stars. The result is that when viewing a star's redshift (the shift of light toward the red end of the spectrum when an object moves away from the observer), which is always visibly equal regardless of its position in the sky, radical ideas like extra dimensions and unbounded cosmos are needed to accommodate the observations. Psalm 14:1 speaks to Einstein's assumption when David says, "The fool has said in his heart, 'There is no God.'"

The option Einstein neglected to entertain was that the earth is a special creation of God, maintaining a position at the very center of what we call the universe. This makes the equal redshift a logical outcome of our observations, even within a simple three-dimensional framework of a bounded cosmology (a view of the universe with a defined end – not infinitely expanding). The resulting math from the Creator-centered assumption shows rational dates within the range of recorded biblical history.

In the same way that the deceiver has us believe things through the use of incomprehensibly large numbers, he does so by going incomprehensibly small. Once an object gets small enough to only be seen by a microscope, the deceiver can start working. If it is small enough only for an electron microscope, he knows that he can really go to town. Bacteria can only be seen through a powerful microscope. Viruses can only be seen through an electron microscope. As a result, very few people ever get to view them firsthand. Because some actually do get to see them, I am not debating their existence, but those who get to be part of the debate about what bacteria and viruses actually are and how they function is very limited, and they are pressured by the funding of an even smaller group with huge financial backing and political agendas.

In their book, *What Really Makes You Ill? Why Everything You Thought You Knew About Disease Is Wrong*, Dawn Lester and David Parker put together a very well researched case against the mainstream "germ theory." It is their claim that neither bacteria nor viruses have any ability to make people sick, and that they in fact do just the opposite. They are found in sick people around diseased cells, and because of this they have been implicated in the crime. However, their function is actually in the repairing of the diseased tissue. They use the analogy of firefighters being found around structure fires and assuming they must be the ones who started it. The real culprits in all communicable and noncommunicable diseases, they say, are toxins in the body creating oxidative stress.

These are pretty bold claims, but this is just a summary of their findings without writing about any evidence for those claims. So, if you believe me based on what I've just said, you have not done your homework. If you go to medical school and look through electron microscopes and then take the textbook's word for what you have just seen, you have still not done your homework. And it will be the same story if you believe germ theory based on what other people in lab coats and talking heads on a screen have told you. You have worshiped someone's opinion as an idol.

Just because I have read their book, I have no right to start proclaiming what they said as absolute truth. What I can do is to realize the possibility that there might be another way of looking at the problem of disease. But now I have two unprovable opinions about a topic on which I am not an expert in any fashion. What am I to do? I can put some of their conclusions to the test by taking their advice on healthy living and cleansing toxins to see how I feel compared to taking the drugs recommended by the medical industry for the same problems, if I have an opportunity to do so. This is part of what is known as testing the spirits.

> Beloved, do not believe every spirit, but test the spirits, whether they are from God; for many false prophets have gone forth into the world. By this know the Spirit of God: every spirit which confesses that Jesus Christ has come in the flesh is from God. And every spirit which does not confess that Jesus Christ has come in the flesh is not from God; and this is the antichrist which you

Two: Images – Gateway to Deception

heard is coming, and now is already in the world. Little children, you are of God and have overcome them, because He in you is greater than he in the world. They are of the world; because of this they speak of the world, and the world hears them. We are of God; the one knowing God hears us. Whoever is not of God does not hear us. From this we know the spirit of truth and the spirit of error (1 John 4:1–6).

The Bible says I should find out where they stand on Jesus Christ coming in the flesh. I don't know these authors personally and neither their book nor their website mention anything on the topic. But John here also relates the idea of Jesus coming in the flesh to being from God and not coming in the flesh to coming from the world. So, we can look at which ideas are obviously based more in the fleshly world.

We can see by looking at our medical and insurance bills that the medical world is absolutely corrupted by money, and that is certainly a worldly thing. I also know that the authors are doing their research independently out of their own pockets without any outside financial backing. I cannot put that on par with proclaiming Jesus Christ come in the flesh, but I can certainly put the two opinions on a balance scale and see which one rises up. So, I have a tendency to lean in the authors' direction, yet I still have some hesitation to think they are completely correct in every conclusion. But that is okay because my main point is in learning how to overcome deception, not to know all truth about every topic.

Let's take the example of a very famous virus from our recent history, the coronavirus. During the entire pandemic, images of the virus were on the television and internet pretty much nonstop for at least three years. People were told that they must believe that the virus they were looking at was the cause of whatever sickness was going around, and they were told in such a way that it was just assumed to be fact. The idea of debating it was not ever brought up so that people might not start thinking. Even the so-called "alternative" media ran on this assumption.

Unfortunately, those images of the virus were an almost complete fabrication. I say almost because even though most of the images that were shown were simply computer generated, it appears that there have been some electron microscope pictures taken of little circles with spots on them inside of cells that we were told were coronaviruses, and, with some imagination, they could be said to resemble the computer graphics shown on television. These electron microscope images may have actually been real viruses. Were they coronaviruses? Maybe. Giving the benefit of the doubt to them indeed being coronaviruses, were they the cause of the illness that many people had? That is very difficult to prove. In fact, just to show that any viruses exist at all, they must first be removed from the patient, then transferred to different cells in a lab and made to replicate in those new cells, usually taken from monkey kidneys or lung cells from a cancer patient[31]. As a result, they have never actually been observed participating in the disease they were implicated in causing.

If the ideas of Dawn Lester and David Parker are correct, then viruses, being trained firefighters, may very well replicate readily in the new cells they are placed into for study, as they attempt to repair the damage to their new homes. That would not say anything about their behavior in whatever disease they were taken out of. When we take larger animals out of their natural habitat and place them into a zoo, their behavior is very different.

But none of that was important to the media blitz about the virus. It was simply talk about a killer virus alongside of computer-generated images of something we were told was a coronavirus. A photo of the thing, or even a fully sequenced genome of it does not

---

[31] https://www.auckland.ac.nz/en/news/2020/11/16/kochs-postulates-covid-and-misinformation-rabbit-holes.html

Two: Images – Gateway to Deception

say anything about its behavior or ability to cause disease. Somebody could plaster a photo of me on every billboard in the United States with the words "Most Wanted Serial Killer" next to it, but just because it is an actual photo of me, it would not make it true. The virus was a false flag—an idol set up to be worshipped in place of the truth.

So, what is the truth about the virus? I have to admit that I cannot say definitively. Being now a few years removed from the pandemic, even the mainstream media is beginning to admit to a certain amount of deception perpetrated on a grand scale. But what the truth is, they are still not letting on. It is often easier to know what is wrong than to know what is right. I've seen enough deception to know how it works and the pandemic fits the pattern to a tee. But that kind of deception, even when discovered, is also very good at concealing what reality is.

Many people claimed that Covid was simply the flu renamed. I was one of them, until I came down with it and it nearly killed me. I've had the flu before, and this was not it. It knocked me on my butt. I had a fever for twelve days in a row and coughed uncontrollably so much that my ribs were extremely sore. I barely ate and had difficulty getting enough oxygen. Most people would have been in the hospital on a ventilator in my state, but I would not go near a hospital. I finally obtained some Ivermectin and immediately started improving.

I do have my suspicions about what Covid actually is, though I cannot prove it. The symptoms of Covid happen to match very closely with certain types of radiation poisoning. The fact that the Covid lockdowns were used to rapidly deploy 5G cell towers across the world is very suspicious.

The same symptoms can also be shown to be a pattern that has happened historically after every new advance involving electromagnetic energy. The Spanish Flu, for instance, occurred as radio towers were being installed worldwide as a result of World War

Part 4: The Ten Ordered Matters

I. Similar outbreaks happened when telegraph lines were spread across the country and again when electrical lines were first installed en masse in major cities.³² Again, I cannot prove that is what caused Covid, but I can follow patterns. Whenever strong radiation is introduced to an area, whether cell towers or strong radio transmitters, there is an outbreak of sickness in the area. You can actually follow the path of where Covid spread, from Wuhan to Italy, then to the U.S. and around the world, and it exactly matches the rollout of 5G installation. Follow the patterns.

The illnesses didn't just affect people either, but also animals. Birds and insects have died off at an alarming rate since these things have been introduced. That is something that I can verify with my own eyes. Before Covid, our yard was full of birds almost every day of the year. We had finches, juncos, bushtits, song sparrows, kinglets, and many more. Many of these would show up in large groups when they came.

But after Covid, we realized that we saw very few birds at all anymore, even though our back yard was still a neighborhood oasis of habitat. It is a big deal now when we see one or two birds show up. I notice the same phenomenon everywhere I go, too. Can I prove that they are gone because of 5G radiation? No, but the patterns do keep repeating. Fortunately, another pattern I've seen is that both humans and animals do seem to eventually adapt to the new sources of radiation after a period of illness and die-off.

There are other theories about Covid as well that I could bring up, but this is not supposed to be a debate about Covid or 5G, but about idolatry. I bring up Covid to show the role that images played in our deception, and how those images can become a form of

---

²⁶ Firstenberg, Arthur. *The Invisible Rainbow: A History of Electricity and Life*. Chelsea Green Publishing, 2020.

Two: Images – Gateway to Deception

idolatry. Remember, if we submit to something, we are worshiping it.

There is another pattern that is even more important, however, when it comes to medicine:

> If you will diligently listen to Yahweh your God's voice, and will do that which is right in his eyes, and will pay attention to his commandments, and keep all his statutes, I will put none of the diseases on you, which I have put on the Egyptians; for I am Yahweh who heals you (Exodus 15:26 WEB).

Yahweh had just brought Israel out of the land of Egypt, where they were surrounded by idols of every sort, and He was explaining to them how to have things go well. (As a quick aside, notice also that this admonition to keep His commandments in Exodus 15 came two months before He even gave them the Ten Commandments in chapter 20! Much earlier than that, Genesis 26:5 says, "Because Abraham obeyed My voice and kept My charge, My commandments, My statutes, and My laws." The Ten Ordered Matters we are discussing seem to have been around since the beginning. How can we think that they are no longer pertinent, and how did Abraham know them?)

God says idolatry begets disease. This thought brings us back around to the first study of this section, that the modern medical system itself causes more deaths than any other leading cause of death. It is time to start thinking of modern medicine as idolatry and realizing the toll it is really having on us.

How much time, energy and money do we spend on it? Or on health "insurance"? Can health insurance ensure anything? No, it cannot, because God tells us that He has every hair on our heads numbered (Luke 12:7), numbers the days of our lives (Job 14:5, Psalm 39:4), and that we cannot add even one hour to our lives (Matthew 6:27). Yet He also tells us here that we can certainly change the quality of the days we are allotted. We do so by keeping His commands, laws, and statutes. Central to those commands is the second ordered matter we are discussing.

It is time to start looking at the Word of God as the only important player in our health. The Bible calls modern medicine witchcraft or sorcery. It uses the word *pharmekia* in Greek, Strong's G5331, which is not coincidentally where we get our word for pharmacy, but the biblical translation is usually witchcraft or sorcery. *Thayer's Lexicon*[33] says of it,

1) the use or the administering of drugs
2) poisoning
3) sorcery, magical arts, often found in connection with idolatry and fostered by it
4) metaphorically the deceptions and seductions of idolatry

Do we really think that we can continue living with one foot in sorcery and witchcraft and another in the Word of God? For those who are already ill, or reliant on the medical system, I realize this is a hard thing to hear. But how did you get to that point of reliance? If what we are reliant on is not from God, it is idolatry!

Recently, I have known way too many people who have had their health decimated by trusting the hospitals to help them get better. Routine checkups turned life-threatening. Run-of-the-mill surgeries were botched, and I wish they were isolated cases.

I have also known some who got over their pharmekia induced illnesses through prayer. Our God understands of our situations, but He is also a rewarder of those who diligently seek Him. We can no longer falter between two opinions.

Sanae had her digestive system destroyed by the drugs that were prescribed to her for the inflammation of an injured shoulder. She has spent the last seventeen years recovering, finding natural

---

[33] Thayer, Joseph Henry, et al. *Thayer's Greek-English Lexicon of the New Testament*. Hendrickson Publishers, 1996.

Two: Images – Gateway to Deception

remedies that God has shown her, often growing in our own garden.

An older gentleman in my fellowship went for a checkup for a previous illness. While there, they used unsanitized equipment, giving him an antibiotic-resistant infection, for which they told him he would have to be on antibiotics for the rest of his life. However, after much prayer by many of us in the fellowship, he is now doing fine without antibiotics.

Personally, I have had back issues since I injured it at eighteen, although my worst injury was shortly after my son was born when I was thirty-five and herniated my disc and could not get out of bed because the pain was so excruciating, as I mentioned earlier in the book.

I did physical therapy for months but could not shake the sciatic pain, so I ended up with surgery to remove the portion of my lumbar disc that had squeezed out. Around the same time, Sanae actually herniated her disc as well. They wanted to give her steroids for hers until they found out she was breast-feeding. Surgery was also an option, but she opted to do nothing, trusting her body could heal on its own.

It took some time, but her body did heal on its own. She was in pain and dealing with a new child, which was very difficult for both of them, but in the long run she has had no significant recurrences of that back injury.

After my surgery, I felt better immediately but regularly re-injured myself, so that I was in severe pain for days or sometimes weeks, a cycle that went on for years. Sanae made the wiser choice.

Of course, my own back was eventually healed, as I described in the chapter, "You are Your Own Analogy." The past two-plus years have been the first time I have been without significant pain for more than six months, even though I've over-worked it many times.

A few years before my own healing, I was being introduced to the power of the Holy Spirit being *real*. The stories I heard of miraculous healings happening today as they did in the Bible truly excited me for the first time in a long time. I wanted to test that new reality myself. If what was presented was true, I should be able to go lay hands on the sick and see them healed! My desire was at odds with my absolute fear of actually going up to someone and attempting this, however. It took me a long time to get up the nerve.

Finally, I did work up the nerve one day when I was on my way home from work and saw a woman in a wheelchair asking for money by the road. I pulled over and talked to her about her situation and asked if I could pray for her. She said she was a believer and had had a dream before about being healed and agreed.

I prayed over her, but nothing happened. I prayed again, still nothing. I felt bad, but she was moved that I had taken the time to care. I was both disheartened and encouraged. I at least saw that even failing to heal someone could still lift their spirits because someone cared.

One day at work, I was doing my normal routine of inspecting fire extinguishers. I was working with a gentleman from the city (it was a city building), and we were walking a lot and had to do a lot of stairs, which his bad knees objected to.

At lunch, he told me that for the rest of the afternoon he'd just let me work on my own because his knees couldn't handle the stairs any longer. I asked if it would be okay if I prayed for him. He agreed, even though he was not really a believer. I prayed and commanded the pain to leave his knees. Then I asked him if they felt any different.

He stood up and tested them out and couldn't find any pain! He walked the rest of the day up and down stairs without issue. We continued working together occasionally for another three years until he retired, and we still remain in touch. He is still without pain to this day, even though he likely needed surgery beforehand.

This gave me confidence and I started praying more for others. Far more often than not there has been no visible healing, yet at this point at least seven people have had instantaneous healing as a result of my praying.

Two: Images – Gateway to Deception

I also started anointing and praying more boldly for my family. My son's childlike faith made him very receptive to being healed. He saw bad bloody noses instantly stop bleeding, headaches go away, and mystery pain vanish. As he has gotten older, this has lessened, but it is nice to see him asking for prayer still when he is in a bind.

This, of course, has had nothing to do with my own abilities other than my taking at face value Jesus' statement that as His disciples we, "will lay hands on the sick, and they will recover." And of those who were not healed, not once has somebody been angry with me for trying or blamed me or God for the lack of success.

We don't need drugs. We don't need surgery. We don't need chemotherapy and radiation. We don't need thousands of dollars of our wages going to insurance companies "just in case." We need *faith*. We need God's healing. We need to trust the instructions He gave us. We need to live a proper godly lifestyle, eating only the natural things of His creation instead of the processed, chemical-laden creations of man. But not just so we can get healthy enough to continue living the same idolatrous lives we've been living.

I'm talking about a lifestyle change that means living for God in everything we do. Analyze any activity and ask yourself if it points toward His original creation or if it points to man's false creation.

We talked earlier in the chapter on Pentecost about holiness—that being set apart means apart from the ways of the world. We are set apart from it when we are in tune to God's Holy Spirit. The Holy Spirit is not limited by the knowledge of men or bound by the physics of science. We are set apart into the spirit realm, the same one the Creator resides in.

From that vantage point, all things are possible. Healing should be expected, for it is nothing to the God who molded us from dirt in the first place. But do we truly have faith that it is so?

I am not saying that there is no legitimate reason to ever see a medical doctor. If I break my leg, after praying, I will certainly head to the doctor or hospital to have it set because that is something they are actually well-trained in. There are other reasons, too, and I am not about to dictate what you should do in your personal situation.

We've also talked about evil things sometimes being redeemed for good. This can certainly happen in the medical system, and I've seen miracles happen through that system as well.

There are also good doctors and bad doctors, but the main problem is not the individuals as much as the system itself. This means that more and more, there is less and less freedom for the individual doctor to do what is right, because funding, quotas, directives, and policies will not allow good doctors or nurses to do so. Personally, I will steer away from any treatment that involves pharmekia or neglects using our bodies' God-given ability to heal themselves.

What if we have faith, but we still get sick or die? I cannot be the one to judge why, except possibly for myself, as much as it has to do with my relationship with Yeshua. But we were never promised that we would not die early. Facing death is part of following God. We cannot live in fear of what might happen but must simply respond appropriately to every challenge that is presented. Dying while doing our best to follow Yahweh is what we are asked to do. We should know that our lives do not end on the earth. In fact, they really will not begin until we leave it! In Philippians 1:21–24, Paul wrote:

> For to me, to live is Christ, and to die is gain. But if I live on in the flesh, this will mean fruit from my labor; yet what I shall choose I cannot tell. For I am hard-pressed between the two, having a desire to depart and be with Christ, which is far better. Nevertheless to remain in the flesh is more needful for you.

He understood that the only reason to live was to do God's will. Dying was preferable because he would be with Christ! Let us not be given to a spirit of fear. The medical industry is very good at making us worry about a million *what ifs*, but we forget to ask, *What if I don't follow Yahweh in faith*? To follow any other way is idolatry.

Three: Don't Bear the Name of Yahweh in Emptiness

> You shall not take the name of Yahweh your God in vain, for Yahweh will not hold him guiltless who takes his name in vain (Exodus 20:7 WEB).

Looking up words in Hebrew is always a great way to gain a better understanding of any passage. Often times translations are made with just as much or more weight on the sound or flow as on the accuracy of the words in English. This is certainly the case with the third ordered matter.

Nasah (Strong's H5375), the Hebrew word for "take" in this commandment, really means to carry, bear, lift up, or exalt. We are not talking about simply using or speaking His name but bearing His name. We are to be ambassadors of the kingdom of God, and as such, we are His representatives on the earth. When we bear His name, it is attached to us. We are physical pictures of what it means to be a member of His kingdom.

Part 4: The Ten Ordered Matters

The word for name is *shem* (Strong's H8035), which is interesting, because Shem was also the name for one of Noah's three sons. Shem was the one whom the lineage went through, creating the lines of the Shem-itic, or Semitic peoples. They were the line that bore the name of Yahweh upon them.

The Semitic peoples include not just Israel's line, but also the lineage of all of Abraham, which includes the Arabic people through Ishmael, Hagar's son. This means that most of the nations that currently surround the nation of Israel, the ones often accused of being "anti-Semitic" are also Semitic themselves. These nations are mostly Muslim, a religion which also espouses belief in Yahweh, the Elohim (pronounced Allah in Arabic) of Abraham. They, fittingly, are also bearers of the name.

The *Ancient Hebrew Lexicon* says of Shem,

> **I. Breath**: The breath of a man is character, what makes one what he is. The name of an individual is more than an identifier but descriptive of his character or breath. **II. There**: Used to identify another place. **III. Sky**: The place of the winds. **IV. Aroma**: A sweet aroma that is carried on the wind or breath (emphasis in original).

The name is also related to the breath, which will make more sense in a little bit, so I'll come back to it.

Vain is a word that I think must not have a good direct translation into English, as the definitions I read seem to have a hard time pinpointing it. It speaks of desolation through loud thunder crashes and the crashing of the sea, and to the emptiness that is caused by it. It also speaks of evil, nothingness, lying, and worthlessness. Wrapping this up into one word seems difficult. Emptiness or desolation may be closest. But conceptually, we start to see the idea of representing God in an empty fashion.

This is not talking about using His name as a cuss word as we often think of, although that would also be a good thing to avoid! It is getting at the very lifestyle of what it means to be a Christian, Jew,

Three: Don't Bear the Name of Yahweh in Emptiness

or Muslim name-bearer. It is attaching identity to ourselves because we are bearing that name. If we do so in a lukewarm way, we have diluted the name and caused it to be empty. Going to church one day a week and thinking we are fulfilling our duty is breaking this commandment.

Churches today are full of empty name bearers, because when we look at their lives outside of the church building, they are no different from anyone else. Somebody who bears His name should look different to the world. They should be set-apart from it—Holy. Yahweh's kingdom is not of this world, so we should look the part!

Where is this found in nature? We talked about set-apartness already in the chapter on Pentecost. Holiness is found in nature in that its character is outside of nature by definition, just as a kingdom not of the world is outside of the world by definition. Yet there is more. If a name is an important thing to us, it was a much more important thing to the ancients. Names had meaning, and to know the name of someone or something was to know their power. So, let's look at God's name.

What is God's name? I have been writing it as Yahweh, for the most part, because that is one common way to vocalize יהוה, the Hebrew Tetragrammaton (literally, four letters). Others say Yehovah, or Jehovah, or Yehuah, or Yohuwah, etc. What His name is certainly not, is the LORD, which is a title meaning master. Lord is a translation of the Hebrew word Adon, or Adonay. When you see lord written in the lower case in your bible, this is what it means, and it is an appropriate use. Whenever LORD shows up in all caps, however, it is used in place of יהוה, which early Jewish translators thought was too holy of a word to pronounce, so to ensure it was not pronounced, they exchanged the name for a title, and for some reason, that method has stuck with us into modern times. The original writers, however, had no issue with either writing or pronouncing the name. And if we start to understand a name's association with power, we might want to question why it has been taken out of the very book that is all about the Name!

But what does it mean? When God appeared to Moses in the burning bush, Moses wanted to know God's identity:

> And Moses said to God, Behold, I shall come to the sons of Israel and say to them, the God of your fathers has sent me to you; and they will say to me, What is His name? What shall I say to them? And God said to Moses, I AM THAT I AM; and He said, You shall say this to the sons of Israel, I AM has sent me to you. And God said to Moses again, You shall say this to the sons of Israel, Jehovah, the God of your fathers, the God of Abraham, the God of Isaac, and the God of Jacob, has sent me to you. This is My name forever, and this is My memorial from generation to generation (Exodus 3:13–15 LITV).

I AM is the Hebrew word *Hayah*, meaning "to be" or "to exist." The *Ancient Hebrew Lexicon* says, "Exist: To exist or have breath. That which exists has breath. In Hebrew thought the breath is the character of someone or something." This seems to tie in directly to the word *Shem*. Both the word for "name" and God's name itself are related to the breath.

This is also interesting because the Hebrew alphabet is one of consonants. There are no vowels in it, so vowel sounds must be inferred (at least in ancient biblical Hebrew. The modern language now uses vowel markers). Yet the name itself has no hard consonant sounds in it! It is a breathy sound in almost all attempts at vocalizing it. Those with a "J" sound (like Jehovah in the Literal Version above) can really be discounted because that sound did not exist in Hebrew (or Greek, later. Thus, those who prefer to say Yeshua instead of Jesus). It seems that the pronunciation itself speaks to its meaning. The word *Yahweh* is a more flushed out form of Hayah, with a meaning that can be taken as "He that was, is, and will always be," or "the Eternal."

Three: Don't Bear the Name of Yahweh in Emptiness

If we try to put all of this together to re-form the commandment closer to its intended meaning, we might get something like, "You shall not bear up the name of the breath of Yahweh, your Elohim, in a manner that brings emptiness or desolation, for Yahweh will not let him be innocent who bears His name in emptiness."

God's name was literally revealed to Moses in the natural world in a bush. It was a bush burning with fire, the breath of God. This fire spoke His name to Moses, a name that refers back to the breath of His eternal character. Have you ever thought of God as being fire-breathing? We usually associate that image with the dragons of the enemy, but that is just Satan, being a thief and liar, trying to appropriate something that belonged first to God.

After the burning bush, during the Exodus, Yahweh continued speaking to Moses and the Israelites from a fire and cloud as the breath spoken from the lungs of the tabernacle between the cherubim on the mercy seat.

> The appearance of **Yahweh's glory was like devouring fire** on the top of the mountain in the eyes of the children of Israel (Exodus 24:17 WEB).

> Be on guard for yourselves, that you not forget the covenant of Jehovah your God, which He has made with you, and make to yourselves a graven image, a likeness of anything which Jehovah your God has forbidden you. **For Jehovah your God is a consuming fire;** He is a jealous God (Deuteronomy 4:23–24 LITV).

> And know today that **Jehovah your God is He who passes over before you as a consuming fire;** He will destroy them, and He will bring them down before you; so you shall dispossess them and make them to perish quickly, as Jehovah has spoken to you (Deuteronomy 9:3 LITV).

> Yahweh will cause his glorious voice to be heard, and will show the descent of his arm, with the indignation of his anger, and the

flame of a devouring fire, with a blast, storm, and hailstones (Isaiah 30:30).

His character did not change in the New Testament. The writer of Hebrews refers to the same thing:

> Therefore, since we are receiving a kingdom which cannot be shaken, let us have grace, by which we may serve God acceptably with reverence and godly fear. **For our God is a consuming fire** (Hebrews 12:28–29).

This is the attitude by which we know that we are keeping this third ordered matter. Grace, reverence, and godly fear are the opposite of emptiness and desolation. They are fruit that will not be consumed by the consuming fire. For even though He is a consuming fire, He will not consume those who are His, who act with reverence and godly fear.

> When you walk through the fire, you will not be burned, and flame will not scorch you. For I am Yahweh your God, the Holy One of Israel, your Savior (Isaiah 43:2b–3a WEB).

Just as the burning bush was not consumed, neither will His people who serve Him with reverence and godly fear be. Shadrach, Meshach, and Abednego would not bow to any god but Yahweh, so were thrown into a furnace stoked to seven times the normal heat.

> Then Shadrach, Meshach, and Abednego came out of the middle of the fire. And the satraps, the prefects, the governors, and the king's officials assembled. And they saw these men on whose bodies the fire had no power, and the hair of their head was not scorched, nor were their slippers changed, nor had the smell of fire clung on them (Daniel 3:26–27).

Their lives were dedicated to serving Yahweh as representatives of His kingdom, so could not be devoured by the consuming fire. Let us also bear the name of Yahweh, our Elohim, without emptiness or desolation, but with reverence and godly fear.

Four: The Sabbath Is for Relationship

> Thus the heavens and the earth, and all the host of them, were finished. And on the seventh day God ended His work which He had done, and He rested on the seventh day from all His work which He had done. Then God blessed the seventh day and sanctified it, because in it He rested from all His work which God had created and made (Genesis 2:1–3).

> Remember the sabbath day, to keep it holy; six days you shall labor and do all your work; and the seventh day is a sabbath to Jehovah your God; you shall not do any work, you, and your son, and your daughter, your male slave and your slave-girl, and your livestock, and your stranger who is in your gates. For in six days Jehovah made the heavens and the earth, the sea, and all which is in them, and He rested on the seventh day; on account of this Jehovah blessed the sabbath day and sanctified it (Exodus 20:8–11 LITV).

We looked at the timing for the Sabbath as part of the mechanisms within the sky-clock but we haven't covered the *how* and *why* portion of the command yet. Functionally, the Sabbath is the ordered matter that gets glossed over more than any of the others. It is not a commandment of moral character, so with the vast majority of Christians keeping Sunday as the day of worship, many would just rather pretend that it didn't exist. The main argument against keeping it is that the Sabbath pointed to Jesus and He was the Sabbath—our rest is in Him, so we do not need to keep the Sabbath. The problem with that argument is that it is a half-truth. Yes, Matthew 11:28–29 tells us,

> Come to me, all who are heavy laden, and I will give you rest. Take My yoke upon you and learn from Me, for I am gentle and lowly in heart, and you will find rest for your souls.

We can certainly find rest in Him. Yet He never told us or the disciples to not keep the Sabbath because of that. He corrected the Pharisees numerous times for adding restrictions to the Sabbath that were never mentioned in the Torah, and for getting the spirit of the Sabbath wrong. In His correction, however, He actually reinforced that the Sabbath should still be kept, claiming His authority as High Priest to know about such matters:

> Yet I say to you that in this place there is One greater than the temple. But if you had known what this means, 'I desire mercy and not sacrifice,' you would not have condemned the guiltless. For the Son of Man is Lord even of the Sabbath (Matthew 12:6–8).

He did not ever claim that keeping the Sabbath was the Pharisees' issue, but that they kept it in a way inconsistent with the command. They treated it as though men were to worship it. It was to be so revered that extra guards needed to be put in place so that they would not accidentally step over its bounds. This is why Jesus was compelled to tell them that the Sabbath was made for man, and not man for the Sabbath. They had turned it into an idol instead of a gift.

So, how *do* we keep the Sabbath? The commandment simply says to keep it holy. It does not give a list of things we cannot do or that we must do. Yes, we read later about the Israelites getting in trouble

Four: The Sabbath is for Relationship

for gathering sticks for the fire, and that they should not be buying and selling on the Sabbath, but that is about all we hear.

I've kept the Sabbath for over twenty-five years now, but for all of that and all of my talk on *when* the Sabbath is, I honestly don't know if I am the best one to teach *how* to keep it holy. For much of that time I have struggled to lead my family in keeping it well, often turning it into more of a stressful obligation than anything. I have seen many blessings from keeping it but have also seen a lot of strife over deciding what should or shouldn't be done on that day.

We would gather for the Sabbath with others and everyone else would proclaim how happy they were for the blessed day of rest, but we would be stressed about the fight we were just having on the way over.

We saw a lot of conflicting advice, too. We were told by brethren that it should not be a list of dos and don'ts, yet if we did something they felt should be prohibited, boy, were we in trouble! Because of this, I really want to avoid preaching about the correct way to do it. I don't think it is fruitful. So, I am just going to cut straight to the reasons it was instituted in the first place and leave the rest up to you.

The Sabbath was to be a rest which was set apart (made holy) as a memorial of creation. How we do that will tell God what state our heart is in. What kind of a creation are we? Are we busy being creators of our own world that we are in control of, or are we submitting ourselves to being the creation of the living God? For too long I was the former.

When Israel was wandering the desert during the exodus, He needed to see that His people would have complete faith in Him that His providence of manna would be sufficient for the day. Gathering sticks to cook with was a lack of faith. Buying and selling was the same—a lack of faith that things could be taken care of in the six working days.

The concept is the same today, but it is possible that the things we do to show our faith may be different. I know people who will not turn on the stovetop or coffee pot on the Sabbath because the Bible specified no cooking (gathering of sticks). There is no issue if that is their heart, yet someone else may have no issue with turning a knob on the stove because it is really not work to do so. It can be quite a restful activity to heat up a leisurely meal or a pot of tea for them.

Avoiding the gathering of sticks and the marketplace were things that made sense for Israel in the context of where they were and what Yahweh wanted of them. But there was a reason that He did not make a list as He did with clean and unclean meats.

The only prohibition given in the command is not to work, and the word *work* refers specifically to servile work or an occupation of some sort. The point of this rest from work is to take us out of the world for one day—to forget about the daily cares that are put upon us. We may eat if we wish, but we are given the example of the day of preparation (Exodus 16: 22–26, Mark 15:42) so that we are not spending unnecessary time on food. We will then have the time to spend focusing on the things of God: prayer, study, worship with others; and for those with children, special time playing and bonding and whatever level of study may be appropriate for them.

These things are critical to our growth, and if it weren't for the Sabbath, few would ever make the time for this focused one-on-one with the Creator. Remember, God made the Sabbath for man, not man for the Sabbath. It is to our benefit to study our Creator and give Him the worship He deserves.

What works best for you or your family will be different from your friend's family. We struggled with this for a long time, feeling obligated to study with certain people or to attend church services. When we attended these things, we often felt we did not have the study time we really needed, and our son did not get the interaction he needed. Church can be a really negative experience for active kids. We would often do much better when we stayed home together.

Four: The Sabbath is for Relationship

We now sometimes even go out hiking on Sabbath, which some really frown upon, because they see it as work. But to us, especially my wife who has little opportunity to exercise during the week, it is a release, and we often end up with very good sustained biblical discussions and even prayer time during our hikes. There is something for us about the combination of moving our bodies and being outside in God's creation that soothes us and feels far more worshipful than sitting inside on a chair for two hours.

This is not to say we don't also appreciate going to a church service sometimes, because we do. We especially appreciate being able to lift up our voices in song in a way that is difficult for us to do by ourselves, and we certainly miss fellowship with others if we isolate too much. The point is that we now realize we have freedom to worship and serve God on our Sabbath in whatever way works best for our growth and relationship with Him. Conforming to others' expectations of what the Sabbath was supposed to be stressed us out. It is an individual matter, and I truly believe this is why the commandment said nothing else but not to work and to keep it holy.

This also does not mean that it is easy. Since Yahweh sanctified the Sabbath for us, Satan hates it. He will definitely attack us and attempt to find a way to ruin the day. As I already said, we have spent far too many Sabbaths fighting with each other for silly reasons. They still sneak up on us when we are unprepared, but we are now more aware of Satan's plots. When we see that Satan is the culprit and not each other, it is easier to place the blame appropriately and come together in strength of prayer instead of tearing each other down as Satan wants.

To keep this short, by all means keep the Sabbath, and keep it holy. Do your work in six days and rest on the seventh. What that looks like, God leaves up to you. When you give your small child a gift, a toy, you may have an idea of how it is supposed to be used, but the child will not know. You will let him or her play with it as they wish, without getting upset that they are "doing it wrong". Even if it takes a little learning, they will get much more out of it when left to figure it out on their own. God gave you a gift; figure it out and enjoy it! Indeed, that analogy will hold true for all of the holy days and the law!

It is actually *impossible* for some to keep the Sabbath to the letter, and this is by design. Paul taught in Romans 7 that we will all fail to keep the law because of the war going on between our will and our flesh, and while this is true, what I am talking about here is different.

We will all mess up, but certain occupations do not allow for work to be suspended on the Sabbath even if there is a will to keep it: A dairy operator would be negligent if he did not milk the cows or goats seven days a week. The animals would face stress and infection, and the milk supply would risk drying up. Farmers do not have the luxury of a complete Sabbath. Certainly, the workload can be lessened so that nonessential duties can be done before or after Sabbath, but there are just things that cannot be done another time. Does this make farmers worse sinners than others? No! Much of the reason for Sabbath keeping is so that we are without excuse in having time for a relationship with our Creator. Farmers by nature are working directly with the creation every day and that gives them a head start in having that relationship. Talk to any farmer and he will have an innate understanding of many of the agricultural analogies and parables of the Bible, ones the rest of us struggle to comprehend.

Other occupations have similar situations. Emergency workers—paramedics, firefighters, emergency room physicians, etc.— are needed at all hours and emergencies can obviously happen even on the Sabbath. These workers see another side of the natural world that keeps them in touch with the fragility of our physical lives, a trait that tends to make people seek out the deeper questions of God and an afterlife, and it is work that requires an attitude of service, another quality that is critically important to God. Again, this is a head start on the relationship that Yahweh desires.

Four: The Sabbath is for Relationship

Our Creator gave us the Sabbath as a gift in order to supply relationship, and those that He knows will not receive the full benefits of that gift He gives different methods to form relationship. So, it is critical for us to not look at the Sabbath from the standpoint of what we cannot do, but from the view of what is to be gained through it. It was a memorial to six days of creation, a day to look back with reverence and awe on the world He made for us to find Him in. If a laborer finds themselves by the demands of their job having to think about the nature of the creation seven days a week, then forcing extra Sabbath restrictions is counter-productive, and hopefully they can have time to take some extra rest, too.

For the rest of us, the nature of working with more worldly things during six days necessitates us having one to focus on finding relationship with Yahweh. This can and should be done through Bible study, but more and more I see that the reason the Sabbath is linked to the creation is because that is where He wants us to find Him!

I want to end this section on a different note. From reading all of this about the Sabbath and the previous section on the sky-clock, even though I've mentioned already that it is not the case, it could be easy to think that I must believe that the Sabbath or holy days are conditional for our salvation. I maintain that nothing could be further from the truth. Remember, all of the law is simply the proper response to the salvation we have already been given.

Understand this, too: *Keeping the Sabbath does not make us God's people.* This is a big lie that I was taught for a long time in the group I studied with, and I still see it being taught in many Sabbatarian organizations. They use Exodus 31:16–17 to make their claim:

> Therefore, the children of Israel shall keep the Sabbath, to observe the Sabbath throughout their generations as a perpetual covenant. It is a sign between Me and the children of Israel forever; for in

Part 4: The Ten Ordered Matters

six days Yahweh made the heavens and the earth, and on the seventh day He rested and was refreshed.

Yes, it is a sign between God and His people. He gave it to His people. However, does this mean that if some of His people cannot see the sign, or even if they choose not to look at the sign, that they are not His people?

I have been told many times that a Sunday keeper cannot possibly have the Holy Spirit because this verse tells them that they are not God's people. However, when I see a non-Sabbath keeper performing miracle healings, or having gifts of prophecy or words of knowledge, or simply giving of themselves with selfless love, I have to question that.

Now, there are cases where demonic deals can be made in trade for miracles or wonders; some examples being Pharaoh's magicians turning water to blood and their rods into snakes, and the great signs performed by the Beast in Revelation 13. Discernment is always needed, and these things should be understood by the fruit of the "miracle." But true miracles, done in selfless love, nobody can do except through the authority of the name of Jesus Christ, Yeshua the Messiah. It is by love for one another that Christians will be known according to John 13:35. How, then, is anyone doing these things not to be considered God's people?

God gave the sign of the Sabbath to a people who were *already* His people, not to a random assembly saying that whoever obeys the sign will become His people by doing so. At this time, two thousand years removed from the time of Jesus walking the earth, I don't believe that anyone has all biblical doctrine and understanding figured out, so if somebody hasn't figured out the Sabbath yet, that cannot possibly preclude them from being God's people more than a Sabbatarian who can't figure out how to love their neighbor, and I know many of those!

The deciding factor in Matthew 25 as to whether one would enter the kingdom and everlasting life or be turned away to everlasting

Four: The Sabbath is for Relationship

punishment was whether they had fed the hungry, given drink to the thirsty, clothed the naked, taken in the sick and visited those in prison. Whether they kept the Sabbath was not on that list because Jesus cares far more about how we show love to each other.

For a Sabbatarian to tell a Sunday keeper that they cannot be God's people until they keep the Sabbath is the same argument that the Pharisees used about circumcision, that it was a requirement for salvation. Paul blasted that argument out of the water when Peter got weak and would not associate with the Gentiles in front of the Jews because of the circumcision (Galatians 2:11–16).

Brethren, the Sabbath is a beautiful thing, but it does not make us God's people!

17

Five: Honor Your Father and Mother

Honor your father and your mother, so that your days may be long on the land which Jehovah your God is giving to you (Exodus 20:12 LITV).

Children, obey your parents in the Lord, for this is right. "Honor your father and mother," which is the first commandment with a promise: "that it may be well with you, and you may live long on the earth" (Ephesians 6:1–3).

There is a line of thinking that the ordered matters are broken up into two parts—the first half being how to love God and the second how to love our fellow man. Usually this is broken up as the first four, then the last six. In such case this would be the beginning of the second half.

There is a pattern in the Bible and creation, however, that gives us five and five: the tabernacle curtains were connected together five on a side (with an extra overlapping), there were five wise and five foolish virgins in the parable of Matthew 25, and our own bodies have five fingers and toes on each side.

Five: Honor Your Father & Mother

Should this commandment, then, in order to make five per side, be looked at as how to love God rather than men? We'll find that it is not hard to do so.

If there is one ordered matter that speaks to us in both a physical and spiritual manner, this is it. I will not deny that it instructs us to honor our physical parents, but the reason for that is inherently spiritual.

Our own physical families are pictures of our eternal spiritual one. This is why Satan is set on the destruction of the family. He cannot stand the idea of having a constant picture in our lives of how we function in God's family. Our family is where we learn everything important as children. We learn how to relate to others, how to solve problems, how to respect authority, and how to become responsible adults. At least that is how it is supposed to be. Whenever we look back at our own childhoods or our experience as parents, we are more likely to see all of the areas we failed in this. We did not learn all of the things we should as kids, and as a result, as parents, we did not teach correctly, either.

We all have a father in our physical families. Traditionally, he has been considered the head of the household. He was the one the child would look to for guidance and expect discipline from when he or she misbehaved. It is no different with our spiritual Father in heaven.

Some children, through unfortunate circumstances, are brought up without their father, and it invariably affects their lives. The Father in heaven has a special place in His heart for those because He understands the spiritual significance of it. This is why the Bible often talks about the orphan and widow. A child or wife left without the father of the household is at a significant disadvantage in the physical realm, but one who does not recognize their spiritual Father is at an even greater risk. There will be a very specific example of this under the eighth ordered matter, "You shall not steal."

A child who has learned to give honor to their physical father is one who can also learn to give honor to the Father in heaven. But it is not a natural thing for a child to be obedient. There are rules that the parents set up that don't make sense to a kid. It takes life experience and time in order to see the wisdom that our parents tried to impart into us.

Yet that is the reason why God requires obedience. He has also given us rules to live by that don't always make sense to us, yet if we obey, then with time we can see the tremendous blessings that came from it. Right now, we are all children in the eyes of God; we just need to recognize ourselves as such. As Jesus said in Matthew 18:3, "Assuredly, I say to you, unless you are converted and become as little children, you will by no means enter the kingdom of heaven."

But what about the mother? It makes sense to mention her in our physical families, but where do mothers fit in the spiritual realm? This question bothered me for a long time. I think the reason it bothered me was because of the ways the world has tried to sneak the feminine into religious worship with things like "Mother Earth" or "Gaia," and we cannot do that with God. The Catholics insert Mother Mary to this end, often revering her as much or greater than Christ. Yet the falsehood of these devices does not mean that there are no feminine aspects to Yahweh's spiritual world.

The Holy Spirit is associated with the same duties as a wife, especially that of a helper. The very first mention of the very first woman is Yahweh giving Eve to Adam, and He said, "It is not good that man should be alone; I will make a helper comparable to him."

Then, when Jesus is explaining to His disciples that it is His time to go, He tells them, "I will pray the Father, and He will give you another Helper, that He may abide with you forever." This Helper would be comparable to Jesus, just as Eve was comparable to Adam, and with the same role.

Now, I don't believe that the Holy Spirit is actually female. Jesus even refers to the Spirit as a He. I don't think the spirit realm necessarily has genders in the same way we think of them. But there are certain roles that are generally assigned to either male or female in the created world, and if we look at those roles, the Holy Spirit aligns squarely with that of a wife or bride.

We can understand this better when we look at the bride of Christ, which is the church, made up of the saints. It is those saints whom the Holy Spirit was sent to. They are both male and female in their physical bodies, but in the spirit, they are collectively female. They are the helpers of Jesus Christ and are to function as His wife, bringing spiritual offspring to Him through becoming one with Him, having left their fathers and mothers in this world (Genesis 2:24).

I find it fascinating that even while we are still flesh and blood, because we are joined to Yeshua, we collectively become a spiritual body. The church or bride is also often associated with and called Jerusalem, of which Paul says, "But the Jerusalem above is free, which is the mother of us all." This is the spiritual sense of the mother that is to be honored in this command.

We are also told that we will be given a reward for our obedience; it was "the first commandment with promise," according to Ephesians 6:2. Exodus 20:12 says that promise is, "that your days may be long on the land which Jehovah your God *is* giving to you." Deuteronomy 6:16 words it a little differently, stating, "that your days may be prolonged, and so that it may be well with you in the land which Jehovah your God *is* giving to you."

Paul emphasizes the latter, but takes it further by stating, "that it may be well with you, and that you may live long on the Earth." Paul's wording is significant because he was specifically talking to physical children, so he emphasized part of the Deuteronomy version and converted the spiritual promise of the command to its physical counterpart for them to understand it: They will live long physical lives.

Exodus had spoken of "the land which Yahweh your Elohim is giving you." What land was that? I believe that it was spoken of unspecifically like that because the answer would change depending on who was being spoken to. To the kids Paul was talking to, it meant that this command could actually have a bearing on how long they stayed alive. To the Israelites at the time the commandment was given, it meant the promised land of Canaan that they would be entering. To an adult member of the bride of Christ today, it refers to eternal life in the kingdom of God!

After raising a son, I can certainly see how disobedience to parents can result in a shorter physical lifespan. Maybe this is why the command not to murder is next! But aside from the occasional temptation to murder our disobedient kids, we as parents have set up rules that will actually protect them. When those rules are not followed, danger, both physical and spiritual, can be the result. When that disobedience becomes a lifestyle rather than an occasional shortcoming, the workings of death have been set in motion. This works both physically and spiritually:

> Because, although they knew God, they did not glorify Him as God, nor were thankful, but became futile in their thoughts, and their foolish hearts were darkened. Professing to be wise, they became fools, and changed the glory of the incorruptible God into an image made like corruptible man—and birds and four-footed animals and creeping things. Therefore God also gave them up to uncleanness, in the lusts of their hearts, to dishonor their bodies among themselves, who exchanged the truth of God for the lie, and worshiped and served the creature rather than the Creator, who is blessed forever. Amen. For this reason God gave them up to vile passions. For even their women exchanged the natural use for what is against nature. Likewise also the men, leaving the natural use of the woman, burned in their lust for one another, men with men committing what is shameful, and receiving in themselves the penalty of their error which was due. And even as they did not like to retain God in their knowledge, God gave them over to a debased mind, to do those things which are not fitting; being filled with all unrighteousness, sexual immorality, wickedness, covetousness, maliciousness; full of envy, murder, strife, deceit, evil-mindedness; they are whisperers, backbiters,

Five: Honor Your Father & Mother

haters of God, violent, proud, boasters, inventors of evil things, disobedient to parents, undiscerning, untrustworthy, unloving, unforgiving, unmerciful; who, knowing the righteous judgment of God, that those who practice such things are deserving of death, not only do the same but also approve of those who practice them (Romans 1:21–32).

It is a hard thing to make a general statement about the longevity of all people and relate all death to this one law. That is not what I am attempting to do, nor is it what the law is saying. Yet we must regard the law as true and not just a quaint way of thinking, or one with which to threaten our children. As such, there must be a real correlation between the promise of the law and reality.

We have all either known or heard of someone who simply lived hard and fast and burned out, dying early in life. This is often the result of an intense focus on self rather than God. Yet we have also known people who lived this way and lived long enough to see their faults and slow down into a more responsible way. Why do some make it through, and others don't? Is the promise selective, or worse, simply false?

First, it is always God's prerogative to do what He may without our understanding. Yet He is also the One who made the promise in the command, so why does He not always follow through on it?

I have an idea which I cannot prove scientifically without a thorough investigation into the lives of large numbers of these people. The idea is simply forgiveness. If there is a child who continually goes down the road of disobedience, the parents, and others in their life, have a choice. Do we condemn them, stop giving our blessing, and eventually kick them out? Or do we forgive them time and again, as Yeshua instructs us to do? If we forgive someone, we have lifted the penalty off of the crime. We have not condoned the behavior and still may have some physical consequences to the action, but we are not holding obedience over them as a prerequisite to receiving our love.

Forgiveness allows for unconditional love, which in turn allows the doorway to repentance to remain open. When we harden ourselves to their disobedience, we close that door and it will lead to their own hardening, closing them off to God. This will lead to more bad choices which ultimately lead to death. It is my contention that continual forgiveness and unconditional love are the keys to raising a disobedient child. Yahweh promises that a long life is the result of obedience to our parents, but when disobedience is forgiven, then the route to receive that blessing remains open.

Spiritually, then, we have a model for our growth as children of God. When Paul talks of the law bringing death, this is what he was referring to. When one is hardened after the pattern laid out in Romans 1, we have hidden our route to forgiveness. This does not mean that forgiveness is no longer possible, for that is always God's will. We cannot completely remove the path, but we can make sure that we will not find it on our own.

God does have a funny way of putting the path to repentance back in front of us over and over again, however, so that some may eventually trip over it. If we do at some point find the route that Yeshua laid out for us of forgiveness, then we can conquer our own disobedience and leave open the route to eternal life in His kingdom. Romans 7:1–8:16 is about this process. Chapter 7:5–6 says,

> For when we were in the flesh, the passions of sin were working in our members through the law for the bearing of fruit unto death. But now we have been set free from the law, having died to that in which we were held, so as for us to serve in newness of spirit, and not in oldness of letter.

To find this path is to honor both our Father in heaven and our spiritual Mother, which is the body of believers called the Church and the Holy Spirit who indwells it. The reward is long life in the land that He is giving us.

18

Six: Murder – Nephilim vs Jesus

You shall not murder (Exodus 20:13).

You have heard that it was said to those of old, 'You shall not murder, and whoever murders will be in danger of the judgment.' But I say to you that whoever is angry with his brother without a cause shall be in danger of the judgment (Matthew 5:21–22).

This one should be a no-brainer. I don't think I need to explain that murder is wrong. Yahweh created all life, and as its Creator it is His right to take it away. Nobody else has that right, unless it is specifically granted to them by God. When we take a life, we are in essence superseding God's right over His Creation. We are acting as gods, and that is idolatry. We may not think that is what we are doing but God would certainly understand it that way.

Most people understand the difference between killing and murder. There are occasions for killing that will not be counted against us, such as self-defense. But the Bible also mentions when God "gives into your hand" during warfare as being acceptable, and there are no shortage of examples to pull from of God doing just that, giving Him a reputation as a violent God among modern thinkers.

Many people, when wanting to criticize the Bible, will point out the violence of the Old Testament as being both incompatible with a loving God and inconsistent with the New Testament teachings of Jesus. But neither of those statements are true, so this seems like a good place to cover some of the things that need to be considered before reaching those conclusions, as they will also shed more light on this sixth ordered matter.

Let's look at God's rules for war. Deuteronomy chapter 20 lays out God's principles for warfare, showing the rhyme and reason behind some of the orders He gave to Israel in their battles. I won't print the whole chapter, so please read it on your own.

These principles show a very caring God in all cases. We must start out first, though, by acknowledging that Israel was surrounded by enemies who wanted to destroy them. Warfare was a reality of life that could not be done away with, and because of that He wanted to show Israel, that even in war, there were rules to follow and things that would set them apart from those around them. This is also a time when Israel did not yet have a homeland, and Yahweh had tasked Israel with entering a "promised land" that was full of their most formidable enemies.

The first thing He let them know (verses 5–7) was that it was not mandatory for all to fight. If you had just built a house but had not yet dedicated it, or had planted but not eaten from your vineyard, or if you had betrothed a woman, but not yet married her, you were to go back and enjoy the fruits of your home, vineyard, or wife, lest you died in battle and another man took these things before you could enjoy them.

Also, if you were fearful and fainthearted of the battle, you were to go return to your house, so that your fear did not spread among the others. These were concessions that none of the nations around

Six: Murder – Nephilim vs. Jesus

them would have made and showed both a heart for the people and wisdom for the battle, for a man whose mind is not focused on the task at hand would be a crutch rather than an asset in war.

Next, He gave them the rules for engagement (verses 8–20). What we will notice is the differentiation He made between the nations they were to inherit and cities that were very far away. Israel was to start by making an offer of peace; killing was not to be the first option. If the offer of peace was accepted, then that people would be placed under tribute and would serve them. But if they rejected it, then Israel was to kill only the males, taking the women, children, and livestock as plunder. It was then explained that these were the rules for cities "very far from you."

He later (chapter 21:10–14) gave rules for how to treat the women taken captive. If a man desired to take one as a wife, she was first to be given a period of mourning for her parents and then treated respectfully. If she did not please him, he would let her go free and could not sell her for money or treat her brutally, because she had been humbled by him.

There were different rules, however, for the land that God had given to Israel as an inheritance which was inhabited by the Hittites, the Amorites, the Canaanites, the Perizites, the Hivites, and the Jebusites. With those nations they were to, "let nothing that breathes remain alive, but you shall utterly destroy them."

Why were these nations singled out for utter destruction? The reason given was, "lest they teach you to do according to all their abominations which they have done for their gods, and you sin against Yahweh your God." What was it about their abominations that made even their women, children and cattle to be deserving of death? We need to piece a few bits of information together to get it, but then it will make perfect sense.

When Israel first sent spies into the promised land, they came back with this description of the people there in Numbers 13:26–33,

> Now they departed and came back to Moses and Aaron and all the congregation of the children of Israel in the Wilderness of Paran, at Kadesh; they brought back word to them and to all the congregation, and showed them the fruit of the land. Then they told him, and said: "We went to the land where you sent us. It truly flows with milk and honey, and this is its fruit. Nevertheless the people who dwell in the land are strong; the cities are fortified and very large; moreover we saw the descendants of Anak there. The Amalekites dwell in the land of the South; the **Hittites**, the **Jebusites**, and the **Amorites** dwell in the mountains; and the **Canaanites** dwell by the sea and along the banks of the Jordan."
>
> Then Caleb quieted the people before Moses, and said, "Let us go up at once and take possession, for we are well able to overcome it."
>
> But the men who had gone up with him said, "We are not able to go up against the people, for they are stronger than we." And they gave the children of Israel a bad report of the land which they had spied out, saying, "The land through which we have gone as spies is a land that devours its inhabitants, and **all the people whom we saw in it are men of great stature. There we saw the giants** (the descendants of Anak came from the giants); and we were like grasshoppers in our own sight, and so we were in their sight."

These were not your regular folks! Four of the five tribes listed were also mentioned in Deuteronomy 20. These are the same people in the same land, and they were all giants. We can learn more about where these giants came from in Genesis 6:1–5:

> When men began to multiply on the surface of the ground, and daughters were born to them, God's sons saw that men's daughters were beautiful, and they took any that they wanted for themselves as wives. Yahweh said, "My Spirit will not strive with man forever, because he also is flesh; so his days will be one hundred twenty years." The Nephilim were in the earth in those days, and also after that, when God's sons came in to men's daughters and had children with them. Those were the mighty men

Six: Murder – Nephilim vs. Jesus

who were of old, men of renown. Yahweh saw that the wickedness of man was great in the earth, and that every imagination of the thoughts of man's heart was continually only evil. (WEB)

These giants were the offspring of the fallen angels who raped human women. They were genetic hybrids of humans and angels whose physical appearance was of giant people. The book of 1 Enoch speaks of this race in more detail, describing these events with no uncertainty or vagueness as some read into the Biblical text. Whether you believe Enoch can be trusted scripturally or not, it is certain that the disciples in the time of Christ read and understood Enoch, as it was quoted in Jude. Regardless, 1 Enoch is not necessary, because the Bible records the same things.

These giants were a complete abomination to Yahweh, so He made a plan to rid the earth of them that involved the nation of Israel, so as to show His glory through His people. The angels that fell were thrown into the bottomless pit, chained until the final judgement because of what they did, but some of their offspring were allowed to live as a test for Israel.

Enoch also relates that after they were killed, their spirits would remain to harass men until the end of the age. These are known today as demons. Although this is not explicitly stated in the Biblical texts, it is again supported by what they do record. Demon possession was not recorded in the Old Testament, but shows up in the new, seemingly out of nowhere. Yet in the context of the Nephilim, it makes perfect sense. Angelic spirit cannot die, so once devoid of a host body, they must go in search of another, which is what demons do.

The reason that Israel was instructed to completely destroy all men, women, children and livestock was to rid the world of this hybrid abomination, who lived specifically in the land they were told to inhabit. These were not human! Their genetic abominations even extended into animal hybrids (Enoch also explains this), so the cattle could not be allowed to survive either. Yahweh was not an inhumane tyrant who wanted Israel to kill others in cold blood. He was a caring God who wanted to give Israel a land flowing with milk and honey, but the route there involved killing giants which were allowed to remain on earth so that Israel could be tested.

Israel did not always follow the rules they were given, however, and took some captives instead of killing all life completely. Those saved were to become thorns in the side of Israel in later times. David found one of those thorns in Goliath and destroyed him as God intended. They were not completely human, and they were also given into Israel's hand, taking this killing out of the realm of murder.

There is actually some comparison to be made between Yeshua and the Nephilim that we are meant to think about in the biblical narrative. The Nephilim were the offspring of fallen angelic spiritual beings and human women. Yeshua was the offspring of the Holy Spirit sent by the Father (a spiritual being) and a human woman. How that occurred in each case was very different, however.

The Nephilim mated because they found the daughters of men beautiful and because they desired power over men and God. They had uncontrolled lusts that caused them to perform an abomination. Remember that lust comes from the unclean area outside of the temple. Their plan was to reproduce and take over control of the earth.

The Father saw a pure heart in Mary and sent His Spirit, saying, "the Holy Spirit will come upon you, and the power of the Highest will overshadow you." (Luke 1:35). His goal was not domination of the earth and there was no lust in Him. It stemmed from the inner part of the Temple, His heart. He was sending His son to die a horrible death at the hands of those who preferred the corruption of the Nephilim. In fact, the Father's act was the final blow to a battle with the fallen angels that began with the temptation in the Garden of Eden and got out of control when they came into the daughters of men in Genesis 6.

Six: Murder – Nephilim vs. Jesus

The fallen angels fought their battle by reproducing with men, something they could not do with their own kind in the spiritual realm. Yeshua was sent to fight His battle by dying, something He could not do in the spiritual realm. And by dying, He overcame the power of the fallen angels and Nephilim over men. He did not have to resort to murder, or even justified killing, but did just the opposite by giving His own life. He gave us "a more excellent way" of love unto death.

We can also look at the overarching purpose for Israel to enter the promised land. Yahweh was essentially using His people to redeem the land that the Nephilim giants had polluted. Israel would be first ridding the land of them, then cleansing and inhabiting it as a permanent homeland.

Today we are in a spiritual battle with the prince of the power of the air, with spiritual wickedness in high places. Yahweh's people are donning the full armor of God and doing spiritual warfare. We will be victorious and will redeem the place in heaven from where the fallen angels, the progenitors of the Nephilim, have fallen.

They had left their heavenly abode to wander to and fro about the earth and will shortly be thrown directly down to earth (no longer able to go to and fro) because there will no longer be a place for them in heaven (Revelation 12:7). This will be a direct result of the seventh trumpet of Revelation 11:15 where "the kingdoms of this world have become the Kingdoms of our Lord and His Christ." It is only after this event that the rest of the events with the bride and the 144,000 can take place because they now have a place to go. It is where Yeshua went to prepare a place for us, and will come back to receive us, His bride (John 14:2–3). The promised land will have been redeemed from the fallen angels once and for all, cleansed and made ready for His bride, after the pattern set forth in the Exodus. This is why men will judge angels (1 Corinthians 6:3), for it is them that we are displacing from their home.

Part 4: The Ten Ordered Matters

Getting back to the ordered matter, what did Yeshua Himself have to say about it?

> You have heard that it was said to the ancient ones, "You shall not murder;" and "Whoever murders will be in danger of the judgment." But I tell you, that everyone who is angry with his brother without a cause will be in danger of the judgment (Matthew 5:21–22).

He is getting at the root of the problem as to why we would think of murder in the first place. This goes all the way back to Cain slaying Abel his brother out of jealousy. His brother's offering had been accepted by Yahweh, while his own was not. His anger led him to wish his brother no longer existed. His logic was that if Abel were not around, then he would be favored by God instead of his brother. Before he killed Abel, but after his offering had been rejected, Yahweh told him why and what he could do about it:

> So the LORD said to Cain, "Why are you angry? And why has your countenance fallen? If you do well, will you not be accepted? And if you do not do well, sin lies at the door. And its desire is for you, but you should rule over it" (Genesis 4:6–7).

We are to rule over our anger. Paul puts it this way:

> For though we walk in the flesh, we do not war according to the flesh. For the weapons of our warfare are not carnal but mighty in God for pulling down strongholds, casting down arguments and every high thing that exalts itself against the knowledge of God, bringing every thought into captivity to the obedience of Christ, and having readiness to avenge all disobedience, whenever your obedience is fulfilled (2 Corinthians 10:3–6).

This is about self-control, one of the fruits of the spirit. With self-control over our thoughts, anger cannot take root to the point of having intention to kill. Jesus quote from Matthew 5 actually points to there being an anger that *does* have a cause. Abel had done

Six: Murder – Nephilim vs. Jesus

nothing directly to or against Cain, so Cain had no justification for his anger. But we do not have to get so extreme to think that any anger in our life makes us deserving of judgment. With self-control and taking our thoughts captive, we are able to discern where our thoughts come from and whether they are appropriate or not.

Paul rightly points out that our battle is spiritual, fought with spiritual weapons of God. The Old Testament used physical examples to teach its lessons. The rules for warfare against the nations of Israel's inheritance in Deuteronomy 20 were the carnal equivalents of Paul's spiritual warfare. They were set up for "casting down every high thing that exalts itself against the knowledge of God." In Deuteronomy, it was giants that were against the knowledge of God.

Think about murder from a spiritual standpoint. When somebody is killed in this world they cease to exist in this world. However, this will not keep them from existing in the next world. The one who does the killing, though, may indeed be kept from inheriting eternal life in the final judgement. Jesus puts it this way:

> And do not fear those who kill the body but cannot kill the soul. But rather fear Him who is able to destroy both soul and body in hell (Matthew 10:27).

What this tells me is that the far more important lesson in keeping this command is the possibility of the murderer losing eternal life. The one who lost their physical life will still have a chance in the judgement of being found righteous. The murderer will also still have a chance, but only if they fully repent of their sin in their lifetime. Do any of us know when our time is up? Jesus can indeed work miracles in the lives of the worst of sinners, but a stubborn, frozen heart can keep Him from coming in and doing so, as Paul tells us:

> And even as they did not like to retain God in their knowledge, God gave them over to a debased mind, to do those things which

are not fitting; being filled with all unrighteousness, sexual immorality, wickedness, covetousness, maliciousness; full of envy, *murder*, strife, deceit, evil-mindedness; they are whisperers, backbiters, haters of God, violent, proud, boasters, inventors of evil things, disobedient to parents, undiscerning, untrustworthy, unloving, unforgiving, unmerciful; who, knowing the righteous judgment of God, that those who practice such things are deserving of death, not only do the same but also approve of those who practice them (Romans 1:28).

Murder is one of the things listed here that is a result of having been turned over to a debased mind; the end result of not wanting to retain God in their knowledge. If we want to keep God out, it is our free will to do so, but the consequences will be loss of eternal life.

Keep your heart set on God, taking every thought captive, because we are our brother's keeper. The battle is spiritual; to engage in murder or any lust of the flesh is to give power back over to those spiritual entities who found their salvation through the flesh. Our salvation is spiritual and takes us out of the lusts of the flesh and into the heart, where God's Words are written, "You shall not murder!"

Seven: Adultery – Idolatry Part 2

You shall not commit adultery (Exodus 20:14).

Therefore a man shall leave his father and his mother, and shall cling to his wife and they shall become one flesh (Genesis 2:24).

He who commits adultery with a woman lacks heart; he who does it is a destroyer of his own soul (Proverbs 6:32).

We saw in the study on the tabernacle, how those things outside of the tabernacle proper represented areas of uncleanness in our bodies, and how that area can become a false tabernacle for us. Adultery is one of the end results of our focus being outside of the tabernacle, in the area below the ribs.

All of nature speaks of two becoming one. Flowers need pollination from another flower to create one fruit. Animals and humans are no different, which is why parents talk about "the birds and the bees" when they are having "the talk" with their kids. When two come together and become one flesh, the result is bearing fruit, or a child. The child is actually the part that tells us that we became one, because he or she is one totally new creature who did not exist before husband and wife came together. Notice, too, that the reason they came together was not to love each other and enjoy each other's presence, but to become one flesh.

Jesus talked about this subject when pressed about divorce by the Pharisees. It is impossible to separate the subjects of adultery, divorce, and sexual immorality biblically, and Jesus brings them all up in this passage:

> Pharisees came to him, testing him, and saying, "Is it lawful for a man to divorce his wife for any reason?" He answered, "Haven't you read that he who made them from the beginning made them male and female, and said, 'For this cause a man shall leave his father and mother, and shall be joined to his wife; and the two shall become one flesh?' So that they are no more two, but one flesh. What therefore God has joined together, don't let man tear apart." They asked him, "Why then did Moses command us to give her a certificate of divorce, and divorce her?" He said to them, "Moses, because of the hardness of your hearts, allowed you to divorce your wives, but from the beginning it has not been so. I tell you that whoever divorces his wife, except for sexual immorality, and marries another, commits adultery; and he who marries her when she is divorced commits adultery." His disciples said to him, "If this is the case of the man with his wife, it is not expedient to marry." But he said to them, "Not all men can receive this saying, but those to whom it is given. For there are eunuchs who were born that way from their mother's womb, and there are eunuchs who were made eunuchs by men; and there are eunuchs who made themselves eunuchs for the Kingdom of Heaven's sake. He who is able to receive it, let him receive it" (Matthew 19:3–12 WEB).

He created us for the very purpose of coming together as one. "What God has joined together, let not man separate." We need to think about this; if we are marrying ourselves to another, we are

Seven Adultery – Idolatry Part 2

doing the will of God, for He joins us together. Why would we seek to break it apart?

There are many ways to break a marriage apart, but only one that Jesus mentions in the above passage that is an acceptable reason for divorce—sexual immorality. The Greek word for this is *porneia* from which we get our word for pornography. It refers to any type of sexual perversion, sometimes translated as fornication. This includes adultery, homosexuality, incest, and yes, even pornography.

Jesus said earlier, in Matthew 5:27–28, "You have heard that it was said, 'You shall not commit adultery;' but I tell you that everyone who gazes at a woman to lust after her has committed adultery with her already in his heart" (WEB).

There is no escaping that porneia encompasses pornography today. The fact that it is so common as to become socially acceptable is no excuse. I don't say this lightly either, as somebody who has had a problem with it and tried hard to justify its use. I can talk firsthand about the problems that it causes in marriage. I could rationalize all day long how I would never physically cheat, but that could not stop my wife from feeling insufficient and insecure by my using it. She had every right to divorce me based on my infidelity with porn. I'm lucky that she didn't and preferred to stay and help me work out my problems.

I talk about porn openly because it is probably the single most common form of adultery today, yet many don't think of it as such, even within Christianity. It is my hope that my story will encourage others to find a way out, even though it is difficult for me to speak about.

I knew in my heart how wrong it was to use porn but could not convince my flesh that it was that bad. I wanted to stop and always regretted using it, but the reality was that it was an addiction. My conviction had to be stronger than my flesh, and that was no easy battle. Those who struggle with it will understand, and there are far more out there than care to admit it.

Part 4: The Ten Ordered Matters

When an alcoholic is in recovery, the first thing he or she does is to remove the alcohol from their house. It is far easier to not drink when there is nothing available. Porn addicts no longer have that luxury today. It is there waiting on the computer or phone with only a few keystrokes or clicks, and these devices are so embedded in our lives for work or school and everyday communication that we cannot just get rid of them. It's like recovering from alcohol while carrying around a flask of whiskey wherever you go.

But there are a few things that have helped me which I'd like to share. The first was making the connection between porn and idolatry. Porn can also be looked at as a fraud, an invitation to live in the synthetic world that Satan is creating on top of Yahweh's real creation. This synthetic world is really just idolatry.

When my porn use was at its worst, God was also moving me to study idolatry, so it was not a great leap to see pornographic images as the images of the second commandment. I realized that looking at those pictures was a form of worship. Even if it was not physical adultery, it was spiritual adultery, which is exactly how God talks of idolatry over and over in the Old Testament.

Around the same time I was making that connection, my family was also being exposed to some people who had the idea that the Holy Spirit still moves today as it did in the Bible. They put their faith into action and saw radical healings take place no differently than Jesus did. It was God's timing.

I had recently been kicked out of a fellowship that did not seem to have God's love. The self-appointed leader was a strict disciplinarian type, or perhaps more of a schoolyard bully. If you disagreed with anything, you were a heretic and you were kicked out. Why we lasted so long there, I don't know, but when we left and did not know where we would go for fellowship, we told ourselves we would go wherever we found God's love.

We were hungry for love and, without knowing it, for the Holy Spirit. So, when we met these friends, we ate up everything they said.

They lived too far away to fellowship with regularly, but we had a new direction to go in our relationship with Yeshua. It was exciting to start seeing the Bible as real again. We were refreshed and growing. And that kept me out of porn for over two years.

Slowly, however, my heart grew colder again. My excitement wore off, even though I had started seeing God heal people directly from my own hands. I started using porn again on and off. I hated myself for it and hated even more knowing how much it hurt Sanae. I did keep learning and growing in other areas and never gave up hope that I would get over porn eventually.

Then another thing clicked with me from a video testimony of someone whom God was training to cast out demons. In this video, the speaker spoke of being with some friends when one of them started manifesting a demon. He started trying to cast it out and could not. The demon laughed and started telling him about all of his sins he'd committed, so that he had no authority to cast it out. This really intimidated him to hear the demon speaking through his friend about things he thought were secrets.

He called an acquaintance who was more experienced in deliverance, hoping this person could do it over the phone. This person also tried, and the demon started telling him how he had just been using porn and masturbating, so he also had no authority, which shut the man up and neither was able to cast it out that day. He ended by saying that he knows that God forgives us, but one thing is for certain, demons will not respect us and will use our sin as ammunition against us.

This somehow hit home with me because deliverance is something I have felt is important to be able to do, since Jesus said we should and will be doing this as His disciples. From all I have studied, demons are masters of legal contracts. They are bound to follow certain rules and laws, but are also masters of coercion and fraud, getting people to make agreements that we aren't aware we are making for the sole purpose of having ammunition to use against us.

Porn or other sins can easily be held over our heads to keep us from walking in the authority of Christ.

Here is the way I saw what happened in his story: Both men in the testimony could have, in theory, stood their ground in Christ's forgiveness and the power of His blood over the sins the demon was proclaiming. But that can be a difficult thing for most people to do because it takes time to remedy sin because forgiveness needs the healing ointment of repentance to take effect. We never actually lose our authority, but the shame from being actively in our sin will make us weak, losing our confidence, putting cracks in our armor, and losing our defenses that God gave us for such occasions.

The men in this testimony had not responded immediately with repentance for their sin and put their armor back on to stay in the battle. Had they done so, they could have prevailed.

This is why forgiveness cannot be used as an excuse to sin. We are fighting against principalities and powers of the air that know the rules of the game better than we do, so it is essential to not give them any ammunition or any holes in our armor.

Just because our salvation is assured does not mean that there are no consequences for our actions. To stand in strength is to stand in righteousness. The armor of God is there to keep us righteous (belt of truth, the breastplate of righteousness), as an aid to keep strong in *the way* (sandals of the gospel of peace, shield of faith), to walk in the strength of our salvation (helmet of salvation), and able to fight the powers of darkness (sword of the Spirit, prayer in the Spirit for the saints). There is no armor of forgiveness. Forgiveness is a bandage for wounds inflicted by the improper use of our armor. We do not go into battle telling ourselves it's okay to have an arrow hit us because we can ask forgiveness and be all better. In a real battle there is no time for that. Prepare ahead and avoid the injury. That is where both men found themselves compromised.

Seven Adultery – Idolatry Part 2

I don't tell that story because I would have done better, but because I'm sure I would have failed as well. I saw myself in the same vulnerable situation, and it scared me.

The argument the spiritual world seems to be making is that because of our adultery, we are actually practicing idolatry, not worshiping the true God. They are not wrong in that assessment. They are well aware that we cannot serve two masters; if we love one, we will hate the other (Matthew 6:24).

The comparison of adultery and idolatry is all over the Scriptures. When Yahweh gave the Ten Commandments to Israel at Mount Sinai, Israel entered into a marriage covenant with Yahweh (Exodus 24:1–11). Their "I do" was in verse 3,

> Moses came and told the people all Yahweh's words, and all the ordinances; and all the people answered with one voice, and said, "All the words which Yahweh has spoken will we do." (WEB)

Then, after he wrote down all the words of Yahweh, offered up sacrifices and reread the words to Israel, they repeated their vow in verse 7, "All that Yahweh has spoken will we do, and be obedient." Then in verse 10, seventy-two elders went up on Mount Sinai with Moses, eating and drinking in a covenant meal with Yahweh, who was standing on a pavement of sapphire. All of this was symbolism from a marriage covenant and ceremony.

When we later read over and over of Israel and Judah "playing the harlot" with other gods, this is why that language was chosen. Jeremiah chapters 2 and 3 tell the whole story of Israel and Judah in the language of two sisters both married to Yahweh, and both committing adultery:

> "Go, and proclaim in the ears of Jerusalem, saying, 'Yahweh says, "I remember for you the kindness of your youth, the love of your weddings; how you went after me in the wilderness, in a land that was not sown. Israel was holiness to Yahweh, the first fruits of his

increase. All who devour him will be held guilty. Evil will come on them,'" says Yahweh." (Jeremiah 2:2–3 WEB)

This was the wedding at Mount Sinai we just mentioned, when Israel was in her youth and went after Yahweh in the wilderness. But things quickly went wrong:

> "Your own wickedness will correct you, and your backsliding will rebuke you. Know therefore and see that it is an evil and bitter thing, that you have forsaken Yahweh your God, and that my fear is not in you," says the Lord, Yahweh of Armies. "For long ago I broke off your yoke, and burst your bonds. You said, 'I will not serve;' for on every high hill and under every green tree you bowed yourself, playing the prostitute." (Jeremiah 2:19–20 WEB)

Even after much adultery, Yahweh still asked Israel to return to Him. She refused, so He eventually divorced Israel, hoping that at least her sister Judah might see the example and turn back to Him. Yet that was not to be the case:

> Moreover, Yahweh said to me in the days of Josiah the king, "Have you seen that which backsliding Israel has done? She has gone up on every high mountain and under every green tree, and has played the prostitute there. I said after she had done all these things, 'She will return to me;' but she didn't return; and her treacherous sister Judah saw it. I saw when, for this very cause, that backsliding Israel had committed adultery, I had put her away and given her a certificate of divorce, yet treacherous Judah, her sister, had no fear; but she also went and played the prostitute. Because she took her prostitution lightly, the land was polluted, and she committed adultery with stones and with wood. Yet for all this her treacherous sister, Judah, has not returned to me with her whole heart, but only in pretense," says Yahweh (Jeremiah 3:6–10 WEB).

Even after His divorce, Yahweh did not give up on Israel:

Seven Adultery – Idolatry Part 2

> "They say, 'If a man puts away his wife, and she goes from him, and becomes another man's, should he return to her again?' Wouldn't that land be greatly polluted? But you have played the prostitute with many lovers; yet return again to me," says Yahweh. (Jeremiah 3:1 WEB)

> "If you will return, O Israel," says the LORD, "Return to me; and if you will put away your abominations out of My sight, then you shall not be moved (Jeremiah 4:1).

I find this to be very moving to know how much He loves us. We have all been spiritually involved in harlotry, having turned our backs to Yahweh, yet He is still willing to have us back. He hates adultery and hates divorce, yet is patiently waiting for us to turn back to Him so that He can receive us back:

> Go, and proclaim these words toward the north, and say, "**Return**, you backsliding Israel," says Yahweh; "I will not look in anger on you; for I am merciful," says Yahweh. "I will not keep anger forever. **Only acknowledge your iniquity**, that you have transgressed against Yahweh your God, and have scattered your ways to the strangers under every green tree, and you have not obeyed my voice," says Yahweh (Jeremiah 3:12–13).

And that is the most important takeaway from all of this: Let us acknowledge our adulteries and fall on His mercy. He will gladly accept us back!

That was also the last thing that I learned on my journey to overcoming porn. It is a biblical concept to "acknowledge your iniquity." Another way to state that is to confess your sins. The book of James says,

> Is anyone among you suffering? Let him pray. Is anyone cheerful? Let him sing psalms. Is anyone among you sick? Let him call for the elders of the church, and let them pray over him, anointing him with oil in the name of the Lord. And the prayer of faith will save the sick, and the Lord will raise him up. And if he has

> committed sins, he will be forgiven. **Confess your trespasses** to one another, and pray for one another, **that you may be healed**. The effective, fervent prayer of a righteous man avails much (James 5:13–16).

This confession is so important! I had read these verses many times, keeping them in the back of my mind, but could not bring myself to be open about porn because of the shame I felt. Society teaches us to hide our faults, but God teaches the opposite. Finally, though, I knew I had to start talking about it. If I didn't, my wife would, and that would be worse! I opened up at our fellowship a couple times, and I was amazed when others that I looked up to started coming forward to me to admit they were struggling with the same problem or had in the past.

In the end, I could not have overcome it without starting to be open about my problem. Admitting our faults to each other takes away the power of the accuser.

James even related confession to being healed. There is a direct link between our physical and spiritual health. It should not be surprising that there was a relationship between my back problems and my porn use. My back was just a physical symptom of my spiritual disease. When I started confessing my sin to others, I was healed and given freedom.

> If we confess our sins, He is faithful and just to forgive us our sins and to cleanse us from all unrighteousness (1 John 1:9).

Praise God!

Eight: Don't Steal – Emmanuel

You shall not steal (Exodus 20:15).

Stealing is one possible end result of failing at the tenth commandment, do not covet. It is taking action on wanting what you do not have a right to own. It is a commandment I don't personally feel I have an issue with, and it feels so obvious to me that I initially had a hard time writing about it. Yet I know that there are many people who do suffer from a compulsion to steal, and I have even known a couple of them closely. What was it about them that made them want to steal what wasn't rightfully theirs? If I had asked them, they would likely say they didn't know. Neither one was so poor as to need to steal to live or even to fit in with society. Neither was on drugs at the time their compulsive theft started, although both did end up on drugs later. They really didn't understand why they wanted to steal stuff even though they knew it to be wrong. One of these was my best friend from the first grade until after I graduated high school. His name was Emmanuel.

Part 4: The Ten Ordered Matters

This section is my testimony regarding my friend. I know that there are other reasons people steal, and I don't mean to take away from those individual stories. I do believe, however that Emmanuel's story illustrates what is often (certainly not always) at the heart of the problem, and since it is the story that Yahweh has given me through my own life, it is the one that I have to share.

Many will experiment with theft of some sort, especially as children, but most will eventually give it up, realizing that the benefits are not worth the repercussions of getting caught. I did this myself. At seventeen, I went out on a shoplifting spree with a couple friends, led by Emmanuel. We were stealing cassette tapes from music stores, but on our last stop before heading home we were caught by undercover security.

We were fortunate that the security folks at the store called our parents and had them come pick us up instead of calling law enforcement. It was humiliating, and that did the trick for two of us. We never stole again. Emmanuel, however, it did not faze. I remember being out with him on a number of other occasions after that when he decided to take stuff, even very expensive items, from stores while I and others present were trying to talk him out of it. He thought it was funny.

Emmanuel did eventually find drugs, too. By the time he was 26 he was dealing drugs and during a deal that went bad he shot and killed someone. He forced his wife to bury the body in the back yard and then fled town. The police caught up with him on a Greyhound bus. When Emmanuel pulled a gun on the officer, the officer shot first and killed him.

For years after this, Emmanuel haunted my dreams. What was it that gets into people to make them go down that road? It is a question that has bothered me for a long time.

When I think of his family, I get some answers, but probably not the whole picture. His parents divorced, I think around first or second grade, and his dad moved about four hours away. His mom

Eight: Don't Steal – Emmanuel

farmed hay and raised cattle and a few horses. They were poor and worked hard. He had a lot of chores that he resented, and he grew to hate his situation. He would get excited when he got to visit his dad, which didn't seem to happen often. They would usually go skiing or do other fun activities that he didn't get to do at home, which I believe only made him more bitter toward his regular home life and his mom. His mother was a strong Christian who I remember teaching the Bible release classes during elementary school. Later, she actually became a minister. His dad was a partier.

I remember having Emmanuel over to stay the night at my house one time, probably around third or fourth grade. We camped in a tent in the back yard and, of course, stayed up late talking and goofing off. Somehow the conversation turned to money. Neither of us grew up in families having much of it, but we agreed that neither of us ever wanted to be rich.

I can't now think of any specific people or instances that made me think that way, but I always saw money as a danger. I thought rich people should do more with their money to help others and since they never did, at least in my limited experience, there must be something about money that made them selfish and uncaring, and I didn't want to be that way. Maybe I pressured or guilt-tripped Emmanuel into thinking that way too, but we made a pact that night that neither of us would ever pursue being rich as a priority.

I've always remembered that pact and kept it in the back of my mind. Looking back at my life now, I've kept my word; my career choices have never been based solely on how much I would be paid.

As we got older, it seemed that Emmanuel's heart was not in the same place. He was a very bright kid with a quick wit and sense of humor, always the class clown. Around the end of our junior year, he got a job at a small software company in town because he was naturally gifted at computer programming. He quickly became the owner's right-hand man and started making good money, at least for our small town. It was the first time in his life he had the ability to buy whatever he wanted, and he started changing. A lot.

He started driving a Mercedes and put a crazy stereo in it and a radar detector. Everything was about his stuff. It was as if he had to prove to the world that he was not poor anymore. It was also during this time that he started shoplifting. Looking back, it makes little sense to start shoplifting *after* he got money, but it seems that after he got a taste of getting what he wanted, it didn't really matter the means of acquiring it.

After graduation, I went off to college, and he continued working for the software company. I'd visit Emmanuel when I came home on breaks and he would show me his new stereo, his new house, his new whatever. He had no interest in what I had been doing in college. He would also introduce me to his new friends, which were all people whom we had gone to school with but were from different crowds, known to be either drug users or dealers.

Now at the time I wasn't so proper or goody-two-shoes to not experiment with smoking pot or drinking, and we did both of those things together at times. But I was starting to see he was experimenting with harder drugs, and I really didn't want anything to do with that.

The last time I saw him, he had lost his job at the software company because the owner was basically forced into retirement, not being able to compete with larger companies taking over his market share. Emmanuel laughed it off when he told me, but I could see his eyes had completely changed. He wouldn't tell me what he was doing for a living or what his plans were. I figured he had started dealing, but I sensed that if I confronted him about it, it could get dangerous. The source of his identity had been cut off and I saw an internal panic to get it back at any cost. Again, the means of acquiring it wouldn't matter.

When I got the call that he had been shot and killed, I probably hadn't seen him in three years.

Eight: Don't Steal – Emmanuel

Everyone who talked about the incident at some point mentioned how dangerous drugs were, assuming they were his main downfall. I saw things differently. The drugs were part of the problem, to be sure, but they did not start the problem. To me, it was his love of money and the identity it gave him. I honestly don't know how advanced his drug use was at the time and wouldn't be surprised if he was not even on drugs when the bad deal took place. His desperation for cashflow was enough drive him that far and, if anything, the drugs just nudged him over the edge.

After he lost his job, I think that drugs became a way to fill the hole left by his misplaced identity. They could at once let him forget the loss, and also act as an immediate replacement of revenue, helping him gain that identity back. It was a counterfeit replacement, right there in front of an impatient and panicked soul, ready for the taking.

To be more accurate, though, the drugs were a counterfeit of something that was already a counterfeit, a lie built on a lie. His identity based on material wealth was already filling a hole where something else was missing.

I defined stealing earlier as taking action to acquire things we don't have a right to own. But there are also things we may not have which we are supposed to desire and have every right to: everlasting life, a relationship with our Creator, and the unconditional love and forgiveness of Jesus Christ. Inside everyone who has a compulsion to steal are holes in the shape of these necessities. It is impossible to steal them because they are freely given, but they are only given when their necessity is recognized and asked for.

When a child is small, the unconditional love of their parents fills these needs until they are old enough to grasp the concepts of a Creator and Savior. Then "a man shall leave his father and his mother, and shall cleave to his wife and they shall become one flesh," which pictures the transferring of responsibilities to our spiritual side.

Part 4: The Ten Ordered Matters

When Emmanuel's parents divorced, he could no longer receive unconditional love properly, even though both parents did love him. His dad leaving left a huge hole that needed filling. He, of course, did not understand that, but instinctually went looking for anything that might fill the hole.

I still don't fully understand what it is that makes some people turn toward God in their hardship and others to trust in riches instead, but I do know the result. Paul wrote to Timothy:

> Let as many as are slaves under a yoke count their own masters worthy of all honor, that the name and teaching of God may not be blasphemed. And those having believing masters, let them not despise them, because they are brothers, but rather let them serve as slaves, because they are believing and beloved ones, those receiving of the good service in return. Teach and exhort these things. If anyone teaches differently, and does not consent to sound words, those of our Lord Jesus Christ and the teaching according to godliness, he has been puffed up, understanding nothing, but is sick concerning doubts and arguments, out of which comes envy, strife, evil-speakings, evil suspicions, meddling, of men whose mind has been corrupted and deprived of the truth, **supposing gain to be godliness**. Withdraw from such persons. But godliness with contentment is great gain. For we have brought nothing into the world, and it is plain that neither can we carry anything out. But having food and clothing, we will be satisfied with these. But those purposing to be rich fall into temptation, and a snare, and many foolish and hurtful lusts, which plunge men into ruin and destruction. **For the love of money is a root of all evils, by means of which some having lusted after it were seduced from the faith, and they themselves pierced through by many pains.** But you, O man of God, flee these things and pursue righteousness, godliness, faith, love, patience, and meekness. Fight the good fight of faith. Lay hold on eternal life, to which you were also called and confessed the good confession before many witnesses. I charge you before God, He making all things alive, and Christ Jesus, the One witnessing the good confession to

Pontius Pilate, that you keep the commandment spotless, blameless, until the appearing of our Lord Jesus Christ, who in His own time will reveal the blessed and only Potentate, the King of kings and Lord of lords, the only One having immortality, living in light that cannot be approached, whom no one of men saw, nor can see; to whom be honor and everlasting might. Amen. **Charge the rich in the present age not to be high-minded, nor to set hope on the uncertainty of riches, but in the living God, the One offering to us richly all things for enjoyment; to do good, to be rich in good works, to be ready to share, generous, treasuring away for themselves a good foundation for the coming age, that they may lay hold on everlasting life** (1 Timothy 6:1–19).

Apparently, there is nothing new under the sun. This chapter starts by speaking of the situation of slaves, and I believe Emmanuel saw himself as a slave who could somehow buy his own freedom. But he could not. In trying to, he could only find the path to destruction, as Paul warned.

When I went to find the quote for this, I was originally just going to quote the, "for the love of money is a root of all evils," part, but the context around it is so good that I could not help quoting almost the entirety of the chapter, so please read through the whole thing carefully if you haven't done so. It is getting at the heart of what makes people steal and the results of doing so. I have witnessed the truth of this in its entirety through Emmanuel.

"A good name is to be chosen rather than great riches, loving favor rather than silver and gold," Proverbs 22:1.

I've often thought of Emmanuel's name, meaning "God with us," and how he chose riches over his name. There are multiple layers to the meaning of "name" in the quote from Proverbs 22:1. It is the word *shem*, which we've looked at before. It refers to the breath, which in turn makes up the character of the person. It is their reputation, especially in the eyes of God, thus it relates to favor, or grace from God, as the second half of the verse implies. Emmanuel's mother chose for him a good name, in giving Yahweh praise for the gift of her firstborn. Yet Emmanuel did not choose for himself a good name in the sense of his reputation or character, or rather thought his reputation could be found in riches instead. But to God, a good name and riches are mutually exclusive, one or the other, choosing both not being an option. The problem was not that God was not with Emmanuel, but that Emmanuel chose to not be with God. God is with all of us always, and He is there urging us to choose the good name—*His* name and favor—over riches. Choosing otherwise will cause us to break the eighth ordered matter, "You shall not Steal."

Nine: No False Witness – The Land Cries Out

> You shall not bear false witness against your neighbor (Exodus 20:16).

In the beginning of the book, I talked about the false "other" creation. This ordered matter is very closely related to that concept and is simply the requirement that we do not follow in the steps of the adversary to create our own false reality, especially through deception of others.

The act of lying is an act of deception. We are putting a thought in somebody else's mind about a reality that we might wish existed but does not. Usually that deception is made to make ourselves look better than we are or to hide our sin. To admit our wrongdoing would make us look bad, so we twist the truth or put a spin on it that is not exactly how things played out in reality.

The word *witness* is the Hebrew *ayd* and comes from a root meaning "to repeat." The *Ancient Hebrew Lexicon* says it is, "An event or person's testimony recounting another event or person." The wording of the command is legal, as of a witness giving testimony to the court. It is about creating a false narrative and repeating that story to others. Satan is very good at it—the father of lies:

> You are of your father the devil, and the desires of your father you want to do. He was a murderer from the beginning, and does not stand in the truth, because there is no truth in him. When he speaks a lie, he speaks from his own resources, for he is a liar and the father of it (John 8:44).

Just as Yahweh spoke and created the heavens and the earth, so Satan spoke lies and created his own world. Yahweh's creation was based on truth and order; it was "very good." Satan's is based on lies and chaos. God made man in His likeness and Satan makes idols in his.

Satan's world began with the lie in the garden of Eden and built his kingdom from there. It infected Cain, instructing him that killing his brother was a good solution, and then that he could not trust Yahweh to protect him, which caused him to build the first city. All of Satan's creation is built on the same lie, that we cannot trust Yahweh.

Israel was later infected, too. They listened to Satan's false witness, so could not trust that Yahweh would protect them from Egypt, provide food or water in the desert, or bring them into the promised land.

We continue to this day, believing that only things that man has made can save us. We look to chemical drugs instead of the plants that God gave us for healing. We look to man-made governments to save us from the evils that they are actually responsible for perpetuating, instead of the one King who sent His Son to save us from our own pitiable selves. And we look to man-made religion to teach us about the God who created the natural world instead of actually looking at the nature that God's fingerprints are all over, fingers that point straight back to Him.

That nature, the created world, cannot tell a lie, because God created it Himself. It is still there to witness to us. It is a true and

Nine: No False Witness – The Land Cries Out

reliable witness and it will testify of the evils that have been done to it by the liar that has tried his best to cover over it with concrete, technology, chemicals, and spilled blood:

> How long will the land mourn, and the herbs of every field wither? The beasts and birds are consumed, for the wickedness of those who dwell there, because they said, "He will not see our final end" (Jeremiah 12:4).

They were deceived by a lie into thinking that anything could be hidden from God. But that wickedness resulted in infecting the land, the herbs, the beasts and the birds. And the land itself mourned as a witness. When Cain slew Abel, it was also the land that cried out as a witness:

> And He said, "What have you done? The voice of your brother's blood cries out to Me from the ground. So now you are cursed from [on account of] the earth, which has opened its mouth to receive your brother's blood from your hand" (Genesis 4:10–11).

The land could not lie like humans can. All of the created things which were called "good" in Genesis 1 are good because they only have the godly nature that Yahweh created them with. They could not know both good and evil. It was man who was given that ability because we were made in Yahweh's image, capable of knowing both. Yet the remarkable thing to me is that our ability to do evil did not lower God's estimation of His creation, but raised it, for afterwards He stated that His creation was "*Very* good!"

His estimation was raised because free will entered into the equation. You see, God wants us to do good, but He wants it through our free will, because it means a lot more. When the capacity to do evil is present but is overcome, that is called love, and it is what God desires from us. When we do not do good, though, there are witnesses against us that cannot lie, such as the land, but also things that are of the land.

Part 4: The Ten Ordered Matters

We read in 1 John 5:8, "And there are three that bear witness on earth: the Spirit, the water, and the blood; and these three agree as one." They agree, so their testimony can convict, as they did in the case of Cain, because, as Deuteronomy 19:15 states, "One witness shall not rise against a man concerning any iniquity or any sin that he commits; by the mouth of two or three witnesses the matter shall be established."

Many things other than people have been called as witnesses before God: heaven and earth (Deuteronomy 4:26), a heap of stones and a pillar of stone (Genesis 31:52), the tabernacle (of *Witness*, as it was often referred to!), a song (of Moses, Deuteronomy 31:19), the book of the Law (Deuteronomy 31:26), an altar (Joshua 22:26–27), the gospel of the kingdom (Matthew 24:14), corrosion of gold and silver (James 5:3), and of course God Himself.

The common thread among all of these things is that they are creations of God Himself. The heap, pillar and altar are all of raw, uncut stone, as God commanded no tools to touch the stones that made His altar. The tabernacle of witness was built by men but designed by God Himself. Gold and silver are of course natural materials. That they were made by God made them trustworthy witnesses. It was men who were not trustworthy, so in our case two or three must agree in order to establish guilt.

When we look outside and see the earth covered in man-made materials—sprawling cities, industrial wastelands, and even farmland treated as if it is an industrial product—we should understand that the earth is crying out as a witness to the things being done to it. The physical and spiritual consequences of bearing false witness can be staggering.

I'm going to give you one example to add to the two that I discussed in the second ordered matter. Fluoride.

When our son was born, Sanae and I had not yet started to discover many of the deceptions that are out there, but we had some intuition that we should at least question some of the standard

Nine: No False Witness – The Land Cries Out

protocols for raising a child that we didn't understand. When we were told that we needed to start our son on fluoride supplements, Sanae immediately sensed something wrong with the idea. It didn't seem natural to do so.

I didn't worry so much and agreed with the doctor to start using fluoride drops so that his teeth could grow in healthy, even though I had heard in passing of people that thought of fluoride use as a toxic conspiracy. But on Sanae's insistence, I agreed to do some research.

I found a book called *The Fluoride Deception*, by Christopher Bryson at the library and started reading. Not far into the book, I had to stop giving the drops to our son. The case against it was just too well documented.

The history of fluoridation of drinking water goes back to World War Two nuclear material production. It is an industrial byproduct that is scrubbed from the smokestacks of heavy industry. Although known from the beginning to be extremely toxic to all life, it was decided that if it was released in small enough amounts into the drinking water supply, they could gradually use up this waste material and claim it to be a beneficial supplement.

It did indeed make the enamel on people's teeth harder. What was never said to the public was that it also makes those same teeth, as well as the bones, extremely brittle. And that is in addition to its being a neurotoxin among many other things, causing long-term health effects for millions of people. It has been the cause of innumerable industrial lawsuits since the mid twentieth century.

The book chronicles the cover-ups that our government implemented to convince dentists and the general public that it was beneficial. One case involved a large-scale cover-up at an industrial facility where the workers were experiencing rapidly declining health, including problems with their teeth. It was a large enough incident that government scientists showed up to study what was going on. They later issued a formal report on their findings, stating that there were no issues, and that their studies actually showed zero cavities in any employees, proving that fluoride was safe and effective for teeth. The part they left out of their study was that the reason there were no cavities was that very few employees had any teeth left at all due to the toxicity they were experiencing.

The information contained in the book is well documented, widely accepted, and backed up by respected scientists the world over, to the extent that 98 percent of European municipalities refuse to fluoridate their water. Even in the United States today, the union that represents the scientists for the Environmental Protection Agency regularly recommends against fluoridation of the water supply. Yet somehow the EPA itself continues to override the scientists, recommending the toxic sludge as an addition to our water.

I can't recommend *The Fluoride Deception* enough. Even if your area doesn't fluoridate the water and you already avoid fluoridated toothpaste, it is a great read to understand the lengths that the enemy will go to deceive us, so you can start to see the patterns elsewhere.

Our lives are filled with similar false narratives that have consumed our educational facilities and newsrooms. Many books could be and have been written on exposing them, so I don't attempt to go into them all here. Just know that there is only one source of truth and that is the Word of God. That Word is written in the Bible and in the creation.

We can view with our own eyes that the land is crying out as a witness against these abominations. When Christ comes back at the final trumpet, those perpetuating the lies will not be spared unless they have truly repented. In the meantime, let none of us bear false witness in any matter, great or small!

Ten: Don't Covet, Give Thanks

> You shall not covet your neighbor's house; you shall not covet your neighbor's wife, nor his male servant, nor his female servant, nor his ox, nor his donkey, nor anything that is your neighbor's (Exodus 20:17).

The first commandment was really a heading or introduction for the next four. It was the thumb on the right hand. This tenth one is the thumb on the left; a bookend summing up the previous four, teaching us how to avoid breaking them. If you covet your neighbor's house, you may be tempted to kill him for it, or to act dishonestly to get it or one like it. If you covet your neighbor's wife, you may be tempted to commit adultery. If you covet your neighbors' possessions you may be tempted to steal them.

And again, we are looking at idolatry. If any of these things have risen in your heart to a level of covetousness, then you have set them up as idols.

The Hebrew word for covet is *chamad*, Strong's H2530. *The Ancient Hebrew Lexicon* says of it, "To want something that is pleasant out of desire or lust." The motivation for wanting it is not pure. In English, covetousness and jealousy are related words, sometimes even interchangeable. If you just bought an amazing new car that I'd love to have, I could say that I am jealous of your new car, or I could say that I am coveting your new car. But this does not hold true in Hebrew.

The second commandment said of idols, "you shall not bow down to them nor serve them. For I, Yahweh, your God, *am* a jealous God." God was jealous because of the idols. I asked a question in the section on that ordered matter whether this jealousy was contradicting the tenth commandment, but I did not answer it there. But the definitions make it clear. Was He jealous out of desire or lust? No. The word for jealous in that context was not *chamad*, but *qanna*, Strong's H7076, "One who is protective over someone or something," (*Ancient Hebrew Lexicon*). Yahweh is protective of His people, not wanting them to fall into idolatry, but He is not covetous, acting out of desire or lust. They are very different things.

It is easy to say not to do something, but in practice that can be difficult. While raising a child, I learned that saying "no" was far more effective if it was reinforced by giving something positive to replace the thing I said "no" to. We need to replace the coveting with something else, preferably its opposite. The opposite of coveting is being thankful. If we are focusing on what we don't have then we can't take the time to look at what we do have or give thanks for it.

> But fornication and all uncleanness or **covetousness**, let it not even be named among you, as is fitting for saints; neither filthiness, nor foolish talking, nor coarse jesting, which are not fitting, **but rather giving of thanks.** For this you know, that no fornicator, unclean person, **nor covetous man, who is an idolater**, has any inheritance in the kingdom of Christ and God. (Ephesians 5:3–5)

Paul actually ties covetousness to idolatry, fornication and uncleanness, and recommends giving thanks as the solution. He promotes the idea again in 1 Thessalonians 5:16–18:

Ten: Don't Covet, Give Thanks

Rejoice always, pray without ceasing, in everything give thanks; for this is the will of God in Christ Jesus for you.

This is so important that Yahweh requests us to give thanks first whenever we come before Him, before asking or petitioning Him for anything.

Enter into His gates with thanksgiving, And into His courts with praise. Be thankful to Him, and bless His name (Psalm 100:4).

Be anxious about nothing, but in everything by prayer and by petition **with thanksgivings**, let your requests be made known to God; and the peace of God which surpasses all understanding will keep your hearts and your minds in Christ Jesus (Philippians 4:6).

I could go on all day about Biblical references to giving thanks; there are over 150 of them. But the short story is that it should be done first and often. If we do that there will be no room left for covetousness.

I haven't brought nature into this section yet, but it is really very simple and straightforward. Have you known people who are thankful and content in everything? They are the ones that everyone wants to be around because they are uplifting and edifying.

They are also healthier. Hundreds of studies have shown that an attitude of gratitude is able to prevent heart disease, diabetes, cancer, influenza, dementia, insomnia, and chronic pain[34]. When we are stressed out our bodies produce toxins and send them all over. It is the culprit to far more disease than we can imagine. Do you think nature is telling us something?

---

[34] Andersen, C. H., MS. (2022, November 28). Feeling Thankful Can Help Prevent These 7 Major Diseases, Says Research. TheHealthy.com. Retrieved October 21, 2024, from https://www.thehealthy.com/habits/how-to-prevent-disease-with-gratitude-from-doctors/

PART FIVE
The End

The Gospel of Death

In Genesis 14, in the battle of the five kings, Abram showed righteousness to God in taking nothing for himself in his victory, but blessed God Most High, giving Him the credit and glory. As a result, God sent Abram a vision. In this vision, which came in his old age, while he was ready for death, life was offered. Against all logic, a child would be born to whom it was promised descendants as numerous as the sands of the sea. Abram believed that offer, and Yahweh called him righteous for it, and father of the faithful, for he ate of the tree of faith instead of the tree of death. Yet he still had another decision to make, another set of trees from which to choose. Would he accept the oneness of his marriage to Sarai, with her dead womb, or was the covenant only through him, for the vision had only come to him, and not to Sarai? In the same fashion that Adam believed Eve who listened to the worldly logic of Satan instead of God, Abram believed Sarai and her logic of the flesh, that her womb was dead. They took God's promise to mean that they had work to do in order to create the plan that God had promised, for they could see no other way. So, Sarai offered her handmaid Hagar to Abram to have this promised child with. They did indeed have a child this way, but God said that this would not be the promised seed because

Part 5: The End

it was not out of faith that Ishmael was born, but of their works. There would be another.

God forgave Abram. Because of his faith previously shown, God had made a promise that could not be broken. Adam had not had a promise made to him which could not be broken because he had not had a previous record of righteousness before he chose death and failed to be a savior to his wife and all their future offspring.

God came again to Abram to tell him the promised seed would not be Ishmael, but would come through Sarai, and again Abram believed. After Isaac was born, he understood that his faith could not come to fruition through his own works. So when God told him to sacrifice this son of promise, he did not question but brought Isaac to the mountain carrying his own tree on which to be sacrificed, and when Isaac questioned him, he replied that God will supply the sacrifice, which He immediately did.

Abram, now called Abraham, had accepted death as the way to follow God, and in so doing he gained both the life of his only son, and his own eternal life.

When, in 1 Samuel 17, David saw Goliath standing in defiance of the Israelites unchallenged, he counted death as nothing in standing up for Yahweh. He died to himself, and Yahweh caused David to live through his faith in Him. David did not receive his faith by ritually keeping the law of Yahweh, but understood that the law pointed to something greater, and died to himself in his search to achieve it. Otherwise, he dared not ask to eat the showbread when he was running from Saul; he knew he and his men were holy before God. He was later called a man after God's own heart and given the lineage which would see the coming of the Messiah.

Moses, being brought up in the grandeur of Pharaoh's own household, did not desire such for himself, but wished only for the right treatment of the Israelite people, going out and striking the

Egyptian who abused his Israelite servant, killing him. He lost the life he formerly had and lived in the wilderness. He had died to himself, which made him useful to God in leading His people out of Egypt.

Even in the Old Covenant times, when someone died to themselves, they were given of the Holy Spirit and performed miracles. Moses, Abraham, David, Elijah, Isaiah, Daniel, and others were those given the Holy Spirit, and would be called saints, which is translated from *hagios*, meaning holy, or set apart one. Having died to themselves in their own lifetimes, they would not be under the penalty of death which the law had pointed to, so the grave would not be able to hold them. And what happened the very moment that Christ died, becoming the first of the first fruits unto eternal life? "The rocks were split and the graves were opened and many bodies of the saints who had fallen asleep were raised." Matthew 27:51–52.

To those who choose their own death to this world, life is granted, and death cannot hold them. But those who value their life, being under the law, must bear the penalty of the law, which is also death.

It doesn't matter which law it is. Adam had only one law and broke it, sending its curse to all people everywhere for all time. God chose Israel as a people to use as the example to the world, to all nations, yet all nations did not have the law of Moses, but some other law. To the Romans, who were never a nation under the law of Moses, Paul wrote:

> Do you not know that to whom you present yourselves slaves to obey, you are that ones slaves whom you obey, whether of sin to death, or of obedience to righteousness. But God be thanked that though you were slaves of sin, yet you obeyed from the heart that form of doctrine to which you were delivered (Romans 6:16–17).

And also:

Part 5: The End

> For when the gentiles, who do not have the law, by nature do the things in the law, these, although not having the law, are a law to themselves, who show the work of the law written in their hearts, their conscience also bearing witness, and between themselves their thoughts accusing or else excusing them (Romans 2:14–15).

This can be a great comfort that those who have never known the law of Moses are not bound by what they have never heard. For who can enter a contract never having heard of the other party? In such cases, God can still look at the heart and its willingness to obey whatever form of law they did have, especially the law of love that can be known in every culture and time, and the law that can be seen written in the creation, making them without excuse.

So, we see that to those who choose to die to themselves in their lifetime, judgment has already taken place, the righteous heart being a constant judge of every action before it takes place. But to those who still need the handwritten law to be enforced because their hearts are still stone, judgment must come after death.

This is why we see in Revelation 20 that there are two resurrections. The first (verses 4–6) is for those who lost their lives for Jesus and as a reward will live and reign with Jesus Christ for the thousand-year period. In the second resurrection (verses 11–15) we see judgment of their works as are recorded in the books before life can be granted, and to those whose works do not measure up, they will be destroyed, because unrighteousness cannot inherit the perfection of the spiritual kingdom of the new heaven and new earth. But in both instances, life is attained through death.

Jesus used the parable of a grain of wheat:

> But Jesus answered them, saying, The hour has come that the Son of Man should be glorified. Truly, truly, I say to you, if the grain of wheat that falls into the earth does not die, it remains alone. But if it dies, it bears much fruit. The one who loves his life loses it, and the one who hates his life in this world will keep it to everlasting life (John 12:23–25 LITV).

The Gospel of Death

He was speaking of Himself to Andrew and Philip, explaining that He was about to be killed and glorified. Death comes first before being glorified, because it must be that way. Nature tells us so. But it is not something that was only for Jesus because He was God. His followers would have the same thing happen to them. When wheat is harvested, its heads are cut off:

> And I saw thrones, and they sat on them. And judgment was given to them, and the souls of the ones having been beheaded because of the witness of Jesus, and because of the Word of God, and who had not worshiped the beast nor its image, and had not received the mark on their forehead and on their hand. And they lived and reigned with Christ a thousand years (Revelation 20:4).

Does it start to make more sense why God used harvest seasons to symbolize His appointed times? God's people are the barley and wheat whose heads are cut off, just as they did to John the Baptist. It speaks to their glorification; they will be resurrected and bear much fruit. It may seem like a dark subject to talk about beheading, but I am not being dark by saying these things. I'm simply repeating what the Bible and nature have already said. It is actually the gospel, good news, that we can be confident in our reward when times of real persecution befall us.

24

Love

I could have ended this book after the last chapter. It would seem natural since death is the end of our lives on earth. But that end is really only a beginning, and the reason for that is because of Love, which is a much more excellent way to end a book.

First Corinthians 13 is often called the love chapter. It was read at my wedding and probably the vast majority of other people's weddings. It is popular for good reason. For context, in chapter 12 Paul was talking to the Corinthian church about spiritual gifts, such as prophecy, tongues, and healings, explaining how they are individually granted, as each person is a unique member of the body, performing different functions. He ends that discussion by saying,

> But earnestly desire the best gifts. And yet I show you a more excellent way (1 Corinthians 12:31).

The spiritual gifts are a good thing. But there is something more important that will give meaning and reason to the tools of the spiritual gifts:

> Though I speak with the tongues of men and of angels, but have not love, I have become sounding brass or a clanging cymbal. And though I have the gift of prophecy, and understand all mysteries and all knowledge, and though I have all faith, so that I could remove mountains, but have not love, I am nothing. And though I bestow all my goods to feed the poor, and though I give my body to be burned, but have not love, it profits me nothing.

Love

> Love suffers long and is kind; love does not envy; love does not parade itself, is not puffed up; does not behave rudely, does not seek its own, is not provoked, thinks no evil; does not rejoice in iniquity, but rejoices in the truth; bears all things, believes all things, hopes all things, endures all things.
>
> Love never fails. But whether there are prophecies, they will fail; whether there are tongues, they will cease; whether there is knowledge, it will vanish away. For we know in part and we prophesy in part. But when that which is perfect has come, then that which is in part will be done away.
>
> When I was a child, I spoke as a child, I understood as a child, I thought as a child; but when I became a man, I put away childish things. For now we see in a mirror, dimly, but then face to face. Now I know in part, but then I shall know just as I also am known.
>
> And now abide faith, hope, love, these three; but the greatest of these is love (1 Corinthians 13:1–13).

I want to focus on the description of love by Paul in verses 4 to 8 and compare it to the creation that was given to us by Yahweh. I think that it will shed some light on the love that He has surrounded us with from the beginning.

Love suffers long: Creation has endured much hardship, pollution, wars, and spilled blood, yet continues to live and provide selflessly.

Is kind: Creation gives good gifts—food and material resources in abundance, sunlight, heat and rain—meeting every need of man, beast, and bug.

Love does not envy: There is nothing for creation *to* envy. There is only nature itself and the imposter, which is trying to smother it out of existence. Nobody envies that which is trying to destroy it.

Part 5: The End

Love does not parade itself: Creation just is. You can notice it or not. It will not shove its flowers under your nose.

Is not puffed up: Again, it just is what it is. It is not a manicured English garden. It does not pretend to be more than it is, because then it would cease to be nature.

Does not behave rudely: Misfortune can happen to humans or animals because of nature, but there is never the intention behind it which defines rudeness.

Does not seek its own: It welcomes both the good and the evil and will send rain and drought equally on both.

Is not provoked: It will not respond to ill treatment with malice. A cut tree will not fight back.

Thinks no evil: It thinks only of what it was created to do—grow and provide.

Does not rejoice in iniquity but rejoices in the truth: The creation will only suffer at the hand of iniquity, so it cannot rejoice. It rejoices when it is understood, because it *is* truth and cannot lie, being created by Him who is "the way, the truth, and the life."

Bears all things: "Bears" in Greek is Strong's G4722 *stego*. It means "cover; to hold off, to hold in; hence, to hold out against, to endure patiently." Picture all of the spilled blood and pollution that has been poured out on the ground. It is covered and unseen, being held in until the land sees its final rest. And, as said above, it will suffer long while bearing it.

Believes all things: All truth, that is. Neither love nor creation believes (*knows* being the better translation) or tolerates deception, but both can spot all truth standing against the sea of lies from miles away.

Hopes all things: Surely creation looks forward to better days, when the land will be given its rest. And it has faith that those days will come. "Faith is the substance of things **hoped** for, the evidence of things not seen."

Endures all things: "Endures" here in Greek is Strong's G5278 *Hypomeno*, meaning, according to Mounce[35], "to remain or stay behind, when others have departed." When all man-made things have been destroyed and even when men have died and deserted the land, creation will stay behind and endure. Have you ever seen grass and weeds coming up through the cracks in the concrete? That is the endurance of creation. With time, that picture turns into a rainforest covering over the ruins of the fraud of civilization. It is also the way of love, which can patiently endure until it has covered over all of the lies and deception.

Love never fails: Seed time and harvest still remain. The sun still rises and sets. These are things we can count on because they never fail. They never fail because of all of the other characteristics that were just listed. Love is the same, a force of nature that will succeed every time it is implemented.

But whether there are prophecies, they will fail; whether there are tongues, they will cease; whether there is knowledge, it will vanish away. These things will fail, cease and vanish because they are not creations of the

---

[35] Mounce, William D. *Mounce's Complete Expository Dictionary of Old and New Testament Words*. Zondervan Academic, 2009.

Part 5: The End

natural world, but a result of man living in the natural world— our responses to it. There are good and bad responses, but all will be gone one day. Yet creation will still only be what it is, even after it has been changed or renewed by God.

We can start to see the creation as God's original manifestation of His love for us, surrounding us with every good thing that we need to not only survive, but to thrive and live joyful, complete lives. Our cups have been overflowing with the goodness He gave us.

We've now read many messages that have been written into the creation, and I hope it is apparent that the conclusion of the matter is that they can all be distilled down to His love for us. Our part in that is to notice this love and then implement it in our own lives, giving selflessly to those in need, physically, emotionally, and spiritually.

Let us all take some time to look around at the created things of this world and appreciate the love that God has intended for us to be surrounded with. He has given abundantly and is waiting for us to help ourselves and give in turn to those who have not yet discovered the abundance.

THE END

For more information about Jeffrey Weitzel
and the testimony written into the creation, visit
gospel.design

www.ingramcontent.com/pod-product-compliance
Lightning Source LLC
Chambersburg PA
CBHW020532030426
42337CB00013B/814